Viva Baseball!

Sport and Society

Series Editors
Benjamin G. Rader
Randy Roberts

A list of books in the series appears at the end of this book.

Viva Baseball!

Latin Major Leaguers and Their Special Hunger

Samuel O. Regalado

University of Illinois Press

Urbana and Chicago

This book is printed on acid-free paper.

Library of Congress Cataloging-in-Publication Data
Regalado, Samuel O. (Samuel Octavio), 1953–
Viva baseball! : Latin major leaguers and their special hunger /
Samuel O. Regalado.
p. cm. — (Sport and society)
Includes bibliographical references and index.
ISBN 0-252-02372-2 (cloth: acid-free paper)
1. Hispanic American baseball players—Biography. 2. Baseball
players—Latin America—Biography. I. Title. II. Series.
GV865.A1R38   1998
796.357'64'098—dc21   97-21066
CIP

For my parents
    Salvaldor and Eva
and my sister
    Sus

Contents

Acknowledgments

My research into the saga of Latin baseball players began during my days as a graduate student in the history department at Washington State University. Starting with my master's thesis and continuing into my dissertation, LeRoy Ashby, my mentor, gave me the intellectual guidance to not only refine this work but also realize my dream of earning a Ph.D. The depth of gratitude and respect I have for him is immense. At the earliest stages of this work, my uncle and former major league player, Rudy Regalado, opened doors through his contacts and good reputation in professional baseball. I also thank Richard Hume, a colleague of my mentor, who first suggested that I investigate the history of these players.

Archivists Tom Heitz and Bill Deane and Senior Photo Associate Darci Harrington, at the library of the Baseball Hall of Fame in Cooperstown, and historian Steven Gietschier, at the *Sporting News* in St. Louis, guided me through their respective collections and were gracious hosts during my visits. Additionally, Art Costas at the interlibrary loan office of California State University at Stanislaus worked hard to acquire the many materials I requested. Financial support from two CSU-Stanislaus awards, the Research, Scholarship, and Creative Action and Affirmative Action Development grants, were of great assistance in the completion of this study. I also extend my gratitude to the following baseball clubs and institutions for allowing me access to their players and coaches and for making the appropriate contacts: the Baseball Commissioner's Office in New York

City, the California Angels, the Los Angeles Dodgers, the Minnesota Twins, the Philadelphia Phillies, the San Francisco Giants, and the West Palm Beach Expos. In addition, Felipe Alou, then of the West Palm Beach Expos, and Luis Rodríguez-Mayoral, the Latin American liaison for the Texas Rangers, generously offered insights and hospitality.

Enormous gratitude goes to Curtis Grant, Richard Crepeau, and Jules Tygiel, all of whom patiently read my manuscript several times, gave important suggestions, and provided constant support. They are great friends and respected colleagues. I also appreciate the services of Marianne Franco, who scrutinized the Spanish-language names, and Michael Schmandt, who provided the maps. At the University of Illinois Press, Dick Wentworth, in his capacity as director, friend, and fellow Dodger fan, patiently dealt with my impatience as the project neared completion. I also thank Benjamin Rader, the series editor, for utilizing his editorial skills in advancing this work. Additionally, I would like to recognize the following students at CSU-Stanislaus for their assistance: Angelina Caballero, Gina Espinosa, Sonja Has-Ellison, and Jodi Netherwood.

Morale and encouragement are important when research projects inevitably run into those difficult periods when doubts about direction and completion surface. On this count, Larry Gerlach and the "baseball bunch" at the North American Society for Sport History never wavered in their support of my career and work on this topic: always prodding me to go forward, always reminding me of the importance of this history. I also thank Joe Arbena, Ron Briley, Richard Crepeau, and Jules Tygiel for their creative book titles during a brainstorming session in New York's Greenwich Village. Peter Bjarkman of the Society for American Baseball Research was generous in sending me materials that contributed to this study. I deeply appreciate the efforts of John Broesamle, my undergraduate mentor at California State University at Northridge, who encouraged a rather wayward student to become a professional historian.

I would also like to thank the following individuals who took the time to share their experiences with me: Felipe Alou, Alex Campanis, René Cárdenas, Orlando Cepeda, David Concepcíon, Al Downing, Tito Fuentes, Rudy García, George Genovese, Preston Gómez, Calvin Griffith, Bob Hunter, Monte Irvin, Jaime Jarrín, Manny Mota, Tony Oliva, Tony Pérez, Nick Peters, Ed Rivera, Luis Rodríguez-Mayoral, Octavio "Cookie" Rojas, Chuck Stewart, Tony Taylor, Richard "Dickie" Thon, and Al Zuniga. I did not mention every Latin player in baseball history, nor did I describe every scenario involving them. But I hope they feel that this work does justice to the courage, skills, and tenacity they brought to American baseball.

Finally, my parents, Salvador and Eva, and my sister, Sus, were always there when I needed them and—my mother, in particular—always managed to place things in perspective during my many moments of frustration. I love them now and always. In closing, I want to acknowledge my late grandfather, Manuel Regalado, who, years ago when I was a young boy, held my hand as I entered not only Dodger Stadium's left field pavilion for the first time but also a world that has, since then, greatly enriched my life.

Preface

With bag in hand, Tony Oliva bid farewell to his father and sister as he boarded a plane leaving Cuba. Recalling his 1961 departure he wrote, "This was something I had thought about, dreamed about, since I was a little boy playing baseball on the field on my father's farm. And now, here I was, actually going to America to become a professional baseball player."[1] Armed with but a few dollars and no knowledge of the English language, the young ballplayer made his way to the training camp in the hope that his dreams might soon become a reality. In doing so, Oliva joined a growing list of those who migrated to the United States to play professional baseball.

Between 1871 and the mid-1990s, over 500 Latin American–born players joined major league clubs. For most, their love of baseball was rooted in makeshift diamonds amidst the sugarcane fields and jungles of the Caribbean. For others it came from the dusty, windswept dirt farms of northern Mexico, while for still others it emerged from the banana- and coffee-growing regions of Central America and Venezuela. For many, their talents developed despite the limited resources—and scarce athletic equipment—available to them. Hence, the opportunity to play baseball in the United States carried great significance. "Many of us came from families who didn't have the money to send us to college or anything like that. So the only way of bettering ourselves and our families was to make it in baseball," explained Cuban Octavio "Cookie" Rojas.[2] But to "make it," as he and others like him learned, required a "special hunger"—the drive need-ed to propel them through the pitfalls that they inevitably encountered as they pursued their dreams. That hunger, to be sure, motivated their exo-dus from regions where the per capita income was often less than a few hundred dollars per year, where "lunch" was as foreign as wealth, where $250 a month was "big money," and where the loss of a ten-dollar bill was a tragedy.

No one questions the success Latins have enjoyed on America's profes-sional baseball diamonds. But behind this success lay a sense of purpose. Baseball was more than a game to them. It was a competition that carried social and economic implications. Baseball was a path out of poverty; it helped to bring distinction to their homelands; it was a means to ease the pain and suffering of kinfolk and compatriots; and it provided a sliver of hope to many younger Latins who might otherwise have envisioned a dim future. Their determination to succeed in the face of an unwelcoming cul-ture reveals the human spirit of Latin players. For they, unlike so many other newcomers, faced these barriers alone, without the aid of support groups. And it was this willingness to break through cultural roadblocks that made their hunger "special."

The history of the Latin player in the major leagues parallels the history of the larger Spanish-speaking community in the United States and serves as a microcosm of it. Like their colleagues on the diamond, Latin leaders campaigned for recognition within the mainstream, struggled to maintain their identity, battled to overcome stereotypes, and adapted to white in-stitutions. Moreover, community leaders came to challenge the discrimi-nation that hindered their quest for socioeconomic and political parity. Through mutual aid societies, social movements, and community devel-opments, Spanish-speaking people exhibited what Felipe Alou called "the spirit of the Latin." This spirit was never more evident than in 1981, when Fernando Valenzuela catapulted the heretofore "forgotten people" into the limelight. "Fernandomania" ignited a celebration of both a baseball hero and Latin cultures.

This phenomenon was timely for my academic career. My graduate stud-ies at Washington State University began the year Valenzuela exploded onto the baseball scene. A native of the San Fernando Valley, I happily joined many other fans in the hurricane the media dubbed "Fernandomania." Even with his national recognition, Valenzuela did not touch anyone deeper than those of Mexican descent. Indeed, the mere mention of his name on the newscasts brought excitement to those like my mother, whose nation-alistic fervor reached new levels with each victory. I was intrigued with the carnival-like atmosphere, the lighting of religious candles, and general euphoria in the Mexican barrios every time Valenzuela took the mound. And I observed mainstream baseball fans leaning over the railing attempting to communicate in their broken Spanish with the Dodgers' Mexican hero. In the evenings, entire broadcasts on local networks repeatedly portrayed Valenzuela's path from poverty to fame.

When I carried this excitement with me to the Pacific Northwest, my mentor, LeRoy Ashby, and his colleagues at Washington State University channeled my enthusiasm as I sought to explore the relationship between baseball and ethnic cultures in American social history. And while my search for the meaning of the Latin special hunger began with Valenzuela, I learned that baseball, culture, and the Latin experience in America were far more closely related than I had initially perceived.

Researching this topic was an odyssey of both years and miles. The thrill of interviewing ballplayers, speaking with journalists and broadcasters, visiting legendary parks, combing through clippings at the Baseball Hall of Fame in Cooperstown and the archives of the *Sporting News* in St. Louis, sitting in big league dugouts and press boxes with a "Member of the Press" tag hanging around my neck, and hobnobbing with baseball greats at old-timers' banquets—all this was pure delight.

But the hard research meant scrutinizing newspapers (in both English and Spanish), laboriously reading seemingly miles of microfilm, reviewing players' files, reading biographies and autobiographies of stars, and pouring over an abundance of secondary materials. Writing *Viva Baseball!* also required me to explore the many facets of Pan-American history, with a special focus on American and Latin American cultures in relation to sports. Most importantly, I wanted to examine the players' experiences within the context of the history of Spanish-speaking cultures in the United States. To omit any of the aforementioned points, I felt, would have rendered the story incomplete.

My ultimate aim, however, was to look at the most crucial stage of the Latin baseball saga, namely, players' physical and cultural transitions from homeland to new country. These moves often required decisions of character and courage because there were no guarantees. Few would make it; most did not. Indeed, many received only travel money and no promise of a contract. All remained separated from their families and friends for months. Cubans suffered even more as they agonized over the possibility of never being able to return to the land of their birth. Such were the gripping scenarios that captured my interest.

The most rewarding aspect of my research, of course, was the inter-

xvi   Preface

views. The players often told their stories with passion. Although most were generous with their time, scheduling conflicts were much greater than I anticipated. Spending weeks on the road, bouncing from one airport to another, utilizing countless hotels as my homebase, rearranging missed appointments—these obstacles sometimes tested my resolve. But my determination—perhaps my obsession—to complete the task at hand greatly overshadowed these minor inconveniences. For as the project took shape, not only did it broaden my knowledge of the Latin experience in the United States, but it also brought me into closer touch with my own cultural background.

As I widened my horizons to embrace the experiences of the Latin players, I became aware that even though many of the men were legendary figures in the history of baseball, they were entirely invisible within historical accounts of Latin cultures in the United States. Indeed, I expected their absence from most works of American social history. But surprisingly, the same lacuna mars most studies that chronicle America's Spanish-speaking past. For instance, although players like Roberto Clemente and Fernando Valenzuela were immensely popular cultural heroes to Puerto Ricans, Mexicans, and Mexican Americans, their contributions to Latin cultures and heritage have been ignored by scholars who study American ethnic history. For that matter, the relationship between sports and the Latin community has yet to be examined in many of these works.

Consigned to historical obscurity, the story of Latin players begged for attention in a manner befitting any group that has hugely affected American culture. The Latins' contribution to American professional baseball warrants greater attention than simply a nostalgic look at an aspect of baseball's past. To that end, my purpose is not only to present the tale of a group driven by a "special hunger" to succeed in America's national pastime but also to help bridge a major gap in our understanding and appreciation of their contributions to American life.

Notes

1. Oliva, *Tony O!* 8.
2. Rojas interview.

Viva Baseball!

• 1

That Special Hunger

They come from the Dominican Republic and Puerto Rico and Venezuela, mostly, but they might as well come from the same place. The same thing drives them. They don't want to go back home to a standard of living they tried so hard to leave. They all had the "special hunger."
Octavio "Cookie" Rojas

Dodger Stadium reverberated with excitement on the warm evening of May 14, 1981. Dodgers fans had come to see a young pitcher's attempt to establish a major league record for the most consecutive wins by a rookie at the start of a season. Moreover, they came just to see him. None of the 56,000 seats was empty as patrons sat impatiently in the ballpark awaiting their hero's attempt to capture his eighth straight victory. As the Dodgers took the field, the roar of the crowd reached a crescendo when Fernando Valenzuela, the twenty-year-old Mexican star, popped out of the dugout on his way to the mound. Throughout the stadium fans shouted encouragement in both Spanish and English as Helen Dell, the Dodger Stadium organist, used the "El Toro" theme instead of the more familiar "Charge" for that evening's battle cry.

In the press box, journalists from around the nation jockeyed for space as they sought to cover the phenomenon dubbed "Fernandomania." Behind their microphones, Dodgers broadcaster Vin Scully prefaced the contest with a dramatic analysis of Valenzuela while Jaime Jarrín, the "other voice of the Dodgers," did the same for his Spanish-speaking listeners, which numbered well into the millions. Indeed, in the next several weeks similar scenes occurred in other National League cities when Valenzuela pitched. The native of Etchohuaquila in Sonora, Mexico, had captured national attention. Fans clamored to get his autograph; reporters groped for new information on him. English-speaking baseball followers were captivated by the young man from a humble background who seemed to spin magic on the pitcher's mound. Their Spanish-speaking counterparts saw him—and the surrounding delirium—as symbolic of Latin influence in the United States. Latins had arrived.

———

Clearly, the attention directed toward Valenzuela was a watershed in the history of Latins in America's national sport. Although prior to 1981 Latins had never received such nationwide acclaim, Fernando Valenzuela was nonetheless simply the most celebrated representative of a distinguished group of athletes who have helped shape major league baseball and American culture. Talented stars such as the Alou brothers, Luis Aparicio, Jorge "George" Bell, Orlando Cepeda, Roberto Clemente, Adolfo Luque, Juan Marichal, Dennis Martínez, Orestes "Minnie" Miñoso, and Rubén Sierra were prominent during their respective years of play. Most were driven by a desperate desire to succeed—what Octavio "Cookie" Rojas described as that "special hunger." "I knew it was going to take a lot of hard work, desire, and determination [to succeed]," reflected Dominican Manny Mota in 1982. "When I came to the United States to play professional baseball, I wanted something that nobody was going to give me. I had to go and get it myself."[1]

As these baseball pioneers explored their frontiers in search of stardom and the financial rewards often denied them in their native lands, they expanded the American national pastime into a truly international sport. Latin ballplayers coming to the United States entered a sporting institution that personified the American dream of opportunity, upward social mobility, and success. They brought to major and minor league baseball not only their remarkable skills but also flair and charisma that enhanced the game's spectator appeal. Ultimately, their achievements motivated clubs and the American media to modify their infrastructures, such as expanding scouting regions and employing bilingual personnel.

The importance of the Latin contingent in American baseball, however, transcended the sport. Players often bridged gaps between Latin America and the United States—and their distinct and often conflicting cultures. Throughout most of the twentieth century, major league rosters included those from Cuba, the Dominican Republic, Mexico, the Commonwealth of Puerto Rico, and other Central and South American countries. Brothers joined brothers and sons followed fathers as generations of Latin players gave America's national pastime an international composition. Often heroes in their own lands, they sought to exhibit their national pride on the diamond. Most Latin players saw themselves as "ambassadors" representing their respective countries and frowned at the stereotypes that homogenized all Latins.[2] At the same time, their Spanish-speaking tongue was a crucial bond between players in spite of their varied nationalities. Their language both shielded them from criticisms and served as an impediment in their quest for recognition.

Moreover, the language barrier highlighted the difficulties of Latin acculturation into the United States. Separated from family and home, players struggled daily with loneliness and the pitfalls of a foreign cuisine. For many, such problems were sometimes complicated by the starting points of their American careers. While some Latins landed in areas with large Hispanic enclaves, others were less fortunate. Rico Carty traveled to Yakima, Washington; Juan Marichal went to tiny Michigan City, Indiana; and Zoilo Versalles was a seventeen-year-old in Elmira, New York, places with almost no Latin residents. In addition, political tensions all too often disrupted the lives of Latin players. In 1961 broken diplomatic ties virtually eliminated recruiting in Cuba, which up to that point had been an important source of talent.

But according to Latin American baseball players, their most troubling encounter was with racism. Brought to the United States because of their skills, most Latin players believed in the great American dream. And they assumed that success came by virtue of merit. Too often, however, they learned otherwise. Professional baseball in the United States mirrored the larger American society. The major leagues had excluded African American players from the late nineteenth century until 1947. After the color barrier was breached, the turbulence created by the civil rights movement in the ensuing decades proved unsettling for Latin players on and off the field. Often singled out because of their background, Latins repeatedly felt the stings of American racial prejudice and discrimination. Finally, while Latins and American blacks confronted racism together, Latins alone dealt with the additional trauma of acculturation.

Yet for many players from Spanish-speaking countries, their negative experiences faded into the background when compared with the poverty found in their own countries. Baseball for many was clearly the only way out. Furthermore, it embodied the Latin virtues of individualism, personal honor, and integrity.[3]

Starting in 1911 Latin players came to the United States with growing regularity, and with each wave their impact in the major leagues enlarged. From 1911 to 1947, they entered the majors almost exclusively via the rosters of the Cincinnati Reds and the Washington Senators, who fostered scouting efforts to recruit low-cost talent, primarily from Cuba. But after Jackie Robinson joined the major leagues, black Latins poured into the United States during the integration years of the 1950s and 1960s. The influx reflected expanded scouting efforts that drew players from Latin regions well beyond Cuba. By the 1970s and 1980s, as incoming talent from Cuba diminished, major league programs, such as those found in the small Dominican town of San Pedro de Macorís, were created to develop talent and orient players to U.S. culture. Early Latin pioneers such as Felipe Alou, Santos Alomar, Tony Oliva, and Manny Mota served within the major league framework to help coach the future stars seeking the gold and glory that their predecessors had achieved. Moreover, Roberto Clemente's legacy proved to be an important inspiration.

Like their African American counterparts, Latins played magnificently. From Roberto "Beto" Avila in 1954 to José Canseco in 1988, Latin players captured the Most Valuable Player award six times, in addition to seven Rookie of the Year titles, three Cy Young trophies, and seventeen batting championships. By the end of the early 1990s the Baseball Hall of Fame inducted five Latins: Luis Aparicio, Roberto Clemente, Juan Marichal, and Rod Carew were honored for their outstanding careers in the major leagues while Martín Dihigo, a Cuban player, represented the American black leagues.

▬▬▬◀

The expansion of baseball's Latin contingent in baseball mirrored the growing importance of Latin cultures in the United States. Victims of racial and cultural stereotypes prior to World War II, Spanish speakers struggled to gain a foothold in mainstream U.S. culture. As the Hispanic population increased, social and political organizations developed to address a variety of urban and rural issues. Benefiting from the gains of the activism of the 1960s, a greater number of second- and third-generation Latins, armed with education and advanced skills, entered the larger corporate and media markets. Many were determined, however, to maintain their cultural heritage. Most certainly the successes of Latins gave rise to optimistic thinking; one Latin leader eagerly announced that the 1980s would be the "Decade for Hispanics."[4]

The achievements and turmoil faced by Latin players coincided with major developments in the larger Spanish-speaking world. Other Latins sought to maintain cultural ties in an unfamiliar and arbitrary environment.

The struggle to achieve recognition and parity in the major leagues was part of the larger Latin quest for equality in the United States. Indeed, the experiences of Latin players in the major leagues provided a unique perspective and often brought into clearer focus the larger Hispanic experience.

Paradoxically, however, Latin ballplayers were the most visible Latins in the United States but the most invisible players in the major leagues. American baseball aficionados could cite their names and statistics, but knew little else about them. At the same time, writers of American twentieth-century cultural history, particularly the experts who delineated the contributions of Spanish-speaking groups in the United States, failed to acknowledge the Latin impact on one of America's most cherished institutions—baseball. Yet, clearly the Latin path that led to baseball's "promised land" was a paradigm of the larger Latin historical experience in the United States. By 1981, patterns apparent both in the baseball world and in the broader Hispanic universe came together in an explosion called Fernandomania. But to understand that special hunger and the long and difficult path culminating in the Valenzuela euphoria, we must begin a century earlier.

Notes

1. Mota interview.
2. Alou interview.
3. Novak, *Joy of Sports,* 59–60.
4. Yzaguirre, "Decade for the Hispanic," 2.

•2

Beginnings

I had heard that Cubans are a deeply religious people. In two days here [in Cuba] I have learned that baseball is their religion.
Sam Lacy, *Baltimore Afro-American*

*E*steban Enrique Bellán probably had little idea of his significance in American baseball history. His 1871 membership on the Troy Haymakers of the National Association of Professional Base Ball Players distinguished him as the first Latin American player in the major leagues. Bellán's trailblazing inaugurated a movement of Latin players to the United States. Most were Cubans until the midtwentieth century, when increasing numbers from all over Latin America had a growing impact. During the pre-integration period, however, Latin players were rarely taken seriously. Their limited arsenal of skills coupled with the difficulty in communicating with them led some managers to feel that they were more trouble than they were worth. Baseball observers in the United States, of course, were not exempt from the large-scale and historical arrogance that most Americans held toward their Latin neighbors. This attitude, compounded by ignorance about Spanish-speaking cultures and racial biases, often polarized the two regions and hindered opportunities to strengthen their common interests. Baseball carried the potential to close the gap. Instead, the prevailing attitudes toward Latins not only forestalled any expansive migration of them into the big leagues but also deprived American fans of enjoying their skills to a greater degree for a half century. Latins, to the surprise of many, were quite passionate when it came to baseball. Indeed, baseball's development in the United States predated the game's emergence in Latin America by only twenty years. Yet, between 1871 and 1911 the big leagues extended an invitation to only one Latin. And invitations on a larger scale were not soon forthcoming.

Between 1871 and 1946 Latins trickled into the major leagues with no great fanfare. Although all of them were considered white, some were deemed a novelty and others became targets of journalistic humor. Their experiences with the press and teammates, moreover, laid the groundwork for American perceptions and stereotypes of Latin players that lasted for decades. Because Latin American players came from cultures that also revered baseball, they were anxious to exhibit their talents in a game that many Americans placed on a pedestal.

Since the end of Spanish rule in the 1820s (save the Caribbean in 1898), sports on the whole in Latin America held varied implications. Similar to the growth of organized sports in the United States, athletics in Latin

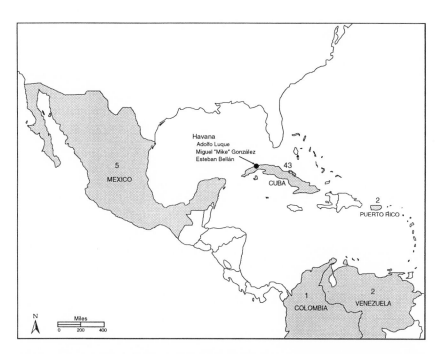

Latin American Origin of Major League Baseball Players, 1900–1950. Numerals denote the total number of players from individual countries. Selected high-profile players noted.

America reflected class lines, both in cultural and financial terms. The rigid social stratification, which was the centerpiece of life during the more than three hundred years of Spanish rule, remained intact. And the development of sporting competitions throughout Latin America served as a microcosm of that tradition. Late-nineteenth-century sports clubs, for instance, emerged not from families of mixed ancestry or from the still-oppressed Indians or from black Latins. They came from the ranks of the urban Creole elite and their European counterparts. Like the status communities found in the United States, the Latin sports clubs were a means of closing ranks to protect cherished positions in the traditional social hierarchy. But the athletic activities that emerged were not distinctively Latin American.

Indeed, Latin America's high profile sports stemmed from what cultural, socioeconomic, and political elites viewed as "progressive" civilizations abroad. As historian Steve Stein pointed out with respect to Peru, its "elite, increasingly integrated into the international economic system, was quick to imitate the cultural patterns of [outside] elites. As with other European imports, soccer arrived in Peru in the 1880s aboard an English ship."[1] Nineteenth-century Latin aristocrats "readily understood what was happening in Europe and ably discussed the latest ideas radiating from the Old World, which they welcomed to the New," according to E. Bradford Burns, until "civilization and the progress that led to it became identified with Europe."[2] Not surprisingly, cricket, polo, cycling, and, by the 1890s, soccer, were reserved exclusively for people of means. "The typical 'sportman,'" claimed Stein in his discussion about Peruvian competitors, "was energetic, athletic, carefree, and the member of a wealthy and prominent family."[3] As for traditional culture, "European thought . . . proved to be an ideological flood, which swept before it most American originality."[4] Native sports were so victimized that by the late twentieth century, argued Latin historian Joseph L. Arbena, "the most popular sports . . . have little connection with traditional society, not much with colonial society, and even less with pre-Columbian civilizations."[5] However, as soccer and other European sports satisfied the urban elite, baseball developed prominence among the other classes.

While the bulk of southern Latin America fancied European sports, U.S. influences penetrated the Caribbean region, Central America, and parts of Mexico. Throughout the mid- to late nineteenth century, U.S. capitalists and speculators poured into these areas in search of profit. Cornelius Vanderbilt opened his overland transit route through Nicaragua in 1850.

The Boston Fruit Company, later the powerful United Fruit Company, started shipping bananas out of Guatemala in 1885. And by the 1890s, Americans had heavily invested in Mexican mines and railroads. As these revenues grew so, too, did American interest in acquiring territory. Manifest Destiny had already victimized Mexico, resulting in the loss of nearly half of its territory to the United States by 1848. And American greed in the Caribbean and Panama continued throughout the nineteenth century. To that end, U.S. diplomats made repeated efforts to purchase such areas as the Virgin Islands and Santo Domingo in 1867 and 1879, respectively. In 1850, the Clayton-Bulwer Treaty between Great Britain and the United States decreed that neither would attempt to acquire exclusive rights to a canal in Central America. In 1901, through careful maneuvering, the United States pressured the British to abrogate the treaty, which ultimately paved the way for the Panama Canal. By then, the United States had defeated Spain and had acquired greater territory and influence in the Caribbean.

Through it all, American arrogance was clear. "We are Americans," proclaimed Secretary of State William Seward in 1869, a chief architect of expansion. "We are charged with the responsibilities of establishing on the American continent a higher condition of civilization and freedom" than seen elsewhere in the world.[6] As American interests expanded, contact between the English- and Spanish-speaking peoples inevitably grew. And within this framework, America's national pastime became an export item.

Several interpretations have been offered to explain baseball's emergence in the Caribbean, Mexico, and South America. Like other Latin American sports that appeared during the nationalistic period of the midnineteenth century, baseball filtered in from outside. As to who imported it— American sailors on leave, Caribbean students home from the United States—remains a cloudy issue. This much, however, is clear: Cuba was baseball's epicenter in the region. Indeed, baseball's development in Cuba was an indirect link to the history of the sport on the other islands. "It's much the same as that which happened with Christianity," claimed Dominican Pedro Julio Santana. "Jesus could be compared to the North Americans, but the apostles were the ones that spread the faith, and the apostles of baseball were the Cubans. Even though the Dominican Republic and Puerto Rico were occupied by the North Americans, the Cubans first brought baseball here."[7]

Although no one is sure who introduced baseball to Cuba, according to Cuban historian Luis Hernández a student named Nemesio Guillot returned home in 1864 with a ball and bat after he had completed his studies in the United States.[8] Two years later, Latin America's romance with baseball reportedly began when a group of American sailors, whose ship was stationed in Havana, invited a few Cubans to participate in a game. At Palmar de Junco the sailors designed a baseball diamond and shortly thereafter games commenced. While there exists no conclusive evidence as to which style of baseball—the New York or Massachusetts game—the Cubans initially adopted, Esteban Bellán's familiarity with the New York brand is suggestive. Although only those of privilege initially competed, various U.S. companies—particularly those in the sugar industry both in Cuba and later in the Dominican Republic—as well as strategically placed American troops helped baseball transcend class and racial lines until it became the sport of choice in Cuba's poorer rural sectors. In 1868, Cuba ushered in professional baseball when a team from Havana defeated a rival from Matanzas 51-9.[9] Interest in baseball spread rapidly in the 1870s and 1880s throughout the Caribbean and eventually onto the Central and South American mainland. The bastion of Latin baseball, however, remained in Cuba, which for nearly one hundred years provided the American big leagues with the bulk of Latin baseball talent.

Known during his career as the "Cuba Sylph," Esteban Bellán was born in 1849 in Havana.[10] In 1866 he came to the United States to attend Fordham University. Already knowledgeable about baseball from his encounters with American sailors in Cuba, Bellán joined the amateur Rose Hill College Baseball Club as a catcher. In 1868 he played with another amateur team until his debut with the Troy Haymakers. During his two-year tenure in the major leagues, first with Troy then with the New York Mutuals, Bellán developed a reputation as a good third baseman. The *Troy Daily Whig*, which appeared to set a precedent in Americanizing Latin names, wrote that "'Steve' has courage and activity, laces the hottest 'liners' [and] 'grounders,'" and was an "accurate thrower to the bases."[11] He fueled further Cuban interest in baseball when he returned home. Bellán, who participated in Cuba's first professional contest, continued as a player-manager until 1886, promoting and teaching the game at every available opportunity.[12] By the late 1880s, Cuban writer and former player Wenceslao Gálvez y Delmonte wrote that "baseball . . . had rooted itself so strongly in this land as proven by the hundreds of clubs in almost all parts of the island."[13] Furthermore, he correctly predicted that the "baseball fields of Cuba will persist longer than the cockfight and the bullring."[14]

As early as 1878, Emilio Sabourín helped to establish that island's first organized league, the Liga de Béisbol Profesional Cubana, in which regional teams competed and intense rivalries formed. The most popular was between Havana and Almendares—teams that fielded the best talent on the island.[15] Other clubs representing towns such as Cienfuegos, Fe, Marianao, and Santa Clara also became part of Cuba's rich professional baseball heritage. Early stars like hitter Wenceslao Gálvez y Delmonte of Almendares and pitcher Adolfo Luján of Havana added to the excitement on that island. Sabourín managed the Havana club to nine championships between 1878 and 1892 before his death at the hand of the Spanish government in 1897. Like Sabourín, many affiliated with baseball garnered praise not only for their skills but also for their patriotism, as monies earned at the gate sometimes ended up in the coffers of the Cuba Libre movement that fought against Spanish oppression.[16]

Cuban players became so skilled that, following the Spanish-American War in 1898, American big league clubs and individual stars visited the island with increasing frequency. The warm weather during winter months, proximity, and an opportunity for added revenue all made Cuba an attractive spot to visit. While Ty Cobb and Christy Mathewson were among the first white American stars to play in Cuba, American black professionals eventually competed in Cuba to enhance their finances and gain a needed reprieve from the torrent of racial abuse in the United States. Cuba was clearly the hub of baseball activity in Latin America. Indeed, one American writer described the Pearl of the Antilles as "stark raving dottily crazy over baseball."[17]

Baseball also expanded into other Caribbean regions. But it did so during an era when many islanders resented U.S. hegemony. By the turn of the century, the military and economic power of the Great Colossus of the North affected all realms of Caribbean life. Encroachment by the United States, had, of course, concerned Latins long before 1900. Seward's 1869 enunciation of prevailing American attitudes brought great discomfort to Latin intellectuals, who readily understood the ramifications of Manifest Destiny. Indeed, as early as 1811 a Cuban writer characterized the United States as "a colossus which has been constructed of all castes and languages and which threatens to swallow up, if not all our America, at least the northern portion of it."[18] Latin nationalists understandably squirmed as North American investments poured into their countries, sometimes by invitation, as was the case in Mexico under Porfirio Díaz in the latter part of the nineteenth century. During the last years of Spanish rule in the Caribbean, the Puerto Rican press corps sharply debated the U.S. presence in the region. Some admired Americans' willingness to intervene on Cuba's behalf for "moral" reasons, while others warned of an impending "Yankee peril."[19]

Those who were uncomfortable with a seemingly unchecked United States could hardly turn to historical precedent to ease their minds. Since 1822, when the United States sent Joel Poinsett to develop diplomatic relations with the court of Mexico's Augustín de Iturbide, Latin observers were already apprehensive about their northern neighbor's appetite for expansion. Throughout most of the nineteenth century, as the United States competed with other neocolonial powers, such as Great Britain and France, American influence into Latin America grew more intense. Perhaps anticipating the inevitable, Cuban patriot José Martí warned, "Once the United States is in Cuba, who will get it out?"[20]

As a result of the Spanish-American War, the United States by the end of the nineteenth century was, indeed, in Cuba as well as in Puerto Rico. Unable to extricate themselves from American militarization or capitalism, Latins learned and used baseball as a means of expression and took great pleasure in beating the "gringos" at their own game. After 1900, baseball continued to blossom in Puerto Rico and, soon thereafter, those serious about the sport formed professional clubs. Though the first Puerto Rican to enter the big leagues—Hiram Bithorn—did not make his appearance until 1942, baseball was already well-entrenched in the new American commonwealth. As islanders gained a reputation for providing formidable competition, visiting clubs from Cuba and the United States began to routinely dock at San Juan to test Puerto Rican talent.[21] American black stars such as Satchel Paige, Josh Gibson, and Buck Leonard also competed there against some of the island's legendary players, including Chato Rivera, Liborio Caballero, Pancho Coimbre, and Perucho Cepeda. Indeed, the Puerto Rican Winter League, founded in 1938, became one of the most popular off-season havens for American big leaguers.

Baseball had already found a home in the Dominican Republic by the time of the Spanish-American War. Cubans who fled the brutality of the Ten Year's War (1868–78) brought baseball with them.[22] The Dominicans learned the game rapidly so that by 1907 they had professional clubs, including a Santo Domingo team called Licey, for which most of that island's best athletes competed. Later other clubs, such as Escogido, rose to challenge Licey's dominance. As the appeal of baseball fanned Santo Domingo's sportive fires, Licey and its rivals drew thousands to their games. More than just sporting rituals, the games crossed class lines as they provided entertainment for both high society and those of lesser income.[23] By 1910 the Dominicans also competed against clubs from neighboring islands.

Like their counterparts in Puerto Rico, many Dominican baseball aficionados viewed their adopted sport as a symbolic show of pride and defiance against U.S. imperialism. During the frequent American occupations following 1916, games with U.S. military personnel provided Dominicans with "a chance . . . to measure themselves against their occupiers."[24] Dominican Manuel Joaquín Báez Vargas claimed with pride that "these games with North American sailors and marines were very important. There was a certain kind of patriotic enthusiasm in beating them."[25] In 1914, for instance, when the popular Enrique Hernández pitched a no-hitter against an American navy team, baseball became a symbol of resistance. Another pitcher, Fellito Guerra, however, reached even greater heights in Dominican lore. According to the story, big league scouts chased the standout pitcher in the early 1920s, and one eventually offered him a contract. But Guerra, in protest of an American military presence in his country, refused the invitation to sign with the "occupiers."[26] Given that the first Dominican to reach the big leagues—Ossie Virgil—did not do so until 1956, it is difficult to fathom that the majors showed the type of interest that accompanied the fable. But to an extant the symbolic nature of the story exhibited the degree of Dominican nationalism seen through baseball.

Juan Bosch, the former president whose path to regain office was blocked in 1965 by American marines sent to restore order, later offered an embittered analysis of early twentieth-century North American baseball influence over his country. Baseball contests between American servicemen and Dominicans, he contended, had little to do with goodwill. "These games manifested a form of the peoples' distaste of the occupation. They were a repudiation of it," he claimed. Contests were fueled with the incentive to go and "beat the North Americans."[27]

Apart from the political connotations, however, baseball was popular in its own right. From the smallest villages to the largest cities, baseball often overshadowed such traditional pastimes as horse racing and cockfighting. Dominican sports historian Tirso Valdez claimed that baseball was a vital part of community life. "Through [baseball] the village experiences moments of happiness, when its team realizes its desires and wins, or passing moments of dejection if a defeat becomes a rout . . . but above all, the village experiences the hope that always prevails in baseball of coming from behind or winning the next game."[28] The passion in the hearts of the Latins for this adopted sport was apparent during the early years of the twentieth century and grew in subsequent decades.

Baseball, in fact, was underscored by its popularity even in moments of revolutionary crisis. In August 1933, for example, during a revolt against the Cuban tyrant Gerardo Machado, the island lost communication with the outside world for a week. When contact was restored, the *San Juan El Mundo,* the country's leading newspaper, wanted to know, above all else, the American baseball scores of the previous week. The *Sporting News* reasoned that "cutting [the Cubans] off from the scores was like sitting them down in a desert." In fact, "they were as happy to hear how the ball games came out as they were in the restoration of peace in their country."[29] In later years, when Fidel Castro conducted his own revolution from the mountains of Cuba, he listened regularly to Spanish-speaking baseball announcer Buck Canel broadcast the 1958 World Series. Shortly thereafter, when Canel tried to interview Castro about the revolution, the Cuban leader wanted to know "why [Milwaukee Braves manager Fred] Haney pitched [Warren] Spahn instead of [Lou] Burdette in the sixth game [of the World Series]."[30] In the Dominican Republic, during the unstable period following the 1961 assassination of Rafael Trujillo, an armed rebel cornered an American journalist to learn how Juan Marichal had fared in the recent All-Star Game.[31] Baseball's hold on Dominicans was such that some claimed "there will never be any political trouble during the . . . season, only afterwards."[32]

Fueling this excitement about baseball were the regular visits made by major league teams to the Caribbean to compete against Latin all-star teams.[33] Between 1890 and 1911, the Cincinnati Reds, Detroit Tigers, New York Giants, Philadelphia Athletics, and Philadelphia Phillies visited the islands but did not always leave unscathed. American League president Ban Johnson, in 1911, however, temporarily halted the Caribbean barnstorming trips after several Cuban clubs defeated their American counterparts. "We want no makeshift club calling themselves the Athletics to go to Cuba to be beaten by colored teams," he remarked.[34] National League teams, however, continued to march into the Caribbean. The 1936 Cincinnati Reds faced formidable competition in a Dominican all-star squad before finally winning 4-2.[35] However, when the Reds traveled to Puerto Rico that year to face the Cuban Almendares squad, Cincinnati lost. The front-page story in Puerto Rico's leading newspaper the next day was the defeat of the American team.[36] For their part, Latins viewed their passion for the game as not solely based on financial gain, but as a labor of love, whereas "the Yankee baseball players came . . . always for speculation, since they do not understand baseball in any other way."[37]

Unlike in the Caribbean, baseball's beginnings in Mexico were not grounded on the notion of humiliating the imperialists. Nor were Americans directly responsible for introducing baseball into the country. In the Yucatán Peninsula, for instance, evidence suggests that Cuban workers introduced the sport as early as the 1860s.[38] If this is true, it is hard to fathom that the game was readily understood by any of the participants, as the Cubans themselves had only just been introduced to it. Baseball, nonetheless, subsequently captured the interest of those in the working- and middle-class communities. There, "boys in their early teens," claimed the historian Gilbert M. Joseph, "spilled into the plazuelas of Santiago and San Juan near the center of Mérida and played ball well into the evening." But baseball during the 1880s and 1890s also grew to be the sport of the elite, for it "fit nicely into the oligarch's roseate turn-of-the-century vision of a grandeur, more modern Yucatán founded upon the virtues of physical vigor and competition."[39] El Sporting Club, a team of young men who learned the game while attending schools in the United States, was the most competitive in the region. Games in which they participated "ranked among Mérida's important social events."[40]

Interestingly, baseball also gained great prominence as a political tool during Mexico's 1910 revolution. Carrillo Puerto, the region's socialist leader, encouraged baseball activities because it "seemed singularly appropriate to the social transition that the [revolutionary] party would carry out in the Yucatán."[41] Joseph argues that, as Puerto's followers saw it, "the individual [in a baseball game] was only part of a larger entity, whose success depended upon the transformation of individualism into collective conscience."[42] Though Puerto's "New Yucatán" did not entirely come to pass, baseball survived, and there, amidst the ghosts of the old Mayan deities, diamonds graced the land. Ironically, and perhaps justifiably, almost a century after baseball took hold of the Yucatán region, Mexico's greatest sports product, Fernando Valenzuela, donned the uniform of the Mérida Leones on the eve of his move into the U.S. professional ranks and almost immediate stardom.

In the northern and central flanks of Mexico, baseball's entry came in a more traditional manner—American influence. Made convenient by what William H. Beezley called "The Porfirian Persuasion," baseball appeared when "Mexicans saw their country zooming into modernization, hence they rushed to adopt the styles, attitudes, and amusements of other modernized western nations."[43] Though records indicate that citizens of Mexico City did not see their first baseball game until the early 1880s, new American arrivals, baseball fans undoubtedly among them, manufactured a tale in which Abner Doubleday, who served as an American officer in the war with Mexico, promoted his game to troops stationed at the old Aztec capital. That an Illinois volunteer used Antonio López de Santa Anna's captured wooden leg for a baseball bat made the story even more outrageous.[44]

Realistically, a combination of factors led to baseball's emergence in the areas beyond the Yucatán: the Mexican elite's familiarity with cricket, previously introduced by the British; the daily contact between Mexican industrial and railway workers and their American counterparts, particularly in Mexico's northern frontier cities like Monterrey and Chihuahua; and Mexican intrigue with all aspects of modernization, a direct result of the positivist ideology during the Porfiriato that emphasized order and progress.

As the game developed throughout the countryside, amateur and semiprofessional leagues formed. In 1906 El Record, Mexico's most popular club, played a Chicago White Sox team that had come to Mexico City for training and added revenues. Though the Americans easily won, Mexican baseball continued to grow. Following the revolutionary period, teams reestablished league play. The Mexican Baseball League, formed in 1925, was the most prominent of these institutions.[45] Mexican baseball, in subsequent years, blossomed and, as a result, came to threaten the more established American big leagues.

Despite the popular notion that baseball in North America greatly predated its spread elsewhere, Latins were playing baseball less than twenty years after Alexander Joy Cartwright established its basic rules in 1845. Cuba's first professional league began operations only two years after the 1876 inauguration of the National League in the United States. And by the 1880s, baseball was nearly twenty years old in Mexico's Yucatán Peninsula. Indeed, even the distant Japanese were playing the game before the end of the 1880s. Clearly, the roots of baseball in the United States were not much deeper than where it was later adopted. One might presume that ballplayers whose countries were so close to the United States, and whose people were "stark raving dottily crazy over baseball," might warrant attention from the American professional clubs. Ironically, American capitalists paid little attention to the notion of incorporating Latins into American professional baseball. Consequently, by the end of 1910 the presence of Latins in the big leagues was sparse.

Notes

1. Stein, "Soccer," 64–65.
2. Burns, *Poverty of Progress,* 18.
3. Stein, "Soccer," 65.
4. Burns, *Poverty of Progress,* 18.
5. Arbena, "Sport," 3.
6. LaFeber, *Panama Canal,* 14.
7. Ruck, "Baseball in the Caribbean," 605.
8. Luis Hernández cited in Wagner, "Sport in Revolutionary Societies," 118.
9. Ruck, "Baseball in the Caribbean," 605. There are discrepancies in reports of the date of the first organized baseball game between Cuban teams. For another estimation, see Brown, "Cuban Baseball," 110.
10. *Troy (New York) Daily Whig,* Mar. 24, 1871.
11. Ibid.
12. Letter by José Jimenez on Esteban Bellán, Bellán file, National Baseball Library, Cooperstown, N.Y.
13. Rogosin, *Invisible Men,* 152.
14. Ibid.
15. Brown, "Cuban Baseball," 110; Ruck, "Baseball in the Caribbean," 605.
16. Torres, *La historia,* 7. Torres has compiled an impressive list of statistics that dates back to the beginning of the leagues.
17. Phelon, "Baseball in Cuba," 33.
18. Dozer, *Are We Good Neighbors?* 1.
19. Carrion, *Puerto Rico,* 139.
20. Suchlicki, *Cuba,* 84.
21. Wagenheim, *Clemente!* 9.
22. Ruck, "Baseball in the Caribbean," 605–6.
23. Ruck, *Tropic of Baseball,* 9.
24. Ibid., 24.
25. Ibid., 25.
26. Klein, *Sugarball,* 17, 19–20.
27. Ibid., 27.
28. Cantwell, "Invasion from Santo Domingo," 59.
29. *Sporting News,* Aug. 17, 1933.
30. Boyle, "'El As,'" 34.
31. Boyle, "The Latins Storm," 24.
32. Ruck, *Tropic of Baseball,* 32.

33. In 1915, while Cuban teams routinely faced American black clubs, the Havana Reds reportedly visited Florida that spring to play the Chicago Cubs and the Philadelphia Athletics. Results of those contests were not reported.

34. Oleksak and Oleksak, *Béisbol,* 22.

35. Cantwell, "Invasion from Santo Domingo," 58.

36. *San Juan (Puerto Rico) El Mundo,* Mar. 2, 1936.

37. Rogosin, *Invisible Men,* 153.

38. Joseph, "Forging the Regional Pastime," 33.

39. Ibid., 34–35.

40. Ibid., 35.

41. Ibid., 49.

42. Ibid.

43. Beezley, "The Rise of Baseball," 6.

44. Ibid.

45. Ibid., 10–11.

• 3

Béisbol in El Norte

They're trash, they're doing no good and they aren't in place here. They don't fit. If I have to put up with incompetents, they must at least speak English.

Bucky Harris

*O*nly Luis Castro followed Esteban Bellán as a Latin representative in the big leagues prior to 1911. The Colombian, who played for the Philadelphia Athletics in 1902 was not recruited from his country, however. Like Bellán years earlier, Castro attended school in the United States. At Manhattan College in New York he pitched three years for the school team. Born to a prominent family from which a relative, Cipriano Castro, presided as president of neighboring Venezuela, Luis Castro's membership on the Athletics did not trumpet a call to search for more Latin players. Castro's tenure in the big leagues was uneventful, and he served Connie Mack only the one season as a utility player "for which position he was eminently fitted."[1]

Nonetheless, as interaction between American and Latin professionals increased, major league clubs gradually expressed interest in Latin players. Some American sportswriters also admired Latin talent. Impressed with what he called "natural born artists" of the diamond, journalist Revere Rodgers envisioned the expansion of baseball's recruitment efforts into Latin America.[2] Within a few short years, unfolding events lent credibility to his insight.

In 1911 the Cincinnati Reds signed two Cuban players, Rafael Almeida from Havana and Armando Marsans from Mantanzas, the latter who also served as Almeida's interpreter. They were the first Latin Americans of any prominence to break into the major leagues during the modern era. Prior to this, both players had reportedly spent some time in the United States touring as members of the Cuban Stars, a club that competed primarily against black teams.[3] The lighter complexion of these Cubans, however, enabled them to pursue professional careers with teams in the white leagues. Almeida, in addition, was apparently a person of means who, at the outset of his tenure with New Britain's club in the Connecticut League, complained that the hotel facilities did not meet with his standards.[4] Initially considered the more talented of the two, Almeida played only sparingly during his two-year tenure with Cincinnati. Marsans, however, turned out to be the better overall player and competed in the big leagues for eight years. He was also the first Latin player involved in a controversy in the U.S. professional leagues. In 1913 he left the Reds to play for St. Louis in the new Federal League. The Cuban described this move as "his inherent right"; after complicated court proceedings freed him from his Cincinnati contract, he joined the St. Louis team.[5]

Marsans was temperamental as well as independent. Perhaps as an omen of future relations between some Latins and the press, Marsans chided New York sportswriters, who "know nothing of baseball; they aren't even in the kindergarten class." At another time he believed the sportswriters "always thought it funny to poke jokes at me."[6] The *Sporting News* reported that "Marsans did not take authority too well and was apt to respond 'go to hell.' All one had to do is agree with him."[7] Indeed, when Marsans left Cincinnati, the paper speculated that he had done so because he "could not get along with manager [Charles] Herzog."[8] But not all agreed with the *Sporting News*'s assessment of the Cuban's character. In 1914, sportswriter Hugh C. Weir described Marsans as "one of the best liked players of the major leagues. He has maintained a clean, untarnished record both as a player and as a gentleman."[9]

Marsans was one of the outstanding players of his time. Daring baserunning and strong defensive play were his trademarks. During Marsans's tenure at Louisville, the *Sporting News* observed that "so new and startling have been the Cuban's stints along the basepaths that comparatively few of the folks hereabouts have yet come to an appreciation" of them. The paper lauded Marsans for his hustle and his ability to stretch singles to doubles and triples. It also pointed out that "many of the spectators . . . withhold from the señor the credit due him and ascribe it to bone-domed base running, blessed with luck." Marsans, claimed the weekly, was not appreciated; fans unaccustomed to his style "think the Cuban must be a bone-head or a nut."[10]

In later years, when other Latins exhibited Marsans's aggressiveness and hustle, the label "hot dog" replaced "bone-head."

In Cuba, however, Marsans's achievements were viewed quite differently. Impressed with their countryman's .317 batting average while playing for Cincinnati in 1912, the city council in Havana bestowed a $200 gold medal on him and pronounced Marsans, a star with the Almendares ball club during the winter seasons, Cuba's "greatest player."[11] The following season Marsans again exhibited his skills with a bat when he averaged .297 for the Reds.

Marsans's success stimulated further interest in Cuban players. The *New York Tribune* acknowledged Latin talent when it reported that "the [Cuban] republic has become recognized as a new drafting field for promising players."[12] In 1912 the Boston Braves signed Cuban catcher Miguel "Mike" González. Although González played with the Braves for only one game, he returned to the big leagues with the Cincinnati Reds in 1914 and stayed in the majors with various clubs until 1932. Used mostly as a backup catcher, he was strongest with the bat in 1924, when he hit for a .296 average. The Cuban was well-liked by his contemporaries and he remained affiliated with the St. Louis Cardinals as a coach—the first Latin to do so—from 1934 to 1946. Though at times he playfully referred to himself as a "smart dummy," González's baseball prowess was well known by his peers. His deep knowledge of the game impressed observers to the point that J. G. Taylor Spink, in his *Sporting News* column, once wrote of the Cuban that "the players and newspapermen who have come in contact with him, know that he is one of the smartest hombres ever to trod a diamond."[13] During this time, González became the first Latin to manage a big league club when the Cardinals chose him to run their team for seventeen games in 1938 and six games in 1940.

More highly skilled, but far less congenial, was González's countryman from Havana—Adolfo Luque. Luque was the most talented of the early Cuban players to perform in the major leagues. Gifted with a superb curveball, the right-handed pitcher spent twenty years in the big leagues. From 1914 to 1935, he compiled a record of 194-179, in addition to one World Series victory with the New York Giants. Known as the Pride of Havana, Luque shone in 1923 when, as a member of the Cincinnati Reds, he led the National League with a 27-8 record and a 1.93 earned run average. Two years later, he again took the crown. A fine athlete, Luque also became the first Latin to have played in both the National and American Leagues. Later, his baseball instincts contributed to a successful career as

Viva Baseball!

a manager in the winter leagues in Cuba. Luque was so impressive that the *Sporting News* referred to him as "Cuba's greatest gift to our national game."[14]

He also gained a reputation for his violent temper. A known beanball artist, he once "tried to take on the entire Giant team with a bat after they jeered him."[15] After his opponents baited him most of the game, Luque

Adolfo Luque. (Courtesy of the National Baseball Hall of Fame Library, Cooperstown, N.Y.)

lost his patience. Reportedly, the Cuban pitcher "calmly stood on the mound, took off his glove, placed the ball in it and put both on the ground. He then walked straight toward the Giant dugout and, without hesitation, walked right in and belted Casey Stengel in the face." Stengel reportedly had been an innocent bystander.[16] Because Luque was clearly not the darling of the press corps, this story may have been sensationalized. Indeed, even some Cuban sportswriters cared little for him. Pepe Conte, a journalist for Havana's *La Noche* who apparently had crossed swords with the pitcher, wrote in a letter to general manager Gary Herrmann of the Cincinnati Reds that Luque was "the most illiterate man [in] captivity." Conte also claimed that "outside his ability to pitch [Luque] was a most perfect jack-ass." The Latin newspaperman then challenged Herrmann to verify his assessment of Luque's character by checking with other Cuban sports journalists.[17] Though there exists no evidence that Herrmann ever followed up on Conte's suggestion, perceptions of Luque's character—hot temperament, ignorance, and lack of congeniality—continued to appear in press reports throughout the pitcher's career.

Adolfo Luque in many ways personified the negative images of Latins held by many in the United States. His reported behavior in the Stengel incident, Peter Bjarkman argues, "suddenly and predictably played a most unfortunate role in fueling the stereotype that has since dogged his career" and those of other Latins.[18] Beyond the baseball diamonds, many mainstream Americans saw Latins as a lazy, passive, and inferior lot.[19] Moreover, nativists downplayed the notion that Latins could ever be bona fide Americans. As early as 1913, the *Los Angeles Times,* caught up in an imaginary subversive plot, even claimed a large percentage of that city's Mexican population was "known by the police to be rabid sympathizers of the outlaw [Pancho] Villa."[20]

In baseball, Latins' supposed athletic shortcomings were often exaggerated. Much of this stemmed from a phrase Mike González used while on a scouting trip in Cuba for New York Giants manager John McGraw; often assessing a prospect, he wired back a brief evaluation that has become a classic in baseball lore: "Good field, no hit."[21] From that point on, González's phrase became a baseball cliché virtually synonymous with Latin players.

But during the pre-integration period, infielder Melo Almada poked holes in this characterization. Boston manager Joe Cronin once touted

Almada, the first Mexican to play in the big leagues, as "a grand defensive ball player. . . . He covers a lot of ground, recovers a ball like a cat, and can throw."[22] An investigation of the sports coverage throughout his early career, however, revealed that not all aspects of his game were profiled. Indeed, not until three years after he joined the major leagues did the *Brooklyn Eagle* remind baseball followers that as a member of the Red Sox Alameda had carried a .291 batting average.[23] Moreover, in 1938 he batted for a .311 average during the 149 games he played. Overall, he played seven years in the major leagues and ended his career with a respectable .284 average.

Sports reporting, of course, was greatly responsible for both the images and the oversights. During the 1920s, for instance, public interest in sports and sports personalities grew to enormous proportions. A reporter from the *Dallas News* observed that the 1920 World Series overshadowed that year's presidential campaign.[24] Sports news, to be sure, captivated millions of readers, who followed their heroes closely. And sportswriters, in turn, often sensationalized players' feats. In some instances fans enjoyed myths more than reality.[25] This "creative" sportswriting usually resulted in "on-the-spot immortality" for players.[26] It also produced lasting images of Latin players for readers—images that, while entertaining, were often uncomplimentary. One of the most prevalent and negative of these stereotypes focused on Latins' inability to communicate clearly.

The press created a comical image of Adolfo Luque's broken English. In the 1933 World Series when manager Bill Terry approached Luque, known as "Pops," during a tense moment, a writer reported their exchange in the following manner: "'Pops,' Terry said to Luque, 'if you get this guy we win the Series. You've got two strikes on him. Can you get him?' Luque responded, 'Beel, you leeson to Poppa. I see you in the clawhouse queek!' Then after the strikeout was recorded, Luque ran to the clubhouse yelling, 'I feexed heem! I feexed heem! I geev heem Numbaire Two.'"[27]

In another instance, the *Sporting News* reported a conversation between Mike González and a hotel clerk when the Cuban attempted to order sauerkraut juice. The conversation in print made González appear stupid: "'Sakaraka juice, sakaraka juice,' Mike bellowed again and again until finally the Cuban slammed down the receiver in disgust. 'Damphool down there . . . ,' Mike finally sputtered. 'I keep tolding her sakaraka juice, sakaraka juice, but no understand English.'"[28]

In 1939, when Alejandro "Alex" Carrasquel arrived at the Washington Senators' spring training camp in Orlando, Florida, Roberto Estalella's description of him was printed phonetically: "Alexander—ooo—gude peetcher. Ver-ry, ver-ry gude. He peetch curve hokay. Yes fast ball, too. Beeg fellow. Strong, smart. Best peetcher in Cuba. I play with heem. He strike out Bobby. Ees gude peetcher, sure."[29] Critics, in fact, chided Carrasquel for not making any effort to learn English. However, he responded—in Spanish—that his inability to understand English shielded him from insulting fans and reporters.[30]

Some Latin players who neither spoke nor understood English clearly were the victims of cruel jokes at times. In one instance, Rafael Almeida, having become fond of a young American woman, sought instruction from his teammates as to the proper form of address. Confident of his newfound bilingual skills, Almeida reportedly presented her with flowers and said, "It geeve me gr-rate plassure to present you weeth these blossoms, and I only weesh I could poonch you in the face to show how mooch I esteem you."[31] Such incidents did little to endear Americans to prideful Latin players.

Uncomfortable episodes aside, the pool of Latins entering the majors continued to grow. By 1930, twenty Latins had competed as big leaguers.[32] And Joe Cambria, a scout for the Washington Senators, did much to facilitate the further flow of Latin talent to the United States. "Papa Joe," as he was affectionately known in Cuba, was one of the most popular baseball figures on the island from the 1930s to the early 1960s. It was Cambria who provided the impetus for the first major wave of Latins to enter American professional baseball.

Cambria's baseball background began in 1930. The owner of a Baltimore laundry, he invested in a semiprofessional club and later purchased the Albany franchise of the International League. Through this venture Cambria met and became friends with Clark Griffith, owner of the Washington Senators. Years later Griffith's son, Calvin, who dubbed his father a "baseball fanatic," recalled that "Cambria could get anything he wanted from Clark Griffith, money-wise."[33] Because of Cambria's limited knowledge of the baseball business, however, he sometimes got into trouble with commissioner Kenesaw Mountain Landis. At one point, Landis fined Cambria $1,000 for postdating a rookie's contract.[34] Yet, each time Griffith rescued Cambria from Landis's wrath.[35] In 1932, Griffith hired the former laundry owner as a scout.

For the next few years Cambria scouted at random in the lowest, most obscure leagues in the United States. While most of the players Cambria discovered at this time were mediocre, two of them, George Case and Mickey Vernon, had long and respectable careers in the major leagues. Vernon, in fact, won the 1946 American League batting championship. Cambria realized early on, however, that he could not expect to find good players where more talented scouts searched. In addition, Griffith did not equip the inexperienced Cambria with bonus money. Hence, the former laundry owner searched for a region other scouts had previously ignored. He found his gold mine in Cuba.

Cambria saw a chance to provide the Senators with good young players. Furthermore, Griffith did not disdain Cubans. While at Cincinnati, Griffith himself had signed Rafael Almeida and Armando Marsans. In Cuba, a host of athletes from families with a low standard of living were anxious for opportunities to enhance their situations. For Cambria and Griffith, the chemistry appeared perfect—good players at a cheap price.

Cambria was forced to rely on his sales ability to draw players. Ray Fitzgerald of the *Sporting News* described Cambria's tactics: "Bonus? Big money promises? Uh-uh. Cambria's carrot was the fame and glory that would come from playing beisbol in the big leagues."[36] Between 1939 and 1947, Cambria lured nineteen Cubans to the United States. After Jackie Robinson shattered baseball's color barrier, "Papa Joe" eventually signed nearly 400 Latins. So popular did Cambria become in Cuba that a cigar was named in his honor.[37]

In 1935, Cambria's first significant Cuban discovery, Roberto Estalella, a stocky third baseman, made his debut. As was the case with many other Latins who followed, Estalella's contract was good only if he made the club. Cambria paid for his transportation to the United States, a mere seventy-five dollars.[38] Estalella so impressed the Senators that they offered him a contract and instructed him to join their affiliates at Albany, New York, and Harrisburg, Pennsylvania, for more work. Described as having a "great arm," Estalella was brought up for the last fifteen games of the 1935 season.[39]

Cubans considered Estalella's debut important because with Adolfo Luque's retirement there were no other Cubans in the big leagues. When Estalella joined the Senators, Cuba's ambassador to the United States attended the game to congratulate the infielder and wish him success.[40] During the season's remaining fifteen games, Estalella played good defense and batted .313.

Estalella gained instant popularity with Senators fans thanks to his impressive start. Supporters also viewed him as a welcome change from the usual mediocrity of the Senators. His celebrity prompted a number of them to call Griffith Stadium prior to the games to inquire if the Cuban was playing.[41] But Estalella was not popular with many opposing players for reasons other than his baseball prowess. Resentment of Latin players apparently had been growing since the arrival of Almeida and Marsans. As Shirley Povich pointed out in 1936, established pitchers were sorely tempted "to aim their pitches at the heads of the islanders who are so bold as to attempt to insinuate themselves into the great American game." Povich also suggested that some pitchers were racially motivated when they aimed at "the swarthy ones like Estalella. . . . Bobby's skin pigments betray the fact that he is not an American, and his broken English is just a bit too smattery."[42] According to another writer, some white players were of the "peculiar big league mold which is almost psychopathically opposed to Roberto and his coffee colored colleagues."[43]

The attitudes toward Estalella and other Latins betrayed a deep American problem: racial nativism. Powerful in earlier decades, this xenophobia was well-endowed as both an ideology and an institution by the time Latins joined the big leagues. "It was the task of the racethinkers," claimed John Higham of the late nineteenth-century nativists, "to organize specific antipathies toward dark-hued peoples into a generalized, ideological structure."[44] Ingrained with the concepts of racial supremacy during the age of social Darwinism, nativists proposed a series of immigration quotas, laws, and literacy tests, some of which were successfully implemented from the 1880s to the 1930s. Within that time, books such as John Rodgers Commons's *Race and Immigrants in America* (1907) and Madison Grant's *The Passing of the Great Race* (1916) spewed claims that non-Nordic people posed the greatest threat to American civilization and culture.

Racial nativism was loudest during periods of economic depression. Hard times during the late 1870s fed into the anti-Asian bigotry of unemployed workers in California. This combination led to the Chinese Exclusion Act of 1882. Other like-minded programs followed into the twentieth century. Five years prior to Estalella's debut, Congress, concerned about overburdened welfare rolls, instituted a plan that led to the repatriation of both Mexican nationals and some Americans of Mexican descent. Nearly a half million people were eventually sent to Mexico during the 1930s.[45] American xenophobia extended to other Latins as well. Puerto Rican laborers, who were American citizens, faced domestic barriers. A prominent member of the Los Angeles Chamber of Commerce, for instance, trying to de-

cide whether Mexican or Puerto Rican workers should be allowed to enter the county, asked his colleagues if they preferred "the man who had
no idea of becoming a citizen or a menace."[46]

The Great Depression intensified animosities. By 1934 some 69 percent
of the black working population in Allegheny County, Pennsylvania, for
example, was out of work.[47] Although the major leagues were still closed
to African Americans, white players, nonetheless, grew concerned about
the competition they faced for jobs. Driven by the fear of unemployment,
racial nativism sprouted among American big leaguers. Players, of course,
commonly hid their injuries and lied about their ages. With veterans ex-
tending their careers, opportunities for newcomers were few and far between. Some, in order to stay on rosters, accepted pay cuts.[48] These conditions, however, also provided the classic ingredients for xenophobic
attitudes in America's pastime.

Because Americans were perpetually concerned about mythical invasions,
the appearance of more than a few "foreign" surnames on a roster was
tantamount to a takeover. Baseball historian David Q. Voigt revealed the
apprehension of one journalist who feared an Italian assault since they
"take to baseball quicker than they take to spaghetti. These Tonies walk
right into baseball."[49] Misgivings toward Latins, known to play for cheaper
wages, also surfaced. Indeed, the animus directed at Latin players had
precedents in baseball.

In 1911, for instance, public clamor pressured the Cincinnati Reds to
provide affidavits as proof that only "Caucasian blood" flowed through
the veins of Rafael Almeida and Armando Marsans.[50] Once this was done,
the local media promoted the Cubans as "two of the purest bars of Castil-
lian soap ever floated to these shores."[51] Suspicions, nonetheless, circulated and simple scuttlebutt led to exaggerated stories about players' backgrounds. Some journalists, for instance, suspected Mike González of having
"Negro blood." The evidence? A Cuban player had told Willie Wells, a
star of the American black leagues, that González's "momma was black."[52]
In other circles, nativists never regarded any Latin as white. One sportswriter, in his profile on Adolfo Luque, "wanted to know how a lad of an
alien race had come to be such a whale of a pitcher."[53]

Most racial controversies during the late 1930s and into the 1940s centered on the Washington Senators, a team that employed a good number
of Latins during the slightly overstated "Latin Era." On the Senators, reported the *Pittsburgh Courier,* "The Cuban [player] has been regarded as
an unsolid horse by his batwaving brethren. He is supposed to be deficient
in the vicinity of the gizzard and prone to collapse in the pinches and his

high-pitched Latin laughter rubs the average ex-ploughboy the wrong way."[54]

The paper also exposed the misgivings manager Bucky Harris held toward his Latin players. "Why don't that Cambria get me some American boys?" exploded the field boss when he learned that in 1939 "Papa Joe" had signed Roberto Ortiz. "Why does he insist on trifling around in Cuba?"[55] Later, he vehemently denounced Latin players: "They're trash. They're doing no good and they aren't in place here. They don't fit. If I have to put up with incompetents, they must at least speak English."[56] Perhaps encouraged by Harris's sentiments, the rumor mill circulated a story in 1940 that a group of American players delivered a severe beating to a Cuban teammate. In their eyes, he had "forgotten his place."[57] Though no hard proof ever emerged that the incident had taken place, stories such as these suggested the discomfort between Latin and white players.

Joe Cambria, however, tenaciously continued to scout Latin players. And the Washington Senators, in spite of Harris's misgivings, continued to employ them. Roberto Estalella, a Cambria success story, eventually played nine full years in the major leagues and finished with a career batting average of .282. Other Cambria signees such as Roberto Ortiz, a 6'4", two-hundred-pound outfielder, and pitcher René Monteagudo also spent time in the big leagues.

In 1939 Cambria brought a Venezuelan pitcher named Alejandro "Alex" Carrasquel to the Senators. Carrasquel, whom Cambria discovered in his headquarters at Havana, was the first South American to play for any extended length of time in the majors.[58] Carrasquel debuted against the New York Yankees, who had loaded the bases and brought Joe DiMaggio to bat. As the Yankee Clipper approached the plate, catcher Tony Guiliani, who spoke Spanish, raced to the mound to remind the rookie pitcher of DiMaggio's fame. Carrasquel responded to his shocked teammate that he never before had heard of this opponent and proceeded to get the Yankee slugger to pop up to end the inning.[59] Although Carrasquel compiled a disappointing 5-9 record that year, the Senators knew he had potential.

Carrasquel joined a hapless Senators team beset with negative racial attitudes toward its Latin players. Even clubhouse attendants openly grumbled when Carrasquel and other Latins desired routine services. Columnist Shirley Povich uncharacteristically reinforced a Latin stereotype when he wrote that "Alex isn't exactly a handsome guy . . . he looked like a guy off a Spanish galleon who wouldn't be out of character climbing up the side of a pirate ship with a knife in his teeth." Not until 1943, when teammates deemed him to be assimilated, did Carrasquel finally receive courteous treatment.[60] But a fair shake for Latins was always tenuous, as a posthumous story on Carrasquel indicates. In 1969, the *Sporting News* remarked that Carrasquel's "career in the big time was hardly sensational."[61]

Carrasquel also came under fire for his moodiness. Unlike some earlier Latins with noticeable tempers, such as Armando Marsans and Adolfo Luque, Carrasquel was thought to exhibit his disenchantment through lackluster performances. According to Washington manager Ossie Bleuge, "When Alex thought he was being overworked, he was pretty useless. He'd go out there and pitch like he was trying to prove he was overworked."[62] Another manager, Bucky Harris, was confused about Carrasquel; he claimed he never knew "whether he's going to hit a home run or pitch one."[63] Carrasquel, however, was not lazy. He once offered to pitch the back end of a doubleheader after throwing a four-hitter in a losing cause in the opener.[64] He also completed nearly half of the sixty-four games he started in the major leagues.

In an effort to gain acceptance, he briefly tried to Americanize himself by changing his name to Alex Alexandra. In 1944, the Senators named Carrasquel as their "official interpreter." This act, according to Daniel C. Frio and Marc Onigman, "was the first attempt by the Washington management to assimilate the Latin players into the mainstream of the club."[65] Carrasquel eventually spent eight years in the big leagues, was 50-39 lifetime, and had a losing record only in his rookie season.

During Carrasquel's career and into the war years of the mid-1940s, Latin players made their greatest inroads. Professional baseball, considered to be a "nonessential industry" by the government, was hit hard by the military draft. Over a thousand major league players eventually joined the service; this loss of talent took a toll on the standard of play. Owners scrambled to maintain rosters by carrying many players considered unfit for military duty. In the last years of the war, the St. Louis Browns even employed a one-armed outfielder named Pete Gray. Desperate for talent, some owners signed players too young to be drafted, including the fifteen-year-old Joe Nuxhall, who played for the Cincinnati Reds.

As a result of the vacuum created by American players on war leave, Clark Griffith encouraged Joe Cambria to increase his recruiting efforts in Latin America. Although many of these countries joined the allies and contributed mightily with raw materials and land bases, those most associated with baseball did not institute a draft. Between the years 1942 and 1945, sixteen players from Latin countries debuted in the major leagues. Of these, seven Cubans donned the uniform of the Senators. Many of them, however, spent a brief time in the big leagues, including infielder Preston Gómez, who played in only eight contests in 1944. Twenty-five years later, Gómez returned to the big leagues as the second Latin-born field manager.

The drive to expand large-scale recruitment efforts into Latin America, however, never fully developed in this period for two reasons: the end of the war and the creation of a rival league in Mexico. As returning veterans regained their positions in the big leagues, opportunities for Latin players dwindled. Also, American club owners saw the emergence of Jorge Pasquel's Mexican League in 1946 as a threat. Big league operators grew angry as Pasquel tantalized and, in some cases, succeeded in recruiting big league talent. In an effort to undermine his maverick league, the owners blacklisted the Cuban winter league and offered to lift the ban only in exchange for exclusive loyalty to the American leagues.[66] This in effect stifled the chances for those Cubans who participated in the winter league from advancing into the majors. Indeed, the ban, along with fewer jobs, seriously impeded Latins hopeful of making a big league roster. While twenty-two Latins debuted between 1940 and 1945, only five entered the big leagues for the remainder of the decade. Luis Orlando Rodriguez, Cuba's national director of sports, bristled at this development: "We in Cuba feel that baseball was perfectly willing to use over 100 Cuban players during the war, when there was a manpower shortage, but now that the war is over they are through with us." Barriers notwithstanding, Joe Cambria continued to search for Latin talent. It was his good fortune that these barriers were shattered by the late forties.

Until 1947, big league segregation of American blacks had also prevented the recruitment of Latin blacks. Former American black league and major league great Monte Irvin pointed out that "you could have all the ability in the world as a Latin playing in Puerto Rico, Venezuela, Santo Domingo, or Panama, but you could not play [in the major leagues]. So as a [Latin]

black you were in the same situation as a American black."[67] Baseball's
unwritten rule of barring blacks gained great notoriety sixty years earlier
when Constantine "Cap" Anson successfully prevented George Stovey, a
heralded black pitcher for the Newark club, from competing against his
Chicago White Stockings.[68] Several teams during this era began to omit
African Americans from their rosters. Talented black players, such as Moses
Fleetwood Walker and Frank Grant, were repeatedly frustrated in their
attempts to compete against white teams. A letter that Weldy Walker, brother of Moses, wrote to Tri-State League president George McDermott, when
that league barred blacks, summed up the feelings of many black players:
"The rule you have passed is a public disgrace."[69]

Segregation had become the order of the day in the United States. Reconstruction period "black codes" and other regional ordinances in the
South quelled any hope of equality. In industry, union members commonly blocked black membership. In agriculture, ever-growing farmer's alli-
ances and subsequent Populist party affiliates allowed African American
farmers to participate—in a separate group. And in public facilities, such
as hotels, saloons, and transportation, blacks were barred. By the late nineteenth century, rigid segregation—"Jim Crow" as it came to be known—
grew as segregationists gained federal mandates to ensure white superior-
ity. The Supreme Court's 1896 decision in *Plessy v. Ferguson* sanctioned
"separate but equal" accommodations.

Ironically, the first Latin player to compete in the big leagues, Esteban
Bellán, was reportedly of African descent.[70] However, he played well before baseball imposed its segregated standards. At home, Bellán never encountered racial discrimination. In Cuba, as in most of Latin America,
baseball remained integrated. During the off-season white players from the
United States who desired to play professionally in Latin America competed with and against blacks. While American players considered Cuban
white players the most talented, Cuban fans held them in no higher regard
than their black counterparts. In the Latin American professional leagues,
baseball truly was a democratic sport. Ability, not skin color, measured
success.

As American racial mores came to influence the thinking of Cuban baseball aficionados, some did not wish to see black and white players compete in the same leagues. Some white Cubans believed that having integrated teams hindered opportunities for professional play in the United
States. One American writer confirmed that "the black players are A-1
performers, but block the path of the Cuban teams to full recognition and

a proper welcome in the United States."[71] Another journalist visiting Cuba added that "the white Cubans . . . are a proud sort of people, who can show pedigrees of purest Spanish strain, and negro [bloodlines are] regarded with the same sentiment as in the United States."[72]

Black Cuban ballplayers were highly talented and competitive. They often upstaged American big leaguers who competed in Cuba. These Cuban players were so popular that a good portion demanded higher salaries. One frustrated Cuban owner lamented, "I wish that some big league team would whip us ten straight games. That would reduce the heads of the black players, make them listen to reason, and also give a better chance for white men to succeed them on local teams."[73] Color did not taint Babe Ruth's opinion of two of Cuba's greatest stars when the American slugger played against them during the 1921–22 winter. In that series, Cristóbal Torrienti hit three home runs to the Ruth's one. In addition, José Méndez struck out the mighty Ruth three times. Later the Bambino simply commented, "Tell Torrienti and Méndez that if they could play with me in the major leagues, we would win the pennant in July, and go fishing for the rest of the season."[74]

José Méndez, known as the "Black Diamond," was Cuba's most popular player during the first two decades of the twentieth century.[75] Armed with a blazing fastball, Méndez victimized not only Ruth but other American stars as well. Pitchers Eddie Plank and Christy Mathewson both lost to Méndez on their visits to Cuba. New York Giants manager John McGraw, after watching Méndez pitch, placed his value at $50,000.[76] In 1908, when the Cincinnati Reds toured Cuba, Méndez threw a one-hit shutout against them.[77] One visiting American writer said that "Méndez is a big league pitcher, there is no doubt about it. He has the goods, and cinches his class by exhibitions of fielding and batting such as few American pitchers ever dream of giving." Impressed with Méndez, the writer added that the Cuban "is every bit as classy as Walter Johnson."[78] In 1908, Méndez accompanied the Cuban Stars on an exhibition tour against black squads across the United States. By the end of that year-long tour the hard-throwing Cuban compiled a record of forty-four wins and only two losses.[79] Méndez continued to play with the Cuban Stars and on teams in the American black leagues until 1926.[80]

Slugger Cristóbal Torrienti, like Méndez, played in the American black leagues. One American teammate of the Cuban recalled, "He hit a line drive in Indianapolis that hit the top of the right-field wall and [bounced back so quickly that] the right fielder threw him out at first base. That's how much power he had."[81] The New York Giants, at one point, considered signing the Cuban but decided against it because Torrienti had "kinky hair."[82] Torrienti, instead, played eighteen years in the American black leagues.

In 1920, when Rube Foster formed the first Negro National League, he eagerly incorporated Cuban players. Foster knew Cuban talent was economically feasible. The shrewd entrepreneur also realized that Latins had star players whose legendary talents meant enhanced ticket sales. Foster's assessments proved correct as players such as José Méndez, who played with the Kansas City Monarchs, and Cristóbal Torrienti gained popularity in black communities.[83]

Many contemporaries considered Martín Dihigo, another popular black Cuban, to be the best all-around ballplayer to emerge from that island during the segregationist period. His impressive performances in the United States led one American to claim that Dihigo's "gifts afield have not been approached by any one man, black or white." Slugger Buck Leonard called Dihigo simply the greatest ballplayer of all time.[84] His baseball prowess was so great that it earned him induction into four baseball halls of fame in the nations where he performed the most: Cuba, Mexico, the United States, and Venezuela.[85]

Dihigo's versatility as a ballplayer was extraordinary. In a highly publicized match in 1923, for instance, he outdueled Adolfo Luque, one of the finest pitchers in Cuba, 1-0. Three years later, Dihigo led the American Negro League in batting with a .386 average.[86] In 1938, he led the Mexican League not only in batting, with a .387 average, but also in pitching, with an 18-2 record, accompanied by an 0.90 earned run average.[87] Three years earlier, in the Negro East-West All-Star Game, he was the league's best center fielder and an all-star pitcher as well.[88] Martín Dihigo played in the black leagues from 1923 to 1945 and finished his career in Mexico during the 1950s.

Other Latin stars were barred because of color from the big leagues in the United States. Some, like Cuban pitcher Luis Tiant, played year-round in Cuba and the American black leagues. Tiant's experience with American discrimination, however, partly explains his attempt to discourage his son Luis Jr. from pursuing a professional career in the United States. Others, like Puerto Rican Perucho Cepeda, refused to play professional baseball in the United States to avoid potentially humiliating racial discrimination.[89] Cepeda's son Orlando gained fame as a big league star in later years.

By the middle 1940s Jim Crow barriers in baseball were weakening. A number of white sportswriters, such as Shirley Povich and Jimmy Powers, together with black reporters, such as Wendell Smith and Sam Lacy, focused on the advantages of integration. Black baseball prowess was obvious. Moreover, the drive toward integration in baseball was foreshadowed by the triumphs of heavyweight champion Joe Louis and Olympic track star Jesse Owens. In the thirties and early forties, these black athletes were viewed by both black and white Americans as national heroes.

Little by little pro-integration writers chipped away at baseball's color barrier. In 1941, Shirley Povich taunted, "There's a couple of million dollars worth of baseball talent on the loose ready for the big leagues, yet unsigned by any major leagues. Only one thing is keeping them out of the big leagues—the color of their skin."[90] In 1944, Bill Veeck, a maverick owner, attempted to purchase the floundering Philadelphia Phillies and stock the team with established black stars. His efforts failed, however, when Commissioner Kenesaw Mountain Landis learned of Veeck's plan and pressured the Phillies to sell to another buyer.[91] Still, it was apparent that the integration of baseball could not be postponed indefinitely.

During this period Dodger president Branch Rickey devised a careful plan to introduce the first black player into organized baseball in the twentieth century. Rickey's scouts searched North America for a player with the right chemistry of talent and temperament to endure the trials that came with being the pioneer. At one point, Rickey seriously considered bringing a talented Cuban infielder named Silvio García to the Dodgers. Although accounts conflict, Rickey, according to one school of thought, shied away from García after the prideful Cuban said he would kill any man who slapped him in the face. Another story has it that Walter O'Malley, in his early years as a Dodgers executive, himself sought out the Cuban but simply could not locate him.[92] Shortly thereafter, the Dodgers president signed Jackie Robinson instead; he believed Robinson possessed the necessary tools to dismantle segregation in baseball.[93]

In 1947, after a year in the minor leagues, Robinson burst into the majors, ending more than fifty years of segregation in America's national pastime. Robinson did more than change baseball; according to historian Jules Tygiel, Robinson's "triumph had ramifications that transcended the realm of sports, influencing public attitudes and facilitating the spread of the ideology of the civil rights movement."[94] The *Boston Chronicle*'s headline read: "Triumph of Whole Race Seen in Jackie's Debut in Major League Ball."[95] Latin players also benefited.

Between 1871 and 1946, forty-nine Latin Americans had played in the major leagues. But even after Joe Cambria's scouting in Cuba, their length of stay in the states was often brief. When Jackie Robinson joined the Dodgers in 1947, the debut of Latin players that year had shrunk to zero.[96] For many Latin Americans, Jackie Robinson's breakthrough offered hope for them for greater opportunities in the United States. The fences of big league baseball now appeared within reach for all Latins.

Notes

1. Article donated to author from Jules Tygiel, Feb. 1994.

2. Revere Rodgers quoted in Seymour, *Baseball,* 83.

3. Ibid.

4. Memo from Louis Heibroner to unknown recipient, Dec. 30, 1910, Rafael Almeida file, National Baseball Library, Cooperstown, N.Y.

5. Weir, "The Famous Marsans Case," 53–59.

6. Untitled clipping, Feb. 13, 1915, Armando Marsans file, National Baseball Library.

7. *Sporting News,* Sept. 19, 1923.

8. Untitled clipping, Jan. 16, 1915, Marsans file.

9. Weir, "The Famous Marsans Case," 59.

10. *Sporting News,* Aug. 9, 1923.

11. Untitled, undated clipping, Marsans file.

12. *New York Tribune* quoted in Frio and Onigman, "Good Field, No Hit," 201.

13. *Sporting News,* undated article, Mike González file, National Baseball Library.

14. *Sporting News,* May 4, 1933.

15. *New York Journal American,* July 17, 1957.

16. Alou, *Alou,* 114–15.

17. Letter from Pepe Conte to Gary Herrmann, Jan. 21, 1923, Adolfo Luque file, National Baseball Library.

18. Bjarkman, *Baseball with a Latin Beat,* 27.

19. García, *Mexican Americans,* 236.

20. Acuña, *Occupied America,* 159.

21. Frio and Onigman, "Good Field, No Hit," 202.

22. *New York World Telegraph,* Apr. 29, 1935.

23. *Brooklyn Eagle,* July 8, 1939.

24. Noverr and Ziewacz, *The Games They Played,* 71.

25. Wills, *Reagan's America,* 117.

26. Rader, *American Sports,* 199.

27. Frio and Onigman, "Good Field, No Hit," 204.

28. *Sporting News,* 1939, González file.

29. *Washington Post,* Feb. 22, 1939, Alfonso "Chico" Carrasquel file, National Baseball Library.

30. *Boston Traveler,* Apr. 23, 1940.

31. Ward, "Gonzalez," 33.

32. These 1992 figures were tabulated by Bjarkman in "Hispanic Baseball Statistical Record," 87–95.

33. Griffith interview.

34. Considine, "Ivory from Cuba," 19.

35. Izenberg, *Great Latin Sports Figures,* 206.

36. Ray Fitzgerald, "Uncle Joe—Senators' Cuban Connection," *Sporting News,* June 21, 1980, 17.

37. Kerrane, *Dollar Sign on the Muscle,* 15.

38. Untitled clipping, Sept. 12, 1935, Roberto Estalella file, National Baseball Library.

39. Untitled, undated memo, Estalella file.

40. *Sporting News,* Oct. 3, 1935.

41. Izenberg, *Great Latin Sports Figures,* 208.

42. Shirley Povich, *Washington Post,* Mar. 14, 1936.

43. Considine, "Ivory from Cuba," 19.

44. Higham, *Strangers in the Land,* 133.

45. Meier and Rivera, *The Chicanos,* 160–61. For the best work concerning the Mexican repatriation, see Hoffman, *Unwanted Mexican Americans.*

46. Hoffman, *Unwanted Mexican Americans,* 28–29.

47. Ruck, *Sandlot Seasons,* 13.

48. Voigt, *American Baseball,* 28–29.

49. Ibid., 219.

50. Brown, "Cuban Baseball," 111; Harold Seymour, in *Baseball: The Golden Age,* points out that before 1911, during Almeida's and Marsans's tenure with New Britain in the Connecticut League, the team manager made a special trip to Cuba to verify the racial background of the players.

51. Bjarkman, "Cuban Blacks in the Majors," 60.

52. Rogosin, *Invisible Men,* 159.

53. Untitled, undated article, Luque file.

54. Frio and Onigman, "Good Field, No Hit," 206.

55. Ibid.

56. Ibid.

57. Alou, *Alou,* 113–14.

58. Izenberg, *Great Latin Sports Figures,* 209.

59. Considine, "Ivory from Cuba," 24.

60. *Washington Post,* Mar. 22, 1943.

61. *Sporting News,* Sept. 2, 1969.

62. *Washington Post,* July 8, 1949.
63. Ibid.
64. *Washington Post,* June 1, 1939.
65. Frio and Onigman, "Good Field, No Hit," 207.
66. Ibid.
67. Irvin interview.
68. Peterson, *Only the Ball Was White,* 28.
69. Ibid., 32–33; Okrent and Lewine, *Ultimate Baseball Book,* 12.
70. Brown, "Cuban Baseball," 110.
71. Phelon, "Baseball in Cuba," 35.
72. Ibid.
73. Ibid.
74. *Miami Herald,* Apr. 30, 1978.
75. Brown, "Cuban Baseball," 110.
76. Peterson, *Only the Ball Was White,* 211.
77. Holway, *Voices,* 3.
78. Phelon, "Baseball in Cuba," 34.
79. Peterson, *Only the Ball Was White,* 212.
80. Ibid.
81. Ibid., 224.
82. Ibid., 245.
83. Rogosin, *Invisible Men,* 155.
84. Peterson, *Only the Ball Was White,* 243.
85. Brown, "Cuban Baseball," 111.
86. Ibid., 112.
87. Ibid.
88. Peterson, *Only the Ball Was White,* 243.
89. Cepeda interview.
90. Tygiel, *Baseball's Great Experiment,* 35.
91. Veeck and Linn, *Veeck,* 171–72.
92. Bjarkman, *Baseball with a Latin Beat,* 13.
93. Brown, "Cuban Baseball," 112.
94. Tygiel, *Baseball's Great Experiment,* viii.
95. Ibid., 178.
96. Bjarkman, "Hispanic Baseball Statistical Record," 87.

•4

In Las Grandes Ligas

Most Latin players are black. I remember when Jackie Robinson came
to our country, in 1948. . . . It was a proud moment. To see Robinson
in the Brooklyn lineup gave us hope. . . . There was a black man out
there with a major league uniform on.

Felipe Alou

The [Latin players] tried harder to succeed. Not only could they have
a good career and make some money, but they would make it easier
for those that followed. They were sort of like pioneers.

Monte Irvin

"*T*hose babies could play out of this world." So spoke
black star Jesse Hubbard of the Latins he faced in Cuba during the 1920s.[1]
Indeed, in the decades prior to World War II many American baseball players—black and white—came away with similar impressions after facing
Latin talent in the winter leagues. However, by the 1950s, only fifty-four
players from Latin countries had appeared in the majors. These numbers
are low in view of the strength of Latin America's baseball heritage. Though
the color barrier accounted, in part, for the low numbers, the American
baseball establishment remained unconvinced of Latin talent. By 1950, only
Adolfo Luque had been a bona fide star. Aside from Mel Almada's respectable hitting career, American baseball observers blindly accepted the notion that Latin players were only "good field, no hit" prospects. Winter
baseball in Latin America, however, provided those who competed with
another perspective.

Throughout Mexico and the Caribbean, American players discovered
intense Latin competition. National championships and civic and regional rivalries were fueled by the powerful loyalties given to both local heroes and American stars brought in to fortify teams. Baseball in Latin America was, indeed, a serious venture. In fact, during the 1940s, the Mexican
multimillionaire Jorge Pasquel, convinced of the prowess of players in his

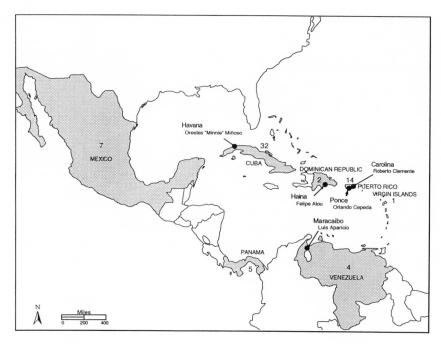

Latin American Origin of Major League Baseball Players, 1950–60. Numerals denote the total number of players from individual countries. Selected high-profile players noted.

country, financed an ambitious attempt to build a powerful league equal to the American majors. The millionaire and his brothers secured the services of a handful of American major and black league players that included Max Lanier, Mickey Owen, Buck Leonard, Satchel Paige, and Josh Gibson. Pasquel also engaged some Latins from beyond Mexico who had previously played briefly in the major leagues. Among them was thirty-year-old Tommy de la Cruz, who, after compiling a 9-9 pitching record, was released by the Cincinnati Reds in 1944.[2] Like most Latin leagues, the Mexican League was racially diverse and seemingly in a position to prosper. American major league baseball, however, fought back in the late 1940s, when owners blacklisted all of the players who participated in the outlaw league. This and poor organization on Pasquel's part led to the league's eventual collapse. While Pasquel's plan failed, the Mexican League, like the Caribbean leagues had done for so many years, provided Latins with further opportunities to test their skills against American stars. Moreover, Latin blacks competed with and against white players on the integrated diamonds of Latin America, something they could not do in the United States to that point.[3]

Jackie Robinson's entrance into the big leagues in 1947 did not immediately change the status of African Americans in baseball. Only a few owners, players, and writers had the courage to support the integration of the game. Furthermore, only four other blacks played major league baseball in 1947. To be sure, no one openly admitted to having racially discriminatory policies. Resistance, however, was sometimes quietly apparent. During the 1947 season, for instance, when the Brooklyn Dodgers first visited St. Louis, a number of the Cardinals reportedly threatened to boycott the series if Robinson played. That the mutiny was never fully proven did not obscure the turbulence within the organization about desegregation.[4] But with the acceptance of African Americans came greater acceptance of Latin American ballplayers. Indeed, the 1950s ushered in a true Latin era, in which Latin players entered the big leagues at an unprecedented rate just as Spanish-speaking populations grew in the United States.

Overall, the Latin population increased in the United States during the post–World War II era. Not since the 1920s had so many Latins entered the Great Colossus of the North. By the end of the fifties over 2 million people had crossed the southern borders of the United States. Many entered legally. Many did not. Once cheaper modes of transportation became commonplace, there was little to keep people in their native lands savaged by unemployment. Upon arrival, Latins sought jobs in both the industrial and agricultural sectors, mostly as unskilled workers, throughout all regions of the United States. Many ventured into urban areas seeking to join compatriots in the already overcrowded and segregated Latin communities. Still others picked berries, harvested lettuce, and processed other farm products in rural areas. And, in contrast to earlier years, they remained in the United States in larger numbers.

Their numerical impact notwithstanding, Latins lacked the political clout needed to attain the social and economic opportunities realized by those in the mainstream. Within the Latin community, however, some groups had already been in America for thirty years. During the 1920s, local groups emerged to provide a political voice for Latins in their quest to assimilate. In 1921, for instance, Mexican Americans who had served in World War I created the Order of the Sons of America. Their goals were noble and,

to say the least, gargantuan: eliminate racial discrimination toward Latins, gain true equality under the law, acquire political representation, and
pursue greater educational opportunities. These aims were ambitious in
the face of an American public hostile to Latin cultures. At the public school
level "they wouldn't let you talk Spanish," recalled César Chávez of his
own elementary school experience in the early thirties. Punishment for
violating language ordinances was routine. Teachers would "make you
write 'I won't speak Spanish' on the board 300 times, or I remember once
a teacher hung a sign [on a student] that said 'I am a clown, I speak Spanish.'"[5] Greater fame as a pioneer to improve the living and working conditions for Mexican American farm hands in California lay in Chávez's
future.

The League for United Latin American Citizens (LULAC) pursued similar goals. Founded in 1929 as a civil rights association for Mexican Americans that paralleled the larger and more high profile National Association for the Advancement of Colored People, this Latin body chose to take
its battles into American courtrooms. In 1946, for instance, LULAC ac-
tivists supported Gonzalo Méndez against the Westminster, California, city
school district, whose racial policies, he charged, led to the segregation of
Hispanic students.[6] Méndez's claims were not unprecedented. In 1931,
parents of Mexican heritage living in Lemon Grove, California, organized
to fight school segregation, sued the school district, and won. According
to historian Rodolfo Acuña, "This was a landmark case that served as a
precedent for school desegregation cases that followed."[7] Fifteen years later
Méndez won his case against Westminster and in doing so not only took
important steps toward Hispanic rights but also magnified the fact that
America's segregation policies were not exclusively aimed at blacks. The
ultimate aim, of course, was to become what Mario T. García described
as "Americans All"—to have parity with the mainstream on all levels. The
1946 *Méndez v. Westminster School District* case notwithstanding, large-
scale political socioeconomic goals remained distant. In 1950, educator
George I. Sánchez reported to a group of his colleagues at a regional conference that the Spanish-speaking constituency in the United States was
"the least known, the least sponsored, and the least vocal large minority
group in the nation."[8]

The experiences of Latin immigrants underscored the saga of those that
played baseball—the "hunger" for work, the confrontation with a strange
culture and racial biases, their "invisibility" as a group, and the struggle
to overcome perceptions. The Latin players were not unimportant to the
many Spanish-speaking communities throughout America. Young Hispan-

ics identified with those who achieved status by being professional ball-players. More than any other Latin group during the first decade following World War II, baseball players were in a position to poke holes in the stereotypes that many Americans came to believe. Early on, like their compatriots beyond the baseball diamond, they remained largely invisible, but perceptions and influence slowly changed.

In the wake of Sánchez's comments, community-based political organizations matured. Just as black Americans joined to bring about civil rights movements, Latins coalesced regionally to fight the lack of equity in such areas as housing, education, and job opportunities. In 1948, Dr. Héctor García, a Mexican American surgeon who had served in World War II, organized the American G.I. Forum. The group members banded together in response to a situation in Three Rivers, Texas, where the only mortician prevented the family of Félix Longoria, a soldier killed in battle, from conducting services in the mortuary's chapel. In Puerto Rico, a demand for better living conditions also began in 1948. Luis Muñoz Marín sparked Operation Bootstrap, a program designed to increase industry on that island and, in turn, provide relief to the unemployed. Far from displaying the stereotypical docility of Latins, this new generation sought to use its increasing numbers as a tool for political strength. Most Latins, however, still possessed few means by which to improve or express themselves. Furthermore, they were truly a "forgotten people," according to Carey McWilliams: "The group is so old that it has been forgotten and so new that it has not yet been discovered."[9] Latin fortitude and overall talent, however, emerged on the baseball diamonds in las grandes ligas.

A spirited black man from Cuba—Saturinino Orestes Arrieta Armas Miñoso—was a catalyst for Latin opportunities in baseball. Born in 1922 on a sugar plantation in the Matanzas Province on the island of Cuba, Miñoso was one of five children in a working-class family. Throughout most of his early years Cuba had been a prosperous land—at least for those receiving favor from the Fulgencio Batista regime, as well as for foreign speculators, plantation owners, casino tycoons, and gamblers. Most, if not all, of the nation's wealth lay in Havana and, according to historian E. Bradford Burns, "failed to trickle down to the impoverished provinces." Poverty, in fact, gripped nearly 90 percent of the population.[10] Miñoso's family was among that vast majority. While young Miñoso wielded a machete in the sugar fields, he learned to play baseball with other plantation youths. He recalled, "My first team was made up of farm boys. We were, indeed, a strange looking team, with our uniforms made of old flour sacks." Their cracked bats and shabby gloves required repair before they saw action. Lack of proper equipment was standard in the poverty-ridden sectors of Latin America. Tito Fuentes recalled using rocks for both bases and balls, while in the Dominican Republic Felipe Alou batted lemons with his arm.[11] As Miñoso put it, "We were forced to use our raw talents more, a necessity which helped many Hispanics break into organized clubs in Cuba, Mexico, the Caribbean and, the ultimate goal, the big leagues in the United States."[12]

At age thirteen, Miñoso managed a team of motley plantation youths while still donning the sackcloth uniform his mother had sewn.[13] As his baseball skills improved, his dreams of becoming a professional quickened. According to Miñoso, "All young Cuban ballplayers had the same dream; first the Cuban League of professional baseball and then the big leagues of the U.S. . . . And we Cubans knew it could be done, because great Cuban stars had already made it in the majors: Alejandro Oms, Armando Marsans, Adolfo Luque."[14] Prior to 1947, however, stardom in the big leagues was reserved for white ballplayers.

In 1944, Miñoso won a spot on the Havana professional team in the Cuban League. Having demonstrated his superior talents, he signed in 1946 with the New York Cubans of the Negro American League.[15] To Miñoso's good fortune, the roster featured not only legendary third baseman Ray Dandridge but also fellow Cuban Silvio García, a veteran infielder. García had played in the American black leagues since 1940 and had originally been seriously considered to break baseball's color barrier.[16] García was familiar with American customs and did his best to orient the rookie from the sugar plantation. Miñoso later said, "He taught me how to live, how to eat, how to play in New York. I owe him much more than I can give him."[17] In addition to García, Rafael "Ray" Noble, who later played with the New York Giants, and Luis Tiant Sr. also played with the New York Cubans during Miñoso's tenure. "I was the youngest player on the team," said Miñoso. "Everyone tried to help me, not only to become a better baseball player, but also to learn English."[18] The young Cuban quickly matured as a ballplayer and earned a spot on the 1947 and 1948 All-Star squads. Miñoso's arrival, as it turned out, coincided with important transitions in the big leagues.

During 1947, the Jackie Robinson saga easily captured the attention of the nation. Scores of black ballplayers realized that their dreams of joining the big leagues might have a chance of fulfillment. Since his youth,

Miñoso had shared that dream, and in that instrumental year he, too, saw an opportunity. The St. Louis Cardinals were holding a tryout camp and all comers were welcome. Miñoso, brimming with excitement and confidence, made his way to the camp. Surely, he believed, two honor-laden years in America's famed black leagues would serve as adequate apprenticeship for the majors. But as he discovered in the United States of the late 1940s merit alone did not always provide a ticket to fortune. Despite his hard-hitting performance the Cardinals bypassed the Cuban. The disillusioned player remembered, "I want[ed] no bonus. I just wanted to play in the big leagues."[19] He added, "My style of play [at] third base was criticized: They said I shouldn't throw so hard to first. I couldn't understand why they wanted to cramp my style." Then, in all innocence, Miñoso said, "It seemed that the Cardinals didn't understand that I was already playing in a strong league and I didn't see why they were making me tryout, as if I were some sandlotter."[20] Miñoso returned to the Cubans. As for the Cardinals, Miñoso's tryout was ill-timed. That same year speculation circulated about the boycott of Robinson's Brooklyn Dodgers. Furthermore,

Orestes "Minnie" Miñoso. (Courtesy of the National Baseball Hall of Fame Library, Cooperstown, N.Y.)

under the ownership of Fred Saigh, the team never fielded a black player. Not until 1953, under August Busch, did the Cardinals finally integrate.

Miñoso enjoyed a fine year with the New York Cubans in 1948. His aggressive play eventually caught the attention of another big league organization, the Cleveland Indians. Owner Bill Veeck, a proponent of integration, signed Miñoso to a contract later that year. Miñoso and a fellow Cuban, José Santiago, joined the Indians' Class A affiliate in Dayton, Ohio. Because the baseball season was nearly over by the time the Cuban players arrived, Miñoso played only eleven games. In his brief stint, however, he batted .525, which eventually prompted Bill Veeck to ask Joe Vosmik, the Dayton manager, if Miñoso was capable of hitting at the big league level. Vosmik quickly replied, "Yes, and if there's anything better than major league pitching, he'll hit that too."[21]

Following a 1949 debut with Cleveland, Miñoso spent the better part of the next two years on the roster of the Indians' minor league affiliate in San Diego. He was spectacular during his tenure in the Pacific Coast League. In the 1950 campaign, he batted in 115 runs, stole 30 bases, and hit for a .339 average. His success in San Diego, combined with his hustle, flair, and good humor, made him a hero in that port city. Of the fans there, Miñoso remembered them as "enthusiastic and 100 percent behind their team. Even though I had confidence in myself, the cheers and the applause of the fans gave me more will and fortitude."[22] Miñoso's achievements in San Diego, however, did not win him a job with the Indians. The parent club was loaded with talent and could not provide an opening. Fortunately for Miñoso, however, another big league team, the Chicago White Sox, found a place for him.

White Sox general manager Frank Lane was in the midst of rebuilding his floundering team and increasing sagging attendance. He sought players who possessed both talent and charisma and recognized that the freedom to recruit black players increased his options. Given the hostility toward integration, however, there was no guarantee that Chicago's first black player on either the White Sox or his National League neighbors, the Cubs, would be welcomed.[23] Further, with Comiskey Park situated in a predominantly black neighborhood, hiring a black player might lead to a cry of tokenism. On the other hand, Lane might have imagined the empty stands at Comiskey Park filled with black fans.

With these factors in play, Lane carefully worked out a deal with the Indians that eventually brought Miñoso to Chicago.[24] The press greeted the move with criticism. In his *New York World-Telegram* column, Dan Daniel suggested that Frank Lane had brought Miñoso to Chicago "to give the Negro customers a player of their race for whom to cheer. Up to this time the White Sox and the Cubs had shown no great eagerness to locate a Negro star."[25] An editorial in the same paper stated that "the Cuban gives the White Sox what they have needed for a long time, a Negro with intriguing possibilities; Comiskey Park lies near the vicinity of Chicago's Harlem."[26]

Chicago, it appeared, was not the ideal spot for experiments in race relations. Since 1919, when a violent race riot left forty people dead and five hundred injured, interracial contacts were virtually nonexistent.[27] So rigid were the racial boundaries that in 1951, the year of Miñoso's arrival to the White Sox, a riot broke out in the all-white suburb of Cicero after a black family attempted to move there. The violent response forced Governor Adlai Stevenson to send four thousand National Guardsmen to restore order in that community.[28] Chicago's Hispanic community was powerless and had grown only minimally between 1920 and 1940. Mexican Americans and Puerto Ricans predominated, but while their numbers rose following World War II, neither the White Sox nor the Cubs at that time needed to cater to the Latin community to gain support for baseball. There is no evidence that the White Sox ever took the Latin population into account when dealing for Miñoso.[29] Hence, Lane brought Miñoso to the White Sox for one reason only—to help make the club a contender.

Miñoso seemed undisturbed by the racial circumstances of the time: "I never felt any really great pressure at being one of the first black players in the major leagues. I concentrated on playing ball and, during the game, put aside personal problems."[30] Miñoso's ability to do so was, perhaps, aided by his character. The Cuban's wit and seemingly carefree personality, which endeared him to most, even came in handy when his English supposedly failed him. While playing in Dayton, for instance, he once missed Joe Vosmik's sign to take a pitch. Instead, Miñoso swung and launched a home run. Vosmik, who understandably had mixed emotions about the turn of events, asked Miñoso if the Cuban had seen his sign. Miñoso smiled and responded, "Oh sure. You say 'take'—so I take big swing." Charm was another Miñoso trait. One year Cleveland general manager Hank Greenberg experienced Miñoso's winsome manner after he threatened to fine the Cuban for being late to spring training. When, in an attempt to reprimand his player, Greenberg asked what Miñoso would do if the roles were reversed, the clever Cuban brightened and said, "I say 'Minnie fine fellow. He always in good shape. He all the time hustle. He work hard during winter. I no mind if he come late.'" Greenberg never issued the fine.[31]

As anticipated, Miñoso's signing stirred some controversy in Chicago. Prior to this, manager Paul Richards moved to temper any potential problems by calling a team meeting. According to Miñoso, Richards maintained he "didn't care what a player's skin color was, but asked if anyone had any personal problems on this matter. No one raised his hand." As for the Chicago fans, Miñoso believed, "I was probably the first black Cuban most of them had ever seen."[32]

After playing professional baseball on two coasts and in a small Ohio city for five years, Orestes "Minnie" Miñoso had learned a great deal about Americans and their country. His English, though still heavily accented, had improved. And certainly his familiarity with America's racial mores and customs had prepared him to break Chicago's color barrier on the baseball fields.

Like Jackie Robinson's, Minnie Miñoso's performances during his first year with Chicago were scrutinized by critics who charged that integration was a bad idea. Not only was he black but his English appeared marginal. Unlike Robinson, however, Miñoso did not face the pressure of representing his entire race or nationality. The White Sox already had white Latin stars such as Alfonso "Chico" Carrasquel and Sandalio "Sandy" Consuegra. But Minnie Miñoso pioneered on two fronts: he was the first black Latin big leaguer when he joined the 1949 Cleveland Indians as well as Chicago's first black in the big leagues.

Miñoso's first full year in the big leagues sensationally vindicated Frank Lane's judgment. He hit for a .326 average, drove in seventy-six runs, and stole thirty-one bases. The Cuban proved to be the catalyst Lane had hoped for, and his hustle and flashy play affected the turnstiles as well. The "go-go" White Sox—as they were affectionately known —set a club attendance record in 1951.[33] Miñoso, the "Cuban Comet," also galvanized Chicago's black community. A group of black citizens pronounced September 23, 1951, Minnie Miñoso Day and showered their new hero with gifts.[34] Miñoso's popularity appeared contagious. One writer claimed that "if hockey officials were really intent on developing speed, they'd put Miñoso on skates." The same journalist declared, "We know of no one in recent years better at sliding into a base safely after a fielder had received a ball." Other "speed" sports were "slow stuff compared to Miñoso on base."[35]

Miñoso's celebrity extended far beyond Chicago. As early as July 1951, one New York writer suggested that Miñoso and National League rookie

Willie Mays were "shoo-ins for Rookie of the Year and crowd pleasers."[36] In light of all this, columnist Dan Daniel wondered "how the [baseball] magnates kept the Negro out of [baseball] so long, and what some of the clubs would do without him." According to the journalist, "Miñoso is not only the Rookie of the Year in the American League, but he may even win the batting championship."[37] As it turned out, Daniel was wrong on both counts—but by the narrowest of margins.

Although Miñoso did not win the batting title that year, he finished second. This accomplishment seemed remarkable given his rookie status. Astonishingly, however, the Baseball Writers Association of America voted Gil McDougald, of the New York Yankees, American League Rookie of the Year. It was a strange turn of events since Miñoso had finished ahead of the Yankee second baseman in most of the major categories, including the Most Valuable Player balloting (Miñoso finished fourth while McDougald ended up ninth). White Sox fans were outraged, none more so than general manager Frank Lane. Lane, in fact, cried out that not only was Miñoso Rookie of the Year but was also an easy choice over Yogi Berra for the Most Valuable Player Award. "It seems you must play on a pennant winner to earn these honors," announced an infuriated Lane. "If that's the way they are picked, both awards might as well be abandoned. It wasn't [Miñoso's] fault that he wasn't on a pennant winner."[38] *The Sporting News,* to its credit, accorded Miñoso its Rookie of the Year honor. As for the baseball writers, tellingly, since the American League inaugurated its own Rookie of the Year Award in 1949, not until 1964, when Tony Oliva won, did the writers select a black player. In contrast, the National League selected eleven black players between 1947 and 1964.

Miñoso's spectacular rookie season did not come without a price. In 1951, the Cuban was struck sixteen times by pitched balls and ultimately held the dubious honor of leading the American League in that category. The normally jovial outfielder began to show frustration toward the end of the year when he declared that only "a bucket of white paint" would terminate the problem. Indeed, after telling a *Sporting News* writer that he even considered wearing headgear to bed for protection, he pondered, "I don't know whatta kind of baseball this is. Yes, you try and get a man out. You brush back. But you not try and keel him."[39]

Although he was neither the first black player to play in the major leagues nor the first Latin, Miñoso's success whetted the appetites of many major league clubs. The Cuban's 1951 season confirmed the suspicion that more outstanding ballplayers could be found competing south of the U.S. border with Mexico. His achievements, indeed, raised eyebrows and provided an important ingredient in generating recruitment of Latin players on a larger scale. This, in conjunction with the integration of major league baseball, widened the path of opportunity for other black Latins.

━━━━━━━━━

By the 1950s, a large influx of Latin ballplayers seemed inevitable. Washington Senators owner Clark Griffith, with scout Joe Cambria, had already proven to other teams that signing Latins was a worthwhile venture. Moreover, many American professionals competed in Latin America during the winter and attested to the talent there. More importantly, many Latins were willing to play for less money to escape the poverty of their countries. With baseball's color barrier no longer a major issue, a golden opportunity arose to draw prospects for a minimum price. Cuban player Sandy Amoros said, "When I see Jackie Robinson play in my country, I say if he can do it, I can do it too."[40] Such incentive stimulated Latin hopes.

To be sure, the trickle of Latin players entering American professional baseball was slow during the immediate post-integration period. During 1947, the year that Jackie Robinson joined the Dodgers, only Fermín Guerra of Cuba and Jesse Flores of Mexico played for major league teams.[41] No Latin players debuted that year. However, between 1950 and 1955, forty-two Latins started in the majors.[42] Given that only fifty-four Latins made the big leagues in over fifty years prior to 1950, this increase was substantial. Within that growth came greater diversity, as players from various Spanish-speaking countries traveled to the United States.

Up to 1950, of the fifty-four Latins who had played major league baseball, forty-three came from Cuba.[43] The 1950s, however, brought dramatic change. Players such as Roberto Clemente, Rubén Gómez, and Vic Power came from Puerto Rico, while others, such as Luis Aparicio and Chico Carrasquel, hailed from Venezuela. In 1956 Ossie Virgil became the first Dominican ballplayer to debut in the big leagues and two years later Felipe Alou emerged as an important pioneer for his country. As the Latin presence in big league baseball became more pronounced, earlier doubts as to their baseball prowess eroded as they challenged the game's leaders for stardom. Stereotypes of the past, such as the "good field, no hit" tag, no longer appeared justifiable. Miñoso's quest for the 1951 batting crown during his rookie season helped in that regard. Three years later, Miñoso again went after the batting crown. Among those he battled was a soft-spoken man from Mexico named Roberto Francisco "Bobby" Avila.

During Avila's upbringing Mexico was not viewed as a reservoir for major league talent. But Mexicans were not exactly clamoring to play baseball in the United States either. Part of this attitude developed when nationalism prevailed on the heels of a traumatic revolution. During the Lázaro Cárdenas rule of the 1930s, Mexicans sought to get out from under the thumb of the larger industrialized powers, many of whom had enriched themselves during the late nineteenth-century Porfiriato. The 1938 nationalization of the petroleum industry symbolized Mexico's goals of creating a strong infrastructure. It also propelled the notion that all that was good was Mexican, including baseball. Hence, many players remained at home and developed strong followings. Not surprisingly, years later a young Fernando Valenzuela, when asked who his hero was, immediately responded, "Héctor Espino"—a Mexican home run champion.

Interest in the major leagues did, of course, exist, but the majors were not necessarily interested in Mexican players. Mexico's post-revolution professional league began operations in 1925, but reaped little attention from major league scouts. Furthermore, Jorge Pasquel's attempt, and subsequent failure, to challenge the North American major leagues during the 1940s undermined the credibility of those who had participated in that organization so that by the 1950s only two Mexicans—Mel Almada and Jesse Flores—had earned spots on major league rosters. Further, with Cubans seemingly all too willing to play for almost any price, there was little reason to scout elsewhere.

Bobby Avila's social origins did not fit the usual profile of poverty-stricken players. With a corporate lawyer father, he was well-educated and fairly well to do. An avid player in grade school, Avila at seventeen earned a professional contract with Cordoba in the Mexican League for 500 pesos (then worth about $100 per month). Five years later in 1946 he garnered a contract of $10,000 per year when he joined the prestigious Almendares team. His consistent .300 plus average drew the attention of Joe Cambria of the Washington Senators.

Already well known for his expertise as a scout in Cuba, Cambria generally scouted players desperate and willing to sign inexpensive contracts. Bobby Avila, however, was not a desperate man. In 1947, when Cambria approached the Mexican infielder with a modest offer, Avila objected: "I tell him no. He offered seventy-five hundred dollars, I shake my head. He tell me how much money I make in the big leagues. I tell him how much money I make in Mexico and Cuba. That end eet."[44] After Cambria left, the Brooklyn Dodgers agreed to match his current salary provided he made the team. As it turned out, the offer may have been part of a scheme by owner Branch Rickey to lessen Jackie Robinson's impact with "one of the swarthier Mexicans," as one reporter described Avila. But neither the Dodgers nor Avila appeared impressed with the other. A man "definitely not big league material," according to journalist Wendell Smith, Avila parted ways with the Dodgers.[45]

Scout C. C. Slapnicka of the Cleveland Indians, one year later, did not write Avila off so quickly. Convinced of his potential, the scout aggressively sought Avila's signature on a contract. The Mexican infielder, however, was not so overwhelmed that he forgot that baseball was a business. Slapnicka, knowing that Avila could be a stubborn negotiator, simply asked the Mexican to name his price. Avila signed a contract for $17,500 and a jubilant Slapnicka wired back to Cleveland that Avila could "do everything except speak English."[46]

Aware that Avila knew no English at the outset of the 1948 spring training camp, Harold Goldstein, the traveling secretary who spoke some Spanish, told the rookie to "get yourself a Spanish-English dictionary and keep it with you all the time." In addition, Goldstein assigned Avila to room with pitcher Mike García, a Mexican American from California who spoke fluent Spanish. At a time when big league organizations exerted little or no effort into orientating their players from other countries, this matchup proved invaluable for Avila's career.[47]

One can only speculate that the Mexican's tenure on the Indians would have been short-lived had it not been for García. Avila riddled the big pitcher with questions and constantly pointed to various objects asking, "Cómo se llama eso? [How do you say that?]."[48] García patiently fielded the inquiries and helped indoctrinate his talented teammate into life both in the big leagues and in the United States.

Cleveland assigned Avila to its top minor league affiliate in Baltimore for seasoning. He stayed in the Maryland city for only one year because of a rule forcing parent clubs to promote all bonus players after one season in the minors. Although he was determined to succeed, from 1949 to 1951 he spent most of his time as a frustrated benchwarmer. When he finally broke into the starting lineup in 1951, he began to hit steadily, ending that season with a .301 average. Mexicans reveled in his success. At one point that year when the Indians visited Washington, D.C., the Mexican ambassador invited Avila to the embassy, pinned a host of medals on

Bobby Avila. (Courtesy of the National Baseball Hall of Fame Library, Cooperstown, N.Y.)

his chest, and said, "Señor Avila, you have brought great renown in athletics to Mexico. All of us are proud."[49] For Avila, greater achievements were on the horizon.

Avila's popularity, however, must be placed in proper perspective. While some Mexican nationals lauded the star from Vera Cruz, he was not a household name in the United States. For one thing, Cleveland was clearly not the center of Latin cultures in the United States. A predominantly European working-class town, Cleveland had no Latin population to speak of. No Spanish-language newspapers or radio stations were available to promote the soft-spoken Avila. Since the bulk of America's Mexican population dwelled in the southwest, Avila remained virtually isolated from Latin cultures. His hitting, however, soon captured national attention.

In 1954, Avila won the American League batting championship with a .341 average, thus becoming the first Latin player to win a batting crown in the big leagues. Miñoso, who gave chase during the year, finished with .320. Their accomplishments served notice to American baseball that Latins could hit as well as field. Many scouts began to dream that perhaps the likes of Miñoso and Avila were only a small sample of the talent to be discovered in Latin America.

By the time Bobby Avila and Minnie Miñoso had established themselves as stars, the Latin presence in the major leagues was increasingly apparent. Only ten years earlier, big league clubs brought Latins onto their teams primarily to fill the war-induced shortage of players. By the mid-1950s, however, Latins were signed onto teams for their potential and the mixture of black and white Latins appeared more balanced. Edmundo "Sandy" Amoros, Roberto Clemente, Félix Mantilla, Héctor López, and Carlos Paula achieved recognition comparable to that of their white counterparts Luis Arroyo and Guillermo "Willie" Miranda.[50] More importantly, the impressive performances of many of the newcomers quelled any doubts as to their ability to compete. As the tide of Latin players in the big leagues continued to surge, standouts broke loose.

Venezuelan Luis Aparicio was among the gifted Spanish-speaking contingency. Born in 1935 in Maracaibo, Aparicio, like Bobby Avila, did not grow up poor. Aparicio's father had been a talented shortstop in the Venezuelan League and tutored his son on the fundamentals of baseball. When young Aparicio turned seventeen, he inherited his father's position on the Maracaibo club. Soon thereafter, he played on another team in Caracas run by former Chicago White Sox manager Luman Harris. Harris, who still worked as a scout for the White Sox, recognized Aparicio's potential and signed him to a big league contract in 1954.

Aparicio spent his first year developing his skills in Waterloo, Iowa, at a White Sox affiliate. He led the league in put-outs, assists, fewest errors, and stolen bases, with forty-eight.[51] Not everything, however, went as smoothly for him.

Coming to the United States was exciting for the young man. Raised by a father who encouraged his pursuit of baseball, Aparicio dreamed all of his life of starring in the United States. But he overlooked the problems associated with the language barrier: "I don't know any English words. So when all the players go out and eat after the games, I just sit there until the lady brings the food, and I point to it, and the lady brings me some of that." A humiliated Aparicio recalled, "I make up my mind right then that I am going to learn English when I get back to Venezuela."[52]

When Aparicio returned for spring training in 1955, he came armed with the basics of English after spending hours with a personal tutor. His ability to communicate enhanced Aparicio's confidence. He told reporters, "It's the same bat, the same ball, the same game as it is in Venezuela. There are the same plays my father taught me. I do not feel so strange, even in this new country."[53] In the following year, the White Sox promoted him.

Sold on the Venezuelan, the Sox made headlines during the spring of 1956 when they dealt away Chico Carrasquel, their skilled shortstop, to the Cleveland Indians for long-ball hitter Larry Doby. In the eyes of many, the Sox had left themselves vulnerable at the shortstop position. However, manager Marty Marion had great faith in the rookie Aparicio. "He's definitely big league," asserted Marion. "What makes you so sure he'll make it?" the manager was asked. "Some players have baseball sense," he replied. "Others don't. Instinct may be a better word. The kid has it. Does everything naturally, effortlessly."[54]

Aparicio had a great rookie season, living up to Marion's expectations. One White Sox coach said Aparicio could make "three kinds of plays—routine, difficult and impossible." Nelson Fox, Aparicio's double-play partner at second base remarked, "The guy makes half my plays. Maybe I oughta give him half my salary."[55] Writer Dan Daniel openly supported the nomination of Aparicio for Rookie of the Year in the American League. The writer, who launched a similar crusade on behalf of Minnie Miñoso in 1951, predicted an Aparicio victory in the 1956 balloting.[56] This time Daniel was correct. Aparicio led the American League in almost all fielding categories, including put-outs, assists, and fewest errors. In addition,

Luis Aparicio. (Courtesy of the National Baseball Hall of Fame Library, Cooperstown, N.Y.)

he led the American League in stolen bases. Indeed, the Venezuelan's talents on the base paths increased as he matured. From 1956 through the 1964 season, Aparicio led the league in stolen bases. In fact, Latins dominated this category with the arrival of Minnie Miñoso. From 1951 through 1972, three Latins—Miñoso, Aparicio, and Dagoberto "Bert" Campaneris—led the league in stolen bases in all but three seasons. Aparicio's success, of course, only highlighted the gold mine that many clubs, by then, realized existed outside the United States.

Throughout the 1950s, expanded scouting efforts brought players from the Dominican Republic, Puerto Rico, and Central America. Many organizations became willing to take more risks on Latin players in light of the accomplishments of Aparicio, Avila, Miñoso, and others. That Latin prospects were equally willing to sign inexpensive contracts tempered the risks.

Joe Cambria continued to work out of his Havana headquarters. No longer hampered by the color barrier, he expanded his search to include all ballplayers. In the early 1950s talented players such as first baseman Julio Bécquer, outfielder Carlos Paula, shortstop Willie Miranda, and pitcher Sandy Consuegra were Cambria products. Later in the decade Cambria added pitchers Camilo Pascual and Pedro Ramos and shortstop Zoilo Versalles to his already impressive list of signees.

Although Cambria continued to monopolize Cuba's baseball talent, other scouts were well known elsewhere in the Caribbean. One very popular figure was Alex Campanis. He began his career with the Dodgers in 1939 as an infielder. While with Montreal, Campanis shared the infield with Jackie Robinson. Following his tenure as a player, he remained with the Dodgers and eventually became their chief scout in Latin America. Campanis was ideally suited for the position; he not only spoke fluent Spanish but he was brought up in a Latin sector of New York City. He thus felt at ease in a Hispanic environment and held a deep appreciation for its people. He later claimed, "I learned baseball through my Latin friends. [Through them] my origins in baseball began. [They] taught me good fundamental baseball. I am very much indebted to them."[57] During the early 1950s Campanis made several trips to the Caribbean in search of new talent. "There were a lot of good Latin baseball players that were beginning to indicate that they could play in the big leagues," he remembered.[58] Chief among his baseball contacts were Puerto Ricans Roberto Marín and Pedrín Zorilla, who directed Campanis to a young player named Roberto Clemente.

Though originally signed by the Dodgers, the Pittsburgh Pirates eventually landed the future star, whose potential was so impressive that general manager Branch Rickey instructed one of his top scouts, Howie Haak, to set his sights on all Latin American prospects: "You're goin to Cuba and the Dominican [Republic] this summer. If there's anymore of those 'creatures' down there, I want 'em!"[59] Haak thus embarked upon the first of many campaigns that made him one of the key scouts in the region: "I went to Venezuela and Panama, and then I started to spend three or four months a year in Latin America. I was the first scout who went to all the countries." According to Haak, "I could probably draw you a roadmap of Latin America—at least where they played baseball. I went lots of places where there weren't any roads. [I] had to take a plane or boat through the jungle."[60]

Until the great influx of scouts, the Latin market was "wide open for a guy who could spot talent," according to Giants scout George Genovese. "A [scout] could be choosy [at that time]. He could go down and take his pick and say 'Well, we'll save this bunch for next year.'"[61] Free to sign players of all races, scouts even opened occasional tryout camps, welcoming all comers.

To be sure, Cambria, Haak, Campanis, and others also pioneered. Their importance, in fact, cannot be underestimated. They were directly responsible for the transition that gave baseball its international constitution. Moreover, they not only represented their respective organizations but also became, in many ways, surrogate fathers to those they signed. Relying solely on faith and the hope that a major league contract might ensure a prosperous future for their offspring, families counted on the scout to take care of their sons and keep them out of trouble. Scouts, in addition to their professional duties, also served as translators, counselors, money lenders, and teachers. They arranged transportation and sometimes took the young Latin hopefuls into their own homes. Good scouts were also good friends. Moreover, many understood that, aside from being major league prospects, their signees were still very young men—some teenagers—who had never been away from home. Latin players understandably clung to these men as the feeling of isolation grew. The familiar face of the Spanish-speaking scout, in times of stress, was always welcome when the weight of loneliness sometimes seemed too much to bear.

Alex Pompez was yet another well-known name during this early period of extended scouting. He eventually brought such players as Felipe Alou, Orlando Cepeda, and José Pagán to the Giants. Pompez also signed Willie Kirkland, Willie McCovey, and Willie Mays. During the late 1950s and 1960s, the Giants had more Latin and black athletes than any other club. Recognizing the problems of adjustment, the New York team placed Pompez in charge of these players during spring training.[62] His experience with Latin blacks dated back to his days as owner of the New York Cubans of the black leagues. During the 1920s, Pompez was also a racketeer whose association with organized crime was well known. In 1937, he fled to Mexico only to return a few years later to inform on members of underworld crime. "He became the only guy who ever snitched on the mob and lived to tell about it," remembered a friend.[63] Pompez then returned to baseball and struck up a friendship with Giants owner Horace Stoneham during the days when Pompez's club used the Polo Grounds. This friendship came in handy when the New York Cubans folded and Stoneham quickly hired Pompez to work for the Giants.[64]

Pompez's task was not an easy one, for he had the immense responsibility of orienting Latin players to American culture within the very short span of spring training. One of his tasks was to educate the Latins about America's racial mores. "When they first come here they don't like it [racism]. Some boys cry and want to go home," Pompez explained. 'But after they stay and make big money they accept things as they are. My main thing is to help them. They can't change the laws."[65] Such was the first lesson in adapting to American culture. Another concerned finances.

———————

Although more Latins were entering American professional baseball, most still received low-paying contracts. Beginning in 1947, baseball management reluctantly signed white free agents to large bonuses as a result of rising postwar attendance, uneven distribution of talented ballplayers, and the impact of Branch Rickey's farm system. Given the rising cost of white ballplayers, teams scrambled for talented players at a low cost.[66] Since Clark Griffith and Joe Cambria of the Washington Senators had successfully recruited inexpensive players from Latin America, it seemed reasonable that Latins, particularly poor blacks, might jump at the chance to join a big league organization, however poor the pay. Their plight, to be sure, was not unlike thousands who had migrated before them.

The demands of the American marketplace have always stimulated the large-scale importation of cheap labor. Indentured servants and African slaves filled the needs of colonial agriculture. In the late nineteenth century European and Asian laborers came in response to the demands of rapid industrialization. These voluntary laborers dreamed of the prosperity that had eluded them in their homelands. Quite often, newcomers were drawn by stories of American success or by letters from friends or relatives who had earlier ventured to the United States and shared the common belief that "America was a far off country where everybody was rich . . . and made plenty of money."[67]

Latins, too, had been imported during the twentieth century to help fill vacant and unwanted jobs. In fact, in each decade from 1900 to 1950, save the depressed thirties, American employers, particularly in the Southwest, sought Latin labor. Mexicans, as well as some Puerto Ricans, toiled in the fields, while other Latins worked on the railroads or in the garment industry. The Bracero Program of the 1940s, in particular, brought thousands of contract laborers from Mexico to perform seasonal agricultural work. Despite these opportunities, the United States frequently adopted rigid policies designed to restrict the influx of Latins. Most notably, repatriation movements during the 1930s and Operation Wetback of the 1950s not only curbed immigration but also symbolized the disparaging attitudes of American policymakers toward Latins. Nonetheless, driven by the quest to improve their financial standing and to fulfill their dreams, Latins continued their exodus.

Latin players, to be sure, were a unique bunch. They were—and remain—the only large group that entered the United States specifically to play an American sport at the professional level. Neither Europeans nor Asians came to the United States with this goal in mind. But the baseball traditions in the Caribbean regions and Mexico by the midtwentieth century were so well entrenched that the baseball fantasies that filled many an American child's head also filled those of young Latins. To that end, many honed their skills in the makeshift fields of their homelands and needed little prodding when American scouts introduced themselves. Cuban Pedro Ramos, who enthusiastically signed with the Senators, remembered that he felt "to go to America and pitch against the blond hero of the 'Jankees' [Mickey Mantle] was incentive enough."[68]

But the excitement and thoughts of grandeur, as well as the meager financial opportunities available to many in their homelands, also left them vulnerable to exploitation. At the outset of his American career in 1955, for example, Ramos agreed to a salary of $150 per month.[69] Another Cuban, Zoilo Versalles, was only slightly better off. After he signed with the Senators, Versalles excitedly wrote home, "My salary is not possible to believe. I will make 175 dollars a month in American money."[70] In 1961, when Tony Oliva joined his first club in the United States, his initial contract covered hotel bills and $3 per diem meal money.[71] After Versalles had gained stardom during the middle 1960s, an inquisitive writer asked him about bonuses given to Latin players. The Cuban responded, "Bonus? Sure we all get bonus. You know the bonus we get? Carfare, that's the bonus." He elaborated, "I tell you, everybody knows us. Everybody knows that we have poverty and hunger. All we want is to play ball. So, okay, no bonus. Latin boys never get no bonus. I don't like this thing but I don't tell you this for complaint. I just tell you so that you will know the way it is."[72]

For the Latins, professional contracts, however, represented the realization of their dreams and, more importantly, their avenue of escape from wretched circumstances. The price for this avenue was often a meager salary, most of which was sent home to their families. Because of limited finances, Latin players sometimes found themselves in the awkward position of having only enough money to dwell in cheap hotels and eat in greasy diners.[73] Zoilo Versalles, for instance, did not foresee the deductions of federal and state taxes from his $175 per month salary. According to writer Jerry Izenberg, "at the end of every pay period he had hardly enough left for a haircut, a movie, or a new glove and baseball spikes, which he had to pay out of his own pocket."[74] Even as a big leaguer, Versalles's money woes continued. He ruefully admitted, "I was a big leaguer with only twenty dollars in my pocket."[75]

After being poor most of their lives, some overspent on luxury items. Braves outfielder Rico Carty, whose prominence came in the early 1970s, once purchased twenty-five pairs of shoes worth $600—in one shopping spree. On another occasion, Carty purchased six suits, twenty-four shirts, and fifteen sweaters. "I go into a beautiful store and I can't help myself," he commented. "I see all the beautiful things and I have to have them."[76] Similarly, Minnie Miñoso's spending prowess was occasionally overshadowed only by his ability to play baseball. In 1955, White Sox general manager Frank Lane visited Cuba to discuss Miñoso's contract. Later Lane claimed, "I had heard talk about a car being given away and I thought Minnie was being honored. Imagine my surprise when I heard it was Minnie who was giving the car away. Now," said a flustered Lane, "he's asking me if he can buy a white Cadillac because he's tired of the green one." Lane concluded, "Minnie is a great player and we offered him a substantial raise but the White Sox are not going to pay for the cars his friends ride around in."[77]

These incidents point to the success of many Latin players that masked their problems of acculturation. Many hopefuls saw only the achievements of their compatriots, which came from talent and perseverance. All too often, however, newcomers overlooked America's diversity in foods, language, and customs and felt only loneliness. Among the factors that affected the Latin ballplayers, none was more traumatic than Jim Crow.

Notes

1. Rogosin, *Invisible Men*, 155.
2. Bjarkman, "Cuban Blacks in the Majors," 61. Bjarkman argues that the Reds

released de la Cruz on the suspicion that he was black. Given that a good portion of the clientele that attended Crosely Field—fans from nearby Kentucky and West Virginia—were traditional southerners, it is conceivable that the Reds wanted to avoid controversy. However, Bjarkman also describes the Cuban as a "young" player. The right-hander, it should be noted, was twenty-nine years old in his only season with the Reds. Therefore, it is also conceivable that the Reds felt that de la Cruz, pushing thirty, might no longer be productive for them.

3. Rogosin, *Invisible Men,* 175.

4. Tygiel, *Baseball's Great Experiment,* 187, 223.

5. Taylor, *Chávez,* 64.

6. García, *Mexican Americans,* 56–57.

7. Acuña, *Occupied America,* 236.

8. McWilliams, *Brothers under the Skin,* 113.

9. Ibid.

10. Aguilar, *Cuba 1933,* 235–36; Burns, *Latin America,* 225.

11. Miñoso, Fernández, and Kleinfelder, *Miñoso,* 12. On Fuentes, see *Sporting News,* July 22, 1967, Minnie Miñoso file, National Baseball Library, Cooperstown, N.Y.; on Alou, see Alou, *Alou.*

12. Miñoso, Fernández, and Kleinfelder, *Miñoso,* 12.

13. *Sporting News,* Apr. 4, 1962.

14. Miñoso, Fernández, and Kleinfelder, *Miñoso,* 13.

15. Peterson, *Only the Ball Was White,* 365.

16. Ibid., 187, 388.

17. Furlong, "The White Sox Katzenjammer Kid," 78.

18. Miñoso, Fernández, and Kleinfelder, *Miñoso,* 36.

19. Ibid.; *Sporting News,* Apr. 4, 1962.

20. Miñoso, Fernández, and Kleinfelder, *Miñoso,* 37–38.

21. Furlong, "The White Sox Katzenjammer Kid," 80.

22. Regalado, "The Minor League Experience," 67.

23. Ibid.

24. Ibid.

25. Dan Daniel, *New York World-Telegram,* May 2, 1951.

26. *New York World-Telegram,* May 1, 1951.

27. For an extensive analysis of the 1919 riot, see Tuttle, *Race Riot.*

28. Oates, *Let the Trumpet Sound,* 414.

29. Gann and Duignan, *Hispanics,* 40–41; Moore and Pachon, *Hispanics,* 47–48.

30. Miñoso, Fernández, and Kleinfelder, *Miñoso,* 41.

31. Furlong, "The White Sox Katzenjammer Kid," 80.

32. Miñoso, Fernández, and Kleinfelder, *Miñoso,* 57–58.

33. Furlong, "The White Sox Katzenjammer Kid," 80.

34. Miñoso, Fernández, and Kleinfelder, *Miñoso,* 67–68.

35. *Chicago Tribune,* Sept. 21, 1951.

36. *New York World-Telegram,* July 1, 1951.

37. Dan Daniel, *New York World-Telegram,* July 18, 1951.

38. *New York World-Telegram,* Nov. 16, 1951.

39. Tygiel, *Baseball's Great Experiment,* 309.

40. Ibid., 343.

41. Author's compilation from *Baseball Register 1947.*

42. Bjarkman, "Hispanic Baseball Statistical Record," 87–95.

43. Ibid.

44. Lewis, "Sensation," 36–37 (quote), 71–75.

45. Tygiel, *Baseball's Great Experiment,* 169.

46. Lewis, "Sensation," 36–37 (quote), 71–75.

47. Mike García, of course, was himself an outstanding pitcher who contributed 19 victories to the 1954 American League champion Indians, a club that won a record 111 games. Furthermore, Al López, an American-born Latin and Hall of Famer whose bilingual skills, no doubt, helped Avila, managed that record-setting club.

48. Lewis, "Sensation," 36–37, 71–75.

49. Ibid.

50. *Baseball Register 1956.*

51. *Christian Science Monitor,* Apr. 13, 1956; Chicago White Sox promotional pamphlet for Luis Aparicio Day, July 19, 1970, Luis Aparicio file, National Baseball Library.

52. Edwin Pope, "Stardom Relative to Aparicio," *Miami Herald,* Mar. 21, 1965.

53. Margery Miller Welles, "Making a Bid for the Big Leagues," *Christian Science Monitor,* Apr. 13, 1956.

54. *New York World-Telegram,* Mar. 3, 1956.

55. *New York Journal-American,* July 21, 1957.

56. Dan Daniel, *New York Journal-American,* July 21, 1957.

57. Campanis interview.

58. Ibid.

59. Kerrane, *Dollar Sign on the Muscle,* 81.

60. Ibid.

61. Genovese interview.

62. Boyle, "Private World," 8.

63. Rogosin, *Invisible Men,* 111–12.

64. Ibid., 117–18.

65. Boyle, "Private World," 18.

66. Scully, "Discrimination," 236–39.

67. Painter, *Standing at Armageddon,* xxxvi; Brownstone, Franck, and Brownstone, *Island of Hope,* 52.

68. George Vecsey, "Pedro Ramos's Biggest Loss," *New York Times,* Mar. 14, 1982, 24.

69. Ibid.

70. Terzain, *Kid from Cuba,* 47.

71. Oliva, *Tony O!* 14–15.

72. Izenberg, *Great Latin Sports Figures,* 79.

73. Irvin interview; Paul MacFarlane, historian for the *Sporting News,* letter to author, Oct. 2, 1982, author's possession; Genovese interview.

74. Izenberg, *Great Latin Sports Figures,* 48.

75. Terzain, *Kid from Cuba,* 82.

76. *Sporting News,* July 22, 1967.

77. *New York World-Telegram,* Aug. 2, 1955.

•5

What Kind of Country Is This?

[Orlando Cepeda and Felipe Alou] told me what to expect. Another coach prepared me mentally to face it and that's what I did. I never realized it was going to be that bad.
Manny Mota

You can't change things there. Those people have lived that way for two hundred years. You are going to play ball. That's all.
Pedrín Zorilla

When Vic Power came to the United States he had never heard of Jim Crow. But in the early 1950s he soon learned about it when the bus of his Kansas City minor league team stopped at a small gas station in Florida. All but one of the players filed out and quickly advanced to the restroom. Only Power, the team's slugging first baseman from Puerto Rico, remained. Shortly thereafter he, too, emerged for some fresh air. He recalled, "I was the only colored one [on the team]. I noticed the gas attendant; he didn't like it, I could tell by the way he looked at me." Nonetheless, Power proceeded to a nearby Coke machine, purchased a drink, and retreated to the bus. Quickly the attendant stormed on board and demanded that he return the bottle. When Power claimed he had purchased the soft drink, the attendant responded, "I don't want your quarter. I want the bottle back." The Puerto Rican returned it along with some angry words. Shortly after the team continued on its journey, a sheriff's patrol car pulled the bus off the road. With the gas station attendant by his side, the sheriff arrested Power for using obscene language. In addition, he asked for five hundred dollars in bail. After his teammates posted bond, he promised repayment following the anticipated trial. But a friend warned him,

"You'd better not go back, Vic—they put you in jail for a long time in that part of the country." "What kind of country is this?" cried Power.[1]

Power and other black Latins entered the United States when institutional segregation faced serious challenges. Jackie Robinson's debut in 1947, of course, marked the end of baseball segregation. But it also marked the beginning of a long siege of resistance on the part of segregationists that extended beyond the national pastime. "The fact is," as Lonnie Wheeler has written, "Jackie Robinson did not desegregate professional baseball in all of the United States—just the northern ones."[2] Jim Crow, until then, was firmly entrenched and integration only a matter of discussion. "Colored people," wrote Richard Klugar in *Simple Justice,* "were plainly aliens in their own nation. And segregation worked to institutionalize that alienation and widen the gap between races."[3] Events on the baseball diamonds in 1947, however, defied that tradition. Integration became a reality. Moreover, if baseball's archaic doors swung open for blacks, segregationists pondered, would other institutions follow suit? The national pastime, in effect, had thrown down the gauntlet before Jim Crow.

By the early 1950s, advocates for civil rights intensified their campaigns. Finally, in a case similar to the long-forgotten 1931 Lemon Grove, California, case and the 1946 *Méndez v. Westminster School District* case, the Supreme Court ruled in the 1954 landmark *Brown v. Board of Education* that segregation in public schools was, indeed, unconstitutional. The ramifications of this decision, of course, transcended the bounds of education. Institutional racism appeared vulnerable. For proponents of integration, the *Brown* decision trumpeted a call to arms. One year later, Martin Luther King Jr. successfully led a coalition of blacks in a peaceful boycott of the segregated city buses of Montgomery, Alabama. Major victories notwithstanding, integration did not come without a cost.

In spite of a federal court order that called for integration to commence "with all deliberate speed," Jim Crow continued to resist. For instance, in Birmingham, Alabama, local lawmakers did not challenge segregation on the grounds that it prevented the "mongrelization" of its citizens.[4] In Indianola, Mississippi, citizens drew up their "Mississippi Plan," designed to bar integration. And throughout the deep South "white citizen's councils" quickly formed as a means to maintain segregation. State-level politicians were equally adamant. In 1957, Arkansas governor Orval Faubus defied a federal court order that called for the desegregation of Central High School in Little Rock. As resistance persisted into the next decade, civil rights leaders broadened their movement to expose discriminatory practices beyond the boundaries of the South. Historian C. Vann Woodward astutely pointed out, "Northern whites were faced with progress in the South accompanied by deterioration and retrogression of race relations in their own backyards."[5]

Discrimination also continued to plague baseball at all levels. In 1955, fifty-three white teams withdrew in protest from South Carolina's little league state championship tournament when they discovered a black club had also qualified. Although the black youngsters were awarded the state championship by default, little league officials there barred them from competing in the regional tournament.[6] In professional baseball, racial intolerance remained apparent. "Whenever there was a lull," recalled outfielder Hank Thompson, "some loudmouth would yell, 'Nigger,' or 'black unprintable' and you could hear it all over the place." Outfielder Leon Wagner, while playing for Greensboro, North Carolina, encountered a shotgun-wielding fan near the fence who yelled, "Nigger, I'm going to fill you with shot if you catch one ball out there." The disconcerted Wagner allowed the first ball hit his way to drop untouched.[7] In 1953, a Hot Springs, Arkansas, team released George Turgeson, a black pitcher, after other teams in the Cotton States League opposed his presence. When Hot Springs brought him back later that year, another opponent, the Jackson, Mississippi, club, refused to play. Later, league administrators awarded Jackson a victory on the grounds that Hot Springs had no right to ask the Mississippians to play against a black person.[8]

Latins in the United States also encountered racial discrimination. Few ventured far beyond their Latin neighborhoods in such cities as New York, Chicago, Miami, and Los Angeles. And as more Latins migrated, white apprehension increased. To begin with, many Americans thought poorly of Latins in general. Data published in 1940 by the Office of Public Opinion Research substantiated, in part, these attitudes. Of those polled, for instance, 49 percent viewed Latins as "quick-tempered"; 44 percent described them as "lazy"; and 34 percent categorized them as ignorant. As for their positive attributes, only 15 percent of those who responded believed Latins to be intelligent; and a meager 5 percent felt Latins were efficient as a people.[9]

Latin stereotypes, to be sure, developed somewhat differently than those for American blacks. While discrimination toward American blacks was largely rooted, according to Gunnar Myrdal, in the "tradition of economic exploitation," the prevailing attitudes toward Latins emerged from ignorance.[10] As early as 1824, pointed denunciations of the Latin capacity to govern competently were apparent. Joel Poinsett, the first U.S. foreign minister to Mexico, was among those who initiated these perceptions publicly when a series of notes he authored that berated Mexico's forlorn emperor, Augustín de Iturbide, were published. Although reasonably accurate about Iturbide's shortcomings, Poinsett unfairly denigrated all Mexican leaders. Less than forty years later, President James K. Polk, whose campaigns often centered around the arrogant philosophy Manifest Destiny, advanced the vision of an archaic Mexico that impeded progress. American politicians targeted other Latin countries, as well. Theodore Roosevelt, for instance, frustrated in his quest to win the Panamanian isthmus legally, constantly and publicly berated the entire Caribbean and Central American regions, portraying them as "banana republics."

The motion picture industry, too, contributed to the public's perception of Latins. In its earliest years, Hollywood produced several "greaser" films—*Tony the Greaser* (1911), *Broncho Billy and the Greaser* (1914), and *The Greaser's Revenge* (1914)—all of which characterized Hispanics as unsavory and villainous. *Barbarous Mexico* (1913), a movie depicting the brutality of the Mexican Revolution, featured Francisco "Pancho" Villa, who, as it turned out, used the residuals to purchase munitions for his army. *Girl of the Rio* (1932), however, was up to that time Hollywood's most controversial of these films. The movie, in which the Latin lead character, a "cold-blooded" man who hated "to have his luncheon spoiled by the noisy victim of a firing squad," won no fans in Mexico. Indeed, the Mexican government, along with several other Latin American countries and Spain, officially repudiated the film.[11] Three years later, *Bordertown* (1935), a movie that clearly contradicted the ideals of the Good Neighbor Policy, cast its Latin hero as a prone to "uncontrollable fits of temper and violent outbursts."[12]

Television's appearance in the 1950s did little to change these demeaning characterizations Indeed, Spanish accents continued to be a target for ridicule. One of the era's most popular programs, "I Love Lucy," was a chief offender. Throughout its entire nine-year run, Desi Arnaz's character, Ricky Ricardo, humored American viewers with his English. "Ricky's thick accent and his vaunted malapropisms—'Birds of a feather smell the same'; 'I'll cross that bridge when I burn it'; 'You can lead a horse to water but you can't make him a drink'—provided an inexhaustible source of cheap laughs," claimed Gustavo Pérez Firmat in his study of the Cuban image. "All Lucy had to do was mimic Ricky's 'dunt's' and 'wunt's' and the audience's amused response was automatic."[13]

Other perceptions were far less amusing. Carey McWilliams, in his 1948 study on Mexican immigration into the United States, revealed that the white mainstream often viewed a Mexican man as "'lawless' and 'violent' because he had Indian blood; he was 'shiftless and improvident' because such was his nature; his excellence as a stoop-laborer consisted precisely in the fact that he did not aspire to landownership."[14] Puerto Ricans, too, were culturally, and most certainly demographically, quarantined. Many ended up in New York City's so-called Spanish Harlem, where over 50 percent lived below the poverty level. Puerto Ricans, believed some American nativists, had only themselves to blame. According to two New York journalists, they were "mostly crude farmers, subject to congenital diseases. . . . They turn to guile and wile and the steel blade, the traditional weapon of the sugar cutter, mark of their blood and heritage."[15] These inferences, at times, appeared to justify unmitigated acts of violence toward Latin communities. In June 1943, for instance, turbulence broke out in the largely Mexican quarter of East Los Angeles. Hundreds of sailors marched into that neighborhood seeking revenge for a comrade who claimed to have been beaten up by Mexican ruffians. Local reporters, who dubbed the conflict the Zoot Suit Riots, inflamed the situation with sensationalistic stories depicting Mexican youths as jabbing "broken bottlenecks into the faces of their victims" and sailors parading freely throughout the district "spreading panic and terror."[16] Police authorities, for their part, promptly announced "that any Mexicans involved in the rioting would be promptly arrested."[17] The Zoot Suit Riots sparked violence later that summer against Mexican Americans in other large cities such as Chicago, Detroit, and Philadelphia.[18]

Racially motivated policies and programs also came in the wake of the riots. Search-and-seizure tactics by law officers and Immigration and Naturalization Service agents were routinely conducted in many Latin neighborhoods between 1953 and 1956; they helped to perpetuate "the image that Mexicans were somehow different." Furthermore, in many regions Latins had been barred from public establishments.[19] "We serve Mexicans at the fountain but not at the tables. We have got to make some distinction between them and white people," stated one food server at a Texas restaurant during the late 1920s.[20] Pauline R. Kibbe's mid-1940s study on Latins in Texas was even more revealing. Mindful that not all Texas proprietors discriminated, she found that many "Anglo-American operators of cafes, beer parlors, barber shops, and theaters are adamant in refusing service to any and all Latin Americans."[21] "We can't have all those dirty, possibly diseased [Mexicans] swimming with our wives and children," cried one Texas politician in 1951.[22] Given these disturbing attitudes, ball-players from Latin America faced a tremendous challenge. Courage beyond the playing field, hence, became a key ingredient for success in the big leagues.

━━━━━━━━━━━

Most black Latin players were unprepared to face America's racial environment. "I didn't even know about the stuff when I get here," claimed a surprised Roberto Clemente. "I don't believe in color; I believe in people."[23] Clemente mirrored the feelings of most Latin players. Indeed, prior to entering the United States, young Latins often perceived American racism as a minor inconvenience in their quest for glory. Older Latins, however, attempted to warn the idealistic young athletes of the pitfalls ahead. "You can't change things there," said baseball coach Pedrín Zorrilla to Clemente. "Those people have lived that way for two hundred years. You are going to play ball. That's all."[24] To many of Clemente's generation, however, racial discrimination in the United States remained nebulous until it was directly confronted. Felipe Alou "did not understand." He claimed, "I never heard of such a thing [as racial segregation]. Back in the Dominican Republic there was never any talk concerning a race problem or racial inequality."[25]

On the Latin baseball diamonds, racism appeared virtually nonexistent. Zorrilla recalled the exploits of Willard Brown, an American black star who won Puerto Rican support with no reference to his color or nationality. He explained that "it was the man . . . the artist . . . it was those things [about him] that they cheered. He didn't have to be Puerto Rican. The Puerto Ricans love baseball, and Willie Brown could play it, and by that very fact he became a brother to us."[26]

The ambiguity of Latin American race relations dates back to the earliest years of the Spanish conquest. Born with the divided roots of Indian and Spanish blood, so-called mestizos, like others of mixed ancestry, faced scorn and were discriminated against throughout the Spanish colonial period. Following the independence movements of the 1820s, however, their growth in numbers improved their opportunities for political and socioeconomic mobility even as it brought about animosity among some members of the white elite. Those of mixed ancestry were, according to Argentine Carlos Bunge in the midnineteenth century, "impure, atavistically anti-Christian; they are like the two heads of a fabulous hydra that surrounds, constricts, and strangles with its giant spiral a beautiful pale virgin, Spanish America."[27] By the late nineteenth century, racial identity had become a minimal factor in social differentiation. Increasingly, the criterion for division was personal wealth. "Race [was] conceived as a thing in itself [to Latin Americans], not as an item of cultural codification," determined sociologist E. Seda Bonilla in an extensive 1961 study of the Puerto Rican social structure.[28] Race alone was not in itself a cause to discriminate. Indeed, those of mixed ancestry made up a large portion of Latin society. Felipe Alou's own family roots were not uncommon in Latin America. "My mother is a Caucasian, the daughter of Spaniard who had migrated to the Dominican Republic. My father is a Negro, the grandson of a slave who had most likely been imported from Africa to work on the farms," he described. "There had never appeared to be anything wrong with a man merely because of the color of his skin."[29] Even as early as the eighteenth century, the Spanish Crown sanctioned interracial marriages, providing that the black or Indian partner was financially stable.

But discrimination did exist in Latin America because "racial identity . . . function[ed] as a barrier to the achievement of high status in the social hierarchy."[30] In Carl Degler's study on race relations in Brazil, one professor of mixed ancestry observed, "Some affirm that the sinister racial problem does not exist among [Brazilians], that the blacks enjoy the same rights, the same prerogatives as the white man. That is a sad utopia. The higher levels of life in the country keep their doors shut against the black."[31] On this count, the discrimination of blacks and those of mixed ancestry in Latin America bore an uncanny resemblance to the Gunnar Myrdal theory of economic exploitation. As he explained in his groundbreaking study, "the very fact that the masses of [American] Negroes, because of economic deprivation . . . are prevented from entering even the bottom of the occupational hierarchy, are paid low wages and, consequently, are poor gives in its turn motivation for continued social discrimination."[32] Latin blacks, though their financial deprivation suggested analogies with their North American cousins, carried more social leverage. "You can go any place you want. You can go to the restaurant, you can go to the movies, and you can go anywhere," claimed Vic Power of his native Puerto Rico. "But the funny thing about it is if you go to a lot of places like a bank or hotel, the white Puerto Ricans—they get the jobs."[33] Tony Oliva's experiences in Cuba reinforced the theory of economic discrimination. "The color of your skin didn't matter as long as you had money."[34] "Although whiteness may be considered desirable, an individual's status is more clearly demarcated by class position," explained sociologist Harry H. L. Kitano with respect to Latin American social stratification.[35] Joseph P. Fitzpatrick, in his research on Puerto Rican society, was even more specific: "In the United States, a man's color determines what class he belongs to; in Puerto Rico, a man's class determines what color he is."[36] Prejudice, claimed one Brazilian black, "is like the dust on the hearth. No one has a clear awareness of its existence, especially among whites."[37] Although Latin players who traveled to the United States were not totally ignorant of discrimination, that skin color might impede their potential, let alone their entire social itinerary, came as a shock to many.

If Jim Crow seemed irrational to most Latins, the manner in which it was practiced further added to their confusion. Americans seemed obsessed with skin color. Puerto Rican–born Rubén Gómez stayed in segregated facilities at the Florida-based spring training facility of the Giants. Gómez, however, found that restaurants seemed selective in their bias. One evening, for instance, after he and a black teammate encountered a "whites only" restaurant, Gómez "went in, but the other guy didn't want to. The owner came over and said 'how are you?' and started to talk to me, and they served me. The other guy saw this through the restaurant window. He came in [but] they wouldn't serve him." Gómez realized "how crazy the whole question of race is in America—if you speak Spanish you're somehow not as black."[38]

Puerto Rican Carlos Bonilla also confronted this racial inconsistency. Upon his arrival at a Florida spring training camp, Bonilla shared facilities with his white teammates. Two weeks later, however, after his skin had darkened in the hot Florida sun, the club reassigned him to live with black teammates. Racial questioning had become so omnipresent that when Italian American Don Mossi joined the Tulsa club, one fan turned to his wife and said, "Good God, Maude, they got three niggers now."[39]

Born in Arecibo in 1931, Victor Pellot Power commenced his professional career in the Puerto Rican League at age sixteen. While he originally planned to pursue a career in medicine, a more promising future on the baseball field developed during his teenage years. After his father's death, Power supported the family by signing with a local Puerto Rican club for $250 a month. In 1950, former American black league great Quincy Troupe, having seen Power perform in Latin America, signed the young player to a nonaffiliated Class D Drummond team in Ontario, Canada. One year later, New York Yankee scout Tom Greenwade, impressed with

Power's .334 average and slugging prowess, acquired the Puerto Rican's contract.

At the time of Power's purchase, the Yankees had yet to integrate. Although a number of other clubs were still exclusively white, the Yankee reluctance to hire blacks was especially embarrassing because the club shared the New York City area with the two most integrated teams in baseball—the Dodgers and the Giants. They faced further ridicule in 1953 when Rubén Gómez, who had been in the Yankee farm system only to buy out his own contract after he had lost hope for promotion, emerged with the Giants and won thirteen games.[40] Moreover, as early as 1945, club president Larry MacPhail had served on Mayor Fiorella La Guardia's city antidiscrimination committee. It was the responsibility of MacPhail and Dodger president Branch Rickey to probe and propose policies designed to eliminate racism in New York baseball clubs.[41]

MacPhail, if anything, undermined the committee's goal, however. At one point, he openly condemned pro-integrationists. He felt they knew "little about baseball and nothing about the business end of its operation." He contended further that they "were talking through their collective hats."[42] MacPhail, in effect, used his influence to water down the committee's recommendation to the baseball commissioner, which included, according to historian Jules Tygiel, "no methods to bring blacks into the major leagues, nor any desire to do so."[43] With no integration more than three years after Jackie Robinson's debut with the cross-town Dodgers, the Yankees faced mounting criticism.

Vic Power, of course, came to play baseball, not to scrutinize Yankee management. Despite his obvious potential, he remained philosophical about the Yankee evaluation of his progress. The team, Power concluded, needed a "left-handed first baseman to get a shot at that right field stand in Yankee Stadium, and I hit right-handed."[44] Unaware of the possible racism at play, Power patiently waited for the parent club to promote him.

Meanwhile, he persevered at the Yankee minor league affiliate in Kansas City, where movie houses, restaurants, and other public facilities bore the sign "White Only." "There was no place . . . to go, just home . . . in the colored section," he recalled. "I made a lot of Spanish friends—some white—but a lot of people didn't like it too much that I [was] a colored player. They [got] mad at me. I remember I was hitting in the ballpark [around] .300 to .350, but they booed me just the same every time I came to bat."[45] When the team was on the road, particularly in the South, he was forced to dwell in different accommodations from those of his white counterparts. "I wasn't allowed to go to the white hotel," recalled Power, whose patience grew thin as he awaited a promotion to the Yankees. "I stayed in the best house in the colored section, and that was usually a funeral parlor. I slept with dead people at night; or let's say I tried to sleep."[46]

Power's productivity on the field also added to his impatience. Moreover, his suspicions increased as criticism of the Yankees grew in intensity. In 1953, he hit .349 for Kansas City and ended up winning the American Association's batting title. Power grew optimistic. "I think, 'Now I can't miss, now I get my break.' Finally, they call me and trade me to Philadelphia before spring training. And they put Bill Skowron, who hit right-handed, like me, at first base."[47]

Prior to the trade, evidence of the Yankee position on integration surfaced. Not only had MacPhail balked at the idea of desegregation but many of his subordinates openly expounded their opposition to integration. Traveling secretary Bill McCorry pledged that "no nigger will ever have a berth on any train I'm running," and manager Casey Stengel often made uncomplimentary remarks about blacks.[48] While the Yankees heatedly denied allegations of racial bias, the Power trade seemed to suggest the contrary. Writer Dan Daniel asserted, "If the Yankees weren't guilty as charged, they were certainly going out of their way to look for trouble."[49] Power's baseball prowess notwithstanding, the Yankees maintained that he endangered their "image." According to the team, that he was prone to exhibit his Latin pride and respond to aggressors regardless of skin color did not help his cause.[50] In short, the Puerto Rican did not possess the "right attitude." At the core of their grievance was Power's apparent relationship with a white woman.[51] The white woman in question turned out to be his wife, a Puerto Rican who enjoyed wearing blond wigs.

Power joined the Athletics for the 1954 season and earned a berth as their regular first baseman. In due course, the Puerto Rican star, whom Yankees president Dan Topping once described as "a poor fielder," won the American League Gold Glove award seven consecutive years after it was initiated in 1958.[52] The team, however, spent its last year in Philadelphia and, in 1955, began operations in Kansas City—a city that he did not hold in high regard. Again he found himself in a place where Jim Crow haunted him and the potential for humiliating circumstances was great. When he drove, city policemen routinely stopped and questioned him about his wife. "Everywhere she went with me the Kansas City people they no like it," he recalled.[53]

But Power's wit sometimes helped him to withstand demeaning treatment. Once, following his arrest for jaywalking in Florida, Power plead-

Vic Power. (Courtesy of the National Baseball Hall of Fame Library, Cooperstown, N.Y.)

ed innocent at the hearing. Asked on what grounds he claimed his innocence, Power replied, "I go to bars, it says whites only. The bathrooms it
says whites only. So when I see people crossing at the green light, I say to
myself, the green light is for whites. The red, that's for colored folks."[54]
On another occasion, when informed by an employee at a Jim Crow restaurant, "We don't serve colored people here," he responded, "That's okay,
I don't eat them."[55]

Nothing, however, could temper the bitter disillusionment of his experiences. "Being a human being I never thought people [were] going to be like that, making me live alone . . . go nowhere," he reminisced. "But what can you do? You can't do nothing except play harder."[56] For Power, his dreams of stardom and, if nothing else, at least a fair shake, with the Yankees succumbed to the reality of a broken promise. "I really thought that if I played for the Yankees I could piss, too."[57]

———

Out of the frustration, however, grew a stubborn perseverance to succeed at all costs. Like Power, other Latins used their racial problems as a springboard to reach their goals. Manny Mota remembered "what happened to other people, but even though I felt bad, I didn't let myself [get] down." According to the Dominican, "I tried harder and harder [knowing] I'd have to suffer. I knew I'd have to take a lot of slaps in the face, something I [didn't] have to take in my own country, but if I was going to make it, I'd have to face all of those things."[58] Mota's countryman, Felipe Alou, shared this dogged determination. "Until [these racial problems occurred], I hadn't been homesick," he explained. "About the only thing that kept me from going home was that I wanted to play baseball more than ever."[59]

For each player, life in American society was far from easy. Discrimination exceeded their worst fears. "I knew of the [racial problems]," Orlando Cepeda recalled, "but I never knew it was going to be that bad. When I finally went [to the United States], I thought that because I was Puerto Rican things would be a little different, but they were still the same."[60] Puerto Rican players were especially bewildered at the treatment they received. Their citizenship, they believed, should have shielded them from resentment. Felipe Alou remembered that "José [Pagán] comes from Puerto Rico. Puerto Rico is part of the United States. José is an American citizen. Yet he is treated the same way as any Latin who is not an American citizen."[61] Many black Latins inexperienced with America's culture initially did not associate race with discrimination. Monte Irvin remembered that Latins of African heritage believed that discrimination in the United States was attributed to "politics, not color." The reality was, of course, different. Irvin explained, "You could have all the ability in the world as a Latin playing in Puerto Rico, Venezuela, Santo Domingo, or Panama . . . but in America, a Latin black was in the same [racial] situation as an American black."[62]

Experienced veterans, such as Roberto Clemente, tried to orient Orlando Cepeda and other incoming Latins prior to their arrival on the mainland. Cepeda recalled, "Clemente [accompanied] José Pagán, Julio Navarro, and myself into the United States. He used to tell us how to behave. If we [saw] a white girl, make sure and not say anything because [white men] used to get mad. But no matter what anyone told us, we had to see it to believe it."[63] Tony Oliva needed no lengthy orientation, for "it didn't take me long to discover that the situation was different in America."[64]

Oliva was an excited twenty year old when he landed in Florida in 1961 to pursue a professional baseball career. Prior to his arrival, he had spent a few days in Mexico City, where his freedom was not impaired by his skin color. Oliva, caught up in optimism, did not anticipate the pitfalls ahead. "After all," he recollected, "we were in America . . . and about to become professional ballplayers." Only minutes after his arrival at the hotel, a team interpreter quickly shuttled him to the segregated facilities reserved exclusively for black players. Oliva claimed that "the only hotel in town said it would accept only the white Cubans; the colored had to find another place to stay." Oliva, nonetheless, remained philosophical at the outset. He rationalized that "if this was the way people were in America, what could I do about it?" Humiliating ordeals, however, followed. As they mounted, Oliva grew less tolerant and his normally jovial attitude disappeared. Finally, at one restaurant, "the owner said blacks couldn't eat with whites— we had to eat in the kitchen so that we would be out of sight of other customers." The Cuban angrily stormed out of the restaurant and retreated onto the bus, where he brooded over the state of affairs. He thought, "If this is the custom in America, it isn't right."[65]

Dominican right-handed Juan Marichal was less vocal but equally as frustrated during the 1958 summer pitching for the San Francisco Giants' minor league team in Michigan City, Indiana. The bigotry he encountered isolated him. He pointed out that "for a Latin American who spoke no English, to travel through the American South was not the most wonderful opportunity in the world." Marichal remembered that "there were no restaurants that would serve the Negroes or Dominicans or Puerto Ricans on the team."[66] His first road trip as a minor leaguer hardened the proud Dominican's resolve to succeed. Denied service from a roadside diner, he vowed, "One day this same restaurant might be honored if Juan Marichal were to enter its doors, but I would pass it by."[67]

Difficulties in adjustments, like for Félix Mantilla, sometimes became dangerous. While playing in Montgomery, Alabama, the black Puerto

Rican and his teammate, Hank Aaron, constantly received death threats. This, in addition to daily beanings, festered within Mantilla. "It wasn't easy for him to turn the other cheek," recalled Aaron. "When [he got beaned], Félix would shout back at the pitcher, mostly in Spanish."[68] Finally, in Macon, Georgia, Mantilla exploded after having been hit with yet another pitch. As the Puerto Rican scuffled with a white opponent an ugly scene developed. "The people from the white section along first base were coming over the railing and people from the colored section were headed to the white section," according to Aaron. "It was real close to being a race riot."[69] Local enforcement officers immediately arrived, wielded tommy guns, and threatened to shoot any spectators who climbed onto the field.[70]

Mantilla experienced trying times during his early years with the Jacksonville, Florida, team in the Sally League. He claimed, "Jacksonville was real bad. I'm talking about 1953. They wouldn't boo you because you were playing bad, it was because you were colored. The whole league was like that." At one point, a death threat that reached Mantilla was forwarded to the Federal Bureau of Investigation. Hank Aaron recalled that within a short time, "there were two FBI guys at the door trying to talk to Félix, who could barely speak English." The following evening, the agents sat in the stands for what turned out to be an uneventful game.[71] Similar to what Vic Power had discovered in Kansas City, Mantilla said of Jacksonville, "The only place you wanted to stay was in your room, but you couldn't stay in your room for six months." Mantilla, among the first of the black Latins to play in the American professional leagues, found it to be a dubious honor: "Me and Hank [Aaron] were the first colored ballplayers in Evansville and then Jacksonville. And then they wanted to send me to Atlanta to be the first there and I told them 'no, I'm tired of being first. Send somebody else. Not me.'"[72]

Incidents in his early big league career also proved rough. During his first spring training in the Milwaukee Braves organization, a club official took the raw rookies into a nearby town to attend the movies. To their misfortune, they were unknowingly left at a Jim Crow theater. "We had to sit on the sidewalk from seven until the bus came back at ten," he recalled. "Right there, a lot of the [Latins] decided to go back."[73]

While the Braves placed Mantilla on their roster, they did little to orient the black Latins about American racial customs. "We used to play a lot of exhibition games down South and nobody used to tell us where we had to go and things like that," he claimed. "We were on our own. I remember times when the white players used to go to the good hotels and we had to find some flea bag somewhere to stay."[74]

In 1956, Felipe Alou received the same treatment. He had been in the United States for only a brief period when the Giants assigned him to his first minor league post in April. As for many other Latins at that time, Alou's early encounters with Jim Crow often tested his fortitude. Although he had been brought up in the small village of Haina, Alou was familiar with foreign travel. As a member of the Dominican Republic's Pan-American team in 1955, Alou impressed American scouts with his hitting performance against a U.S. club they faced in Mexico City. His success as an amateur, however, did little to prepare him for the treatment he encountered as a professional in the United States only one year later. In April 1956, Alou spent several days at the Giants' training facility in Melbourne, Florida, as management decided at what level to place him. As part of an experiment, the Giants sent Alou and five other players to initiate integration of their Lake Charles, Louisiana, club. At that time a state mandate barred competition between black and white players. League officials met and, according to Alou, decided that "the law had to be upheld and that colored ballplayers were no longer welcomed in the Evangeline League."[75] After only five games, as Alou claimed, "they drove us out."[76] Moreover, his trip from Lake Charles to his new team in Cocoa, Florida, turned into a primer on American racial mores. "Wherever I looked during the frequent bus stops in Mississippi, Alabama, Georgia and Florida there was always a sign that I couldn't read but which I was beginning to grasp the awesome power of. It screamed at me from everywhere: COLORED. There were lines at the lunch counters for whites, separate lines for colored people and there is no use in going into details of who got better service and food."[77]

His tenure with the Single A Cocoa team provided little comfort. During road games "the team always split into two groups, the whites going to one hotel, the colored to another. I have no idea what sort of hotel the whites stayed in. All I know is that the one we were sent to was in the colored section of town and that the floors in our second story rooms were so rickety that we were afraid to walk on them for fear they would collapse."[78] Soon, more trouble arose.

Following an evening home game, Alou, accompanied by two American black players, drove to a restaurant for a snack. Unfortunately, they entered a segregated establishment. The owner immediately called the police. The officers, however, did not speak Spanish and a standoff ensued. The Dominican, who correctly deciphered the problem, refused to leave the automobile. Tensions rose. "I wasn't going to get out, no matter what. Too often had I been humiliated. Too often had I been made to feel ashamed of the color of my skin." he charged. "A fleeting thought crossed my mind and I vowed that, if need be, I was willing to die right there rather than make any further concessions." As the policeman reached for Alou's arm, the Dominican "rattled some strong Spanish words to him. He backed away."[79] When he returned to his room, the trauma of that evening brought "a loneliness and despair that made me ache all over."[80] Other disheartening incidents on the ball field and in the locker rooms followed. Alou was a constant target for white pitchers. In one instance, the Dominican discovered some teammates attempting to sabotage his progress by disclosing his batting weaknesses to opposing pitchers.[81]

Other Latins were equally subject to racism. In Georgia, Leo Cárdenas, according to state law, was prohibited from dressing in the same area with whites. To comply with the guidelines, a separate cubicle was built for Cárdenas and his black teammate, Curt Flood.[82] Veteran pitcher Luis Tiant recalled, "There is a lot of stuff I will never forget. I remember when I first broke in, driving forty hours on the bus from Mexico City to Tulsa, and I couldn't even get into a restaurant." To make matters worse, "Me and other Latin players had to sit on the bus and our teammates [had to] bring the food out to us."[83] Former Pirate Manny Sanguillen remembered similar incidents at the outset of his professional career in the United States. "Once we were in Fort Meyers, Florida, . . . and we wanted to eat in a Howard Johnson's. There was Clemente, Manny Mota, Mateo Alou, José Pagán, and me. They made us wait for more than an hour because we were colored and speaking Spanish." On another occasion, Sanguillen noted, "I tried to stay at the Howard Johnson's in Bradenton, Florida, and they told me I had to have a letter from the governor of the state."[84]

Latin players did, at times, find field managers who were sympathetic allies. Buddy Kerr, who managed in the Giants' minor league organization, developed fond relationships with his Latin players. According to Juan Marichal, "Perhaps the toughest part of my life in organized baseball was made easy for me by him." When encountering Jim Crow diners, "Kerr himself would go inside and bring us food."[85] Felipe Alou also spoke highly of Kerr: "He kept me in baseball. I could sense that Kerr was somewhat embarrassed about [racial problems]. He used to take me aside and encourage me. Buddy would tell me I was a good prospect and if I didn't let the race situation bother me I would make it to the majors."[86] George Genovese, 1962 El Paso manager, claimed that Jim Crow attitudes demoralized Latins because they "didn't have the discrimination in their countries as it was here. The big job for a manager was to deal with this lack of understanding." He remembered that "one night in Pecos, Texas we stopped to get some cokes. A few minutes later a man chased two of my black players out with a pistol." Genovese's Latin players were shocked. He, however, had his own methods of battling discrimination and maintaining team unity. To mitigate their humiliation, the El Paso manager always joined his Latin and black players when they were forced to dine in kitchens. And when diners refused service, Genovese simply searched for eating establishments more accommodating.[87]

———

Such episodes were not uncommon during the period the historian Carl Brauer has referred to as America's "Second Reconstruction." Not surprisingly, the civil rights movement increased racial tensions in the 1960s. Freedom bus rides, sit-ins, and desegregation issues led to explosive encounters on college campuses, churches, and ethnic communities throughout the decade. One thing, however, was clear: social "outsiders," such as blacks and Hispanics, had demonstrated their unwillingness to submit to racism any longer.

Baseball, as it had so many times in the past, served as a microcosm during this critical period. During the 1950s the process of integrating the game was slow and rocky. Only a handful of blacks appeared on major league rosters in the early fifties. By the latter part of the decade American and Latin blacks alike became important components for their respective clubs. Moreover, throughout the decade, baseball observers saw a correlation between the success of certain teams and their utilization of black and Latin stars. Yet, off the field black Latins continued to experience racial harassment. And, like those who crusaded for civil rights on the streets, they, too, were less tolerant of American attitudes toward them.

By the 1960s, their supposed quality of play no longer kept Latins from the major leagues. Strengthened by their positions, a number of veteran players, such as Roberto Clemente, Orlando Cepeda, and Felipe Alou, not only defied the status quo but grew more outspoken. They especially challenged the stereotypes that often led to racial indignities. Defiantly, Al McBean of the Virgin Islands pronounced, "We've come a long way, and we're not going to put up with this, but we want to be treated like human beings. We're proud."[88]

Stereotypes of Latins as hypochondriacs angered many players. Roberto Clemente claimed, "If a Latin or an American Negro is sick, they say it is all in his head. Felipe Alou once went to his team doctor and [he] said, 'You have nothing wrong.' The next day he went to a private doctor and the doctor [told] him, 'you have a broken foot.'"[89] Clemente himself was a popular target of writers for his alleged fictitious ills. Unfortunately, his pains were all too real. At one point during the 1963 season the Pirates star was struck by food poisoning and had to have his stomach pumped. Although weakened, he attempted to play but was unable to complete the game. Pirate manager Danny Murtaugh, who had grown increasingly impatient, finally exploded, "You're making too much money to sit on the bench. The next time you feel like playing, you'll play every day until *I* say you won't play." His integrity in question, the Puerto Rican reacted sharply, "You talk like I don't want to play." Clemente later claimed that Murtaugh "didn't believe anything was wrong with me. If I am sick, I do not deny it. If my back is hurting and I am forced to punch the ball with no power, I tell the truth."[90]

Orlando Cepeda's knee problems and slightly malformed leg did not prevent him from a successful career with the San Francisco Giants and later with the St. Louis Cardinals. Born in Ponce, Puerto Rico, in 1937, Cepeda grew up surrounded by baseball. His father, Perucho Cepeda, was a legendary ballplayer in Puerto Rico and acknowledged as one of the most competitive performers in the Caribbean. Though his skills, according to Puerto Rican baseball aficionados, were of major league caliber, the star chose to bypass professional baseball in the United States—about which he had heard tales of vicious discrimination from the mouths of his black American teammates.[91] His son, years later, decided to take the risk. Young Cepeda was so determined to succeed that he appeared at the Giants' 1955 spring training camp with a conditional contract. Scout Alex Pompez had signed Cepeda and fellow Puerto Rican José Pagán with the understanding that payment was contingent on their making the organization.[92] A desire to emulate his legendary father provided added incentive in his quest to succeed in professional baseball. Cepeda's climb took only three years before the organization promoted him to the parent club. By then, the Giants had moved their operations from New York to San Francisco. For the Puerto Rican, the move was timely. Anxious to establish their own major league roots in the west, Bay Area fans quickly adopted the Latin rookie as a San Francisco product. Perhaps more than any other Latin to that time, Cepeda met with unprecedented popularity. "I thought that was kind of an interesting phenomenon because when Willie Mays came out everybody knew he was great," recalled journalist Nick Peters, "but [Mays] had this reputation of being a New Yorker."[93] Giants fans clearly did not take to "imports" and favored those players not "tarnished" with eastern influence. Hence, they looked toward the future and supported Giants players that "they could call their own. And," as Peters pointed out, "Orlando was the first and the best of these young guys."[94]

Orlando Cepeda. (Courtesy of the National Baseball Hall of Fame Library, Cooperstown, N.Y.)

Cepeda delivered. In his rookie season, the Puerto Rican slugged twenty-five home runs, batted in ninety runs, and hit .312. In addition, he led the National League with most doubles. As a result of his accomplishments, the Baseball Writer's Association of America unanimously selected Cepeda for the 1958 Rookie of the Year Award. Giants manager Bill Rigney claimed that "Orlando was the best young right-handed hitter I ever managed. He had phenomenal power."[95] San Franciscans loved him and, partly to spite the New Yorker Mays, voted Cepeda that year's Player of the Year in a popularity contest. Even the great Mays, who was somewhat chagrined over the vote because of his fine season, resigned himself that "Orlando was theirs from the scratch. They didn't inherit him."[96] As he matured, Cepeda provided more power for the Giants. In 1961 he blasted 46 home runs and led the National League with 146 RBIs while helping his club overtake the Los Angeles Dodgers to win the pennant. Yet for all his achievements, managers Bill Rigney and Alvin Dark constantly targeted the "Baby Bull" for criticism. Dark, in particular, had his own perceptions of race.

As a star second baseman with the New York Giants in the 1950s, Dark was a fiery competitor. This demeanor carried over into his managing days, when he made exacting demands upon his team. Most players took his competitive spirit in stride, but he remained a curious personality to the American black and Latin players on the Giants squad. Raised in Lake Charles, Louisiana—the same Lake Charles that was so inhospitable to Felipe Alou years earlier—Dark's perceptions of race appeared to bias his managerial decisions. Ironically, during Dark's 1961–64 tenure, the Giants rostered more American blacks and Latins than any other club. This chemistry proved explosive.

The 1964 season started off on a sour note for the Latin players on the Giants. Dark, in an effort to unify his team, placed signs in the locker rooms instructing all personnel to speak English. Though critics said he was insensitive, Dark was not alone in implementing this type of policy. Paul Richards of the Chicago White Sox also banned his Latin players from speaking Spanish. "The only language I want spoken around here" he announced, "is 'Chicago White Sox.'" Minnie Miñoso, the quick-witted Cuban, took the ban lightly and humored the stern Richards by always ending his Spanish-language conversations with the words "Chicago White Sox."[97]

Unlike Miñoso, however, Cepeda did not find this mandate amusing. To Cepeda, the ban was irrational. Must Felipe Alou, he wondered, converse only in English even with Mateo, his own brother? Outraged by Dark's insensitivity, Cepeda stormed into the manager's office and said, "Listen, I'm Puerto Rican and I'm proud of my language. I would feel foolish if I talked to [José] Pagán in English. First of all we won't be able to communicate because we don't speak [English] that well and secondly, I'm Puerto Rican and I'm going to speak my language." Cepeda remarked that Dark "became bitter" after the incident.[98]

Not all of the Latin players totally disagreed with Dark's approach to team unity. Felipe Alou claimed that the manager "broke up the arrangement of lockers in our clubhouse, seeing to it that there was more of an intermingling between races."[99] Alou reasoned that Dark's approach at racial harmony made sense. The low-key Dominican believed that "the more we chatted together the more we found out about each other's family, hopes, aches, ills and beliefs."[100]

Cepeda's pride at being Puerto Rican, however, was clear. Often he referred to his culture and people as a source of inspiration. "I am very proud of my people," stated the slugger. "When they do big things, important things, it gives me a good feeling."[101] Observers, nonetheless, knew that Cepeda's good nature might turn aggressive when he believed his dignity and heritage were slighted.

Dark and Cepeda had a history of misunderstandings. The skipper, in his autobiography, acknowledged his role in their turbulent relationship. "He was a favorite son in San Francisco, and I shouldn't have diminished him," he recalled. "I didn't handle Orlando very well."[102] In 1962, Dark's problems with Cepeda compounded when he revealed that he kept a "book" of evaluations on his hitters. That Dark maintained such a record was entirely appropriate; that he questioned and demeaned Cepeda's hitting prowess, which he apparently did during the season, seemed ridiculous. Appraised of Dark's judgment, Willie Mays, Cepeda's teammate, replied, "Shit, a man hits .300 and bats in 100 runs, how you gonna say he can't hit?"[103]

Dark also lacked diplomacy. Given that the Giants were a racially diverse team, Dark, who properly insisted upon a high standard of performance, often seriously miscalculated the nature of his statements and policies. With Cepeda, the Giants manager could not fully compliment the sensitive Puerto Rican without reminding observers about his shortcomings. For instance, after praising Cepeda for "popping a ball into right field to drive in the winning run," Dark added that "he had popped out so many times in that situation."[104] During the 1963 season the skipper further aggravated his already tainted image when he told writer Dick Young that "baseball is not ready for colored managers."[105] Forgetting about the American black leagues, Dark qualified his statement by suggesting that blacks, to that point, had little or no experience as field bosses. He also failed to point out that opportunities for blacks as managers literally did not exist. "I didn't run down anyone racially," he said in retrospect. "I said as far as running a baseball club was concerned, which implied a necessary intelligence, I just didn't think blacks were ready." The following year, Dark added more fuel to his own fire.[106]

He often appeared callous by denigrating Cepeda's injury claims as mere lack of desire. In doing so, he also questioned the slugger's integrity. Cepeda later wrote, "With the Giants if you were Willie Mays, you played with a broken hand. If you were Juan Marichal, you pitched with a broken foot. To complain meant you didn't have 'pride.'"[107] Dark's relationship with Cepeda worsened when he suggested in *Look* magazine that the Puerto Rican "lacked hustle." The Puerto Rican, in turn, sued Dark for his allegations. The manager, relentless in his criticism, went on to claim that "Cepeda was a moody athlete who had to be pampered."[108] At one point, Dark allegedly ordered Coach Herman Franks to tell Cepeda not to bother coming to the ballpark.[109] Cepeda believed Dark's attitude reflected a racial bias: "Dark thought I was trying not to play. He treated me like a child. I am a human being, whether I am blue or black or white or green. We Latins are different, but we are still human beings. Dark did not respect our differences."[110]

In July 1964, the tension crescendoed when, during an interview with writer Stan Isaacs of *Newsday*, Dark reportedly said:

> We have trouble . . . because we have so many Spanish-speaking and Negro players on the team. They are just not able to perform up to the white ball player when it comes to mental alertness. . . .
>
> You can't make most Negro and Spanish players have the pride in their team that you can get from white players and they just aren't as sharp mentally. They aren't able to adjust to situations because they don't have mental alertness. . . .
>
> One of the biggest things is that you can't make them subordinate themselves to the best interest of the team. You don't find pride in them that you get in the white player.[111]

Dark's allegations failed to correspond with the facts. His own Latin players were rarely out of the line-up. Felipe Alou averaged 137 games between 1960 and 1964; Cepeda, 151 games between 1958 and 1964; and José Pagán, 145 games between 1961 and 1964. Pitcher Juan Marichal, during the year of Dark's criticism, completed 22 of 33 games and led the league in that category. Other Latin stars consistently played. Luis Aparicio, Minnie Miñoso, and Tony Oliva, for instance, all averaged over 145 games per year during their careers. Moreover, pitcher Camilo Pascual led the American League in complete games for three different seasons. Even the National League's most celebrated hypochondriac—Roberto Clemente—was an example of durability. Between 1955 and 1972, he averaged 135 games per year.[112]

Understandably, Dark's comments met with outrage from Latins and blacks. Indeed, the controversy undoubtedly contributed to his firing at the end of the season. In retrospect, Monte Irvin saw Dark's comments as simply the "tip of the iceberg"; race prejudice was not confined to one manager. "Knowing the history of [American racism]," Irvin reasoned, "I'm sure there were others who felt the same way Alvin did. He just got caught. [But] you can't root out all the evil at once—it's a slow process."[113] Too slow for the likes of many Latins. Though Dark claimed he was misquoted, Latins, like Cepeda, simply viewed this incident as a tiny example of a much larger problem that centered on race. Baseball did not shield them from racial controversies. Hence, even their dream of playing in the majors left them with bittersweet memories.

The racial discord that had ripped American society did not leave baseball untouched. While the special hunger continued to lure them to North American professional baseball, black Latins felt the brunt of American prejudice. Their limited knowledge of bigotry in the United States hindered their ability to fully calculate the depth of the hatred they were to face. To survive, they needed to be able to distinguish differences in the people and regions where they played. However, no amount of orientation could temper the humiliation many black Latins endured. In addition to the racial climate, the uncertainties that all Latins faced coming to America reinforced the notion that they were, indeed, strangers in the land.

Notes

1. Robinson, *Baseball Has Done It,* 169.
2. Aaron and Wheeler, *I Had a Hammer,* 4.
3. Klugar, *Simple Justice,* 306.
4. *Time,* June 14, 1954, 4, 6.
5. Woodward, *Strange Career of Jim Crow,* 324–26.
6. Foreman, "Discrimination," 33.
7. Tygiel, *Baseball's Great Experiment,* 303, 282.

8. *New York Times,* May 22, 1953.

9. Regalado, "'Image Is Everything,'" 103–4.

10. Myrdal, *American Dilemma,* 208.

11. Woll and Miller, *Ethnic and Racial Images,* 244.

12. Ibid., 245.

13. Pérez Firmat, *Life on the Hyphen,* 28.

14. McWilliams, *North from Mexico,* 213.

15. Moore and Pachon, *Hispanics,* 34.

16. McWilliams, *North from Mexico,* 248–49.

17. Ibid., 249.

18. Meier and Rivera, *The Chicanos,* 194.

19. Marden, *Minorities in American Society,* 143.

20. Ibid., 135.

21. Pauline R. Kibbe quoted in ibid., 143.

22. García, *Operation Wetback,* 149.

23. Musick, *Who Was Roberto?* 111.

24. Ibid., 75.

25. Alou, *Alou,* 29.

26. Izenberg, *Great Latin Sports Figures,* 4.

27. Keen and Wasserman, *History of Latin America,* 243.

28. Bonilla, "Social Structure," 147.

29. Alou, *Alou,* 29.

30. Bonilla, "Social Structure," 142.

31. Degler, *Neither Black nor White,* 157.

32. Gunnar Myrdal quoted in Klugar, *Simple Justice,* 313.

33. Robinson, *Baseball Has Done It,* 166.

34. Oliva, *Tony O!* 9–10.

35. Kitano, *Race Relations,* 184.

36. Joseph P. Fitzpatrick quoted in ibid., 185.

37. Degler, *Neither Black nor White,* 157.

38. Wagenheim, *Clemente!* 88.

39. Tygiel, *Baseball's Great Experiment,* 166.

40. Ibid., 296.

41. *Sporting News,* Nov. 25, 1945.

42. Tygiel, *Baseball's Great Experiment,* 82–83.

43. Ibid., 85.

44. Robinson, *Baseball Has Done It,* 166–67.

45. Ibid., 167.

46. Kiersh, *Where Have You Gone,* 305.

47. Robinson, *Baseball Has Done It,* 166–67.

48. Tygiel, *Baseball's Great Experiment,* 294.

49. Dan Daniel quoted in ibid., 295.

50. Ibid., 297.

51. Ibid.

52. Ibid., 296.

53. Robinson, *Baseball Has Done It,* 168.

54. Kiersh, *Where Have You Gone,* 179.

55. Boyle, "The Latins Storm," 29.

56. Robinson, *Baseball Has Done It,* 167–68.

57. Kiersh, *Where Have You Gone,* 175.

58. Mota interview.

59. Alou, *Alou,* 29.

60. Cepeda interview.

61. Alou, "Latin American Ballplayers," 77.

62. Irvin interview.

63. Cepeda interview.

64. Oliva, *Tony O!* 9–10.

65. Ibid., 11, 23.

66. Marichal, *A Pitcher's Story,* 98.

67. Devaney, *Marichal,* 59–60.

68. Aaron, *I Had a Hammer,* 81.

69. Ibid.

70. Tygiel, *Baseball's Great Experiment,* 282.

71. Aaron, *I Had a Hammer,* 83.

72. *Sport,* Aug. 1965, Félix Mantilla file, National Baseball Library, Cooperstown, N.Y.

73. Ibid.

74. *Sports Collector's Digest,* July 19, 1985, Mantilla file.

75. Alou, *Alou,* 29.

76. Cantwell, "Invasion from Santo Domingo," 54–61; Alou, *Alou,* 29.

77. Alou, *Alou,* 30.

78. Ibid., 33.

79. Ibid., 35–36; *New York Post,* Apr. 29, 1956.

80. Alou, *Alou,* 36.

81. Ibid.

82. Flood, *The Way It Is,* 43.

83. "All Latins Want Is an Equal Chance," *Eugene (Oregon) Register-Guard,* May 1, 1979.

84. Wagenheim, *Clemente!* 161.

85. Marichal, *A Pitcher's Story,* 97.

86. Alou, *Alou,* 35.

87. Genovese interview.

88. Boyle, "The Latins Storm," 26.

89. Musick, *Who Was Roberto?* 191.

90. Ibid., 168–69.

91. Cepeda interview.

92. *Sporting News*, Oct. 13, 1962.

93. Peters interview.

94. Ibid.

95. *San Francisco Giants Yearbook*, 22.

96. Mays, *Say Hey*, 111.

97. Alou, *Alou*, 109.

98. Cepeda interview.

99. Alou, *Alou*, 102.

100. Ibid.

101. Rosenbaum, "Leader of the Latins."

102. Dark and Underwood, *When in Doubt*, 91.

103. Einstein, *Willie's Time*, 175.

104. Dark and Underwood, *When in Doubt*, 93.

105. Ibid.

106. Ibid.

107. Einstein, *Willie's Time*, 208.

108. *New York Journal American*, Aug. 7, 1964; *New York World-Telegram*, Oct. 13, 1964.

109. *New York Post*, Oct. 1, 1965.

110. Mulvoy, "Cha Cha," 20.

111. Einstein, *Willie's Time*, 207; Dark issued a rebuttal in the *Sporting News* on August 22, 1964, in which he commented, "I'd have to be the stupidest man on earth to say the things Stan writes I said if I wanted to stay in baseball." However, Isaacs had already testified that the Dark interview was accurately reported. *San Francisco Chronicle*, Aug. 8, 1964.

112. Author's compilation from Reichler, *Baseball Encyclopedia*.

113. Irvin interview.

•6

Strangers in the Land

It was a unique sensation to realize that I was in a land I had heard so much about but which held not a single known friend.

Felipe Alou

I couldn't speak English. Not to speak the language . . . that is a terrible problem. Not to speak the language meant you were different.

Roberto Clemente

"Loneliness had . . . the painful depth of isolation," wrote Oscar Handlin in his Pulitzer Prize–winning book *The Uprooted*. "The man who once had been surrounded with individual beings was [in America] cast adrift in a life empty of all personal things."[1] Handlin's description of the late nineteenth-century immigrant experience spoke equally to the Latin ballplayer. For many, like Felipe Alou, entering America was traumatic.

Arriving from the Dominican Republic on April 7, 1956, Alou began his American baseball career in the Giants' spring training facilities in Melbourne, Florida. His pocketbook held all of ten dollars and he spoke only Spanish. Moreover, dinner that evening foretold the increasing sense of isolation he would feel as the days passed. His menu included "no rice; no beans." He remembered, "they kept feeding me steaks, a food that I found to be very rich and one which I had eaten only on rare occasions in the past. And I faithfully drank my cold, cold milk. Back home we always boiled it and drank it warm."[2] Alou's unfamiliarity with his new diet caused a radical weight loss in just one week. His unfamiliarity with a new world and its characteristics lasted much longer.

Assigned to the Class C farm team in Lake Charles, Louisiana, Alou soon discovered the adverse racial climate of the Deep South. In only five days he was reassigned to a Class D affiliate in Cocoa, Florida, because Louisiana law barred integrated athletic contests. His two-and-a-half day ride from Lake Charles to Cocoa deepened his discouragement. He not only encountered the rigid Jim Crow system of the South but also discovered the consequences of the language barrier. Unable to read the menus and discouraged by the racial circumstances, Alou spent only fifty cents of the twelve dollars given to him for meal money. The tired and hungry Dominican arrived in Cocoa at 4:30 in the morning only to ask himself, "'Where do I go now?' Since I had no answer and didn't know how to go about getting one, I did what came naturally—curled up on a bench and went to sleep."[3]

To many Latins, particularly those from small impoverished villages, the United States was not simply another country, it was another world. They were separated from family, friends, and culture for lengthy periods. Some never returned home. For others, homesickness became too great an obstacle to overcome. "It took a lot of guts for us to come here," reflected Orlando Cepeda.[4] Cuban pitcher Camilo Pascual pointed out that "it's a terrible hard thing for us from another country. Until we feel comfortable, we no can play our best."[5]

The influx of Spanish-speaking ballplayers forced the echelons of America's national pastime to face acculturation. Big league clubs, unfamiliar with Hispanic cultures, sometimes appeared insensitive in their dealings with Spanish-speaking players. They conducted no seminars on American culture, habits, and language. Much of what Latins knew of the United States came from the scouts and ballplayers who had come before them. There were, in fact, no programs to assist Latins in their day-to-day encounters in America. Indeed, management's social Darwinistic approach hindered the development of struggling, young Latin hopefuls and created awkward circumstances that left them vulnerable to ridicule from the mainstream press. As more players from Latin America joined the major leagues, misunderstandings between them and reporters, management, and peers also increased. Consequently, barriers formed that stemmed from a misunderstanding of cultures. This gap typified the relationship between established Americans and Latin newcomers.

With his description of "the puritanical efficiency north of the border and the bumbling and passionate disorder. . . south of it" Paul Theroux characterized the long-held misperceptions of two separate people and worlds.[6] But the depth of misunderstanding clearly went beyond an assessment of organizational skills. Reflecting on this in a 1925 article, foreign correspon-

dent Carleton Beals claimed, "We are accustomed to paying more attention to a dog fight in Yugoslavia than to a first class revolution in Latin
America."[7] Indeed, the cultural chasm between U.S. and Latin societies,
which included historical, religious, ethnic, and language differences, was
formidable and sometimes impassable.[8] To students of Pan-American history this came as no surprise. Time and again during the twentieth century American foreign policy measures toward Latin America bespoke ignorance. Woodrow Wilson's first secretary of state, the often incorrigible
William Jennings Bryan, once assigned "an appointee to a Nicaraguan post
[who] could not find his assigned country on the map." Moreover, historian LeRoy Ashby pointed out that "the new ministers to Latin American
countries could not speak Spanish." (Americans seem not to have learned
from their mistakes. President Jimmy Carter, years later, appointed non-
Spanish-speaking Patrick J. Lucey as ambassador to Mexico and vice president Dan Quayle outrageously claimed that Latin Americans spoke Latin.)[9]

While the good neighbor approach of the thirties healed some old
wounds, cold war initiatives opened new ones. Eisenhower officials, for
instance, instead of working to understand Latin American countries, "reacted according to the scale of the American economic interests involved
and the prevailing domestic and international conditions."[10] Armed with
only these attitudes, U.S. institutions, from politics to baseball, constructed guidelines toward their Latin constituents with neither a working knowledge of nor a concern for Hispanic cultures.

Indeed, this blindness came at a time when Latin cultures had already
become entrenched in the United States. Yet, in spite of their flourishing
communities, Latins, particularly in the American Southwest, wielded limited influence. New Latin arrivals knew that some conformity to mainstream culture and guidelines—found in city councils, schools, and local
police forces—was essential if they were to comfortably co-exist. But even
acculturation did not guarantee access to equity. In 1953, after repeated
incidents of police brutality in the East Los Angeles Latin community,
Chicano activist Ralph Guzmán wrote, "It is becoming more and more
difficult to walk through the streets of Los Angeles—and look Mexican!"[11]
Racial differences and nativism clearly continued to impede attempts to
adapt.

Still, most migrants were protected during their transitional period.
Strangers in a new land, they turned inward to form "island communities"
for support, particularly in times of crisis.[12] By the 1950s and 1960s, many
Spanish-speaking communities were well established in such cities as Los

Angeles, Chicago, New York, and Miami. Thanks to Latin neighborhoods, isolation from their homelands was somewhat alleviated. "There was the comforting presence of relatives and friends, or, at the least, fellow countrymen," claimed L. H. Gann and Peter J. Duignan. "There were clubs, barbershops, and corner stores where Spanish was understood. [Moreover, they cultivated a] political consciousness to set against nativistic campaigns among Anglo-Americans."[13] Whether they dwelled in urban communities or agrarian communes, they ate traditional foods, read Spanish-language newspapers and ads, attended their own churches, celebrated and mourned with each other, and carried on daily routines reminiscent of old folkways.

For most Latin ballplayers, however, no such support system awaited them. Because they came individually, to disparate cities across the United States, most of which had no Latin neighborhoods, they were islands unto themselves. Further, most were teenagers who had never left their regions for any length of time. "Where is Michigan City, Indiana?" asked Juan Marichal in 1956 upon learning of his destination after he signed with the Giants. Such questions were common.

The Latin players really were "strangers in the land" and signs of familiarity were too often out of reach. Felipe Alou found no Latin restaurants while in Shreveport, Louisiana. Roberto Clemente did without fried bananas and Spanish newspapers when he played in Montreal. Orlando Cepeda found Latin dance clubs absent while toiling in Minneapolis. "The living conditions [in North America] were so different. I had to adjust," remembered Manny Mota. "I tried to do it little by little. And I knew that from the beginning I might be uncomfortable. That can happen to you if you go to another country and don't speak the language."[14] Such were the ingredients of loneliness and homesickness. Only the sanctuary of the game could relieve them from their involuntary solitude.

Not surprisingly, when they encountered each other, the bonds were strong. "They were gregarious among themselves," claimed former Giants outfielder Monte Irvin; "they had more in common with their own. They talked about being back home and things they used to do."[15] Tony Oliva rejoiced when he joined the Minnesota Twins in 1964 and found other Latins on the roster: "When I got there Julio Bécquer, Camilo Pasqual and Zoilo Versalles were all there and they helped me a lot. So I was real lucky."[16] Clubs such as the San Francisco Giants sometimes kept Latins without major league potential on their minor league rosters to comfort others who held great promise. According to George Genovese, who managed a Giants affiliate in El Paso in the early 1960s, "When José Cardenal played with us we kept a Latin player of lesser ability on just so José, who was homesick, would not return to Cuba. Given the political atmosphere of those times, José would have never gotten out of Cuba had he returned there."[17] When Felipe Alou joined the Giants' minor league affiliate in Phoenix, his new teammate, Orlando Cepeda, made adjusting to a strange culture easier for the Dominican. Alou recalled that "just listening to Orlando chatter in Spanish was enough to make me feel at home."[18] As he explained, "Most Latins stuck together, a camaraderie that was inspired more by a similarity in language and habit than anything else."[19] Like Irving Howe's description of nineteenth-century Jewish settlers in New York City in whom "homesickness coursed through their days like a ribbon of sadness," Latin players plodded through a strange land in search of success and, of course, comfort.

Although Latins bonded, they needed to do so voluntarily. Vic Power made it clear that although the players enjoyed being with each other, "they have to do it themselves. If you [non-Latins] put them together you are prejudiced." But Power also believed there were drawbacks to this voluntary segregation. "They have a complex," he admitted. "They think the world is against them. They stick together. The Puerto Ricans stick with Puerto Ricans, and Cubans run around with Cubans. But as a group they are very sentimental."[20] Support and loyalty, to be sure, fed this unity. Vic Power, for example, noted that for the 1965 All-Star roster the Latin players "wanted to vote for Félix Mantilla. I asked them, 'don't you think Bobby Richardson is a better second-baseman?' They said, 'Yes, but Mantilla is one of us. And we have to vote for [Bert] Campaneris [as well].'"[21]

The company of other Latins, however, did not always help. Although Roberto Clemente joined Felipe Montemayor of Mexico and Cuban Román Mejías on the 1955 Pittsburgh Pirates, he remained withdrawn. To compensate for his loneliness, the Puerto Rican filled his time by signing autographs. A close friend of his recalled, "At first, when he didn't know a lot of people, we'd leave the ball park and he'd sign autographs for two or three hours."[22] Of this Clemente himself said, "I was lonely [and] had nothing else to do."[23]

Baseball at the minor league level almost always guaranteed isolation. Puerto Rican José Pagán spent a year in El Dorado, Arkansas, with no Latin companions, as did Cuban Leo Cárdenas during his stint in Charlotte, North Carolina.[24] Cuban Tony Taylor almost quit baseball for want of Latin companionship during his first year as a professional in the United States. In 1954, at the age of eighteen, Taylor was the only Latin player on the Texas City, Texas, club: "I had no one to talk to. The only English word I knew was 'okay,' and I would order meals by pointing at the food."

Taylor grew so despondent that he decided to return to Cuba. His financial needs at the time, however, preserved a career that later blossomed into
big league stardom. "If I [had] ten more dollars, I would have quit," he
declared. "I was so homesick. The fare to Havana was seventy-two dollars. I looked in my pocket. I had only sixty-two dollars, so I stayed."[25]

Joining the majors did not put a sudden end to the isolation either. In
1964, for example, Cuban Dagoberto "Bert" Campaneris joined the Kansas City Athletics, a team devoid of other Spanish-speaking players. Campaneris "spoke no English, lived by himself, and carried on no social life."[26]
By then the twenty-two-year-old native from Pueblo Nuevo had been away
from his parents and large family since 1962. Contact with them, moreover, was sparse. "It takes about three weeks for me to get a letter," he
said at that time. "We write to each other. Maybe I get a letter every three
or four weeks. I can send them medicine, but no food or money. You try
and send money, somebody steal it."[27] Hesitant to return to Castro-con-
trolled Cuba during the winter months, Campaneris remained in the United
States and stayed with his cousin, José Cardenal, by then another flourishing major leaguer. During the season one writer speculated that the quiet
Cuban "must be depressed by his solitary life."[28]

When Diego Seguí, another Cuban, joined Campaneris on the club in
1968, however, reporters for the *Sporting News* pronounced the pair "in-
separable."[29] The same publication reported that both Cubans "were often mistaken for each other. Seguí often would allow fans to assume he
was Campaneris to avoid long explanations." Seguí's presence boosted
Campaneris's career, since "Campy had his best year in 1968 when Seguí
was with the club from start to finish."[30] His numbers, to be sure, reflected that assessment. The Cuban batted .276 in 1968 compared to .248 in
1967. Furthermore, he led the American League with 177 hits and 62 stolen
bases. In a career that eventually spanned nineteen seasons, these were
personal bests. Seguí, who appeared in fifty-two games that year in relief,
also established a career low 2.39 earned run average. Seguí's subsequent
trade at the start of the 1969 season left many to wonder how "this will
affect Campy."[31] At season's end, while he equaled his 1968 stolen base
numbers, his average fell to .260, while he totaled 142 hits. He rebounded in the following year with 168 hits, a .279 batting average, and a league-
leading 42 stolen bases.

Perhaps not so coincidentally, that year the shortstop, like his cousin had
done earlier, married an American white woman just prior to the season.
"Marriage has filled an immense void in his life," reported one journalist.[32] "I had no one in the United States," Campaneris noted. "I was so

lonely. Now I got somebody to take care of me."[33] Campaneris and Cardenal, however, took an unusual approach, since Latin players rarely married outside of their cultures.

Like Campaneris, Julián Javier stoically endured his isolation as a member of the St. Louis Cardinals. From 1960 until 1969, he anchored second base but spoke very little. Inside, however, his anguish left him prone to fits of depression. Felipe Alou revealed his similar solitude: "There is a unique power to the aloneness that comes from not being able to communicate. It is always possible to use sign language to establish a rudimentary acquaintance, to exploit the few words one *does* know, but when these shallow wells of contact are evaporated there remains only the uneasy helpless shrug, the look of futility, the nod, wave or handshake of goodbye."[34]

Orlando Cepeda's arrival to the Cardinals in 1966 saved Javier. "Julián was shy before Orlando came to us," remembered manager Red Schoendienst. He "would rarely contribute anything on his own, perhaps because of his limited understanding of the English language. But Orlando has opened him up." The manager then pointed out how Javier's play had progressed: "He was great on the field [after Orlando came]—probably his finest year all around."[35] Javier's batting also showed considerable improvement. In the season prior to Cepeda's first full year with the club, the Dominican contributed only 7 home runs, 105 hits, 31 RBIs, and a .228 average. Remarkably, during the 1967 season, a more jubilant Javier almost doubled his output. At season's end, along with a .281 average, he posted 14 home runs, 146 hits, and 64 RBIs. Their American teammates encouraged the camaraderie between the two Latins. "They're good for each other," noted infielder Dal Maxvil.[36] Cepeda, a normally jovial and always prideful Latin, remembered how Javier used to "get depressed. Now, he has a friend for the first time. Me. We go out with my friends. We go where there is music. It makes him feel different."[37] Like Seguí and Campaneris, "Cepeda gave Javier what he needed most, a cheerleader. The slim Dominican never had a chance to succumb to drooping spirits as was his wont in the past." According to the *New York Times,* "Big Orlando is a locker mate and his gushing enthusiasms [in Spanish] flow next door and give his little buddy a lift."[38]

More than anything, language unified the Latin players. As Al McBean from the Virgin Islands put it, "As long as you can speak Spanish, you're in the clan."[39] Orlando Cepeda added, "We just talk fun. How you say? 'kick it around.' It's a nice feeling to meet friends that talk your language and that you have gone up through the minors with."[40] Julio Navarro, Felipe Alou, and José Pagán, for instance, formed an "inner circle" while playing in Springfield, Massachusetts. Spanish reinforced their personal loyalties. Moreover, it gave them an outlet to air frustrations that might otherwise have been repressed or gone unnoticed.[41]

The sanctuary afforded by language, however, sometimes proved to be a snare. For instance, when Tony Oliva first joined the Twins, he found a number of Latins already on the roster. "I had a lot of people to talk to," Oliva said, but "that hurt me because I had tried to learn English in Wytheville, where no one had spoken Spanish. Now that there were so many Spanish-speaking players, I forgot about English."[42]

Most Latins, understandably, clung to each other for encouragement. Because they were united by a common tongue, their clubhouse gatherings and banter, according to Bill Veeck, were unique. "This clique speaks in a foreign tongue. This is a foreign colony setting itself up in the last American stronghold, the baseball clubhouse," claimed the maverick owner. "You see them there, chattering away in Spanish, and every once in a while you are left with the uneasy feeling that these foreigners are talking about you and laughing at you. If they want to play here and take home our money, you think to yourself, why don't they speak English like everybody else?" But Veeck then warned, "if you are half intelligent you don't carry that kind of thinking too far."[43] That some American players resented the banter did not go unnoticed by their Spanish-speaking teammates. Felipe Alou pointed out that it had "caused considerable resentment among American players. . . . They feel that the moment we begin speaking Spanish we are talking about them. This is not so." Alou explained that through Spanish, they were "free of the uneasiness that so often bothers us when we continually have to think about which word is right or wrong in English."[44]

Joe Garagiola observed, "When these Latins talk English they have to stop and think about what they are going to say next. Immediately, though, when they see one of their own kind, they spit out their Spanish like a Viet Nam machine gun. I don't blame them; I would do the same thing." Garagiola then drew an interesting analogy: "When American ballplayers over in the Japanese leagues see one another I doubt that they get together and try to talk things over in Japanese."[45] Years later Randy Bass, a virtual career minor league player in the United States who found stardom in Japan, not only balked at learning any phrases in Japanese but also utterly refused to have anything to do with the culture that subsidized his life-style. *Sports Illustrated,* which ran a story focusing on his loneliness, sympathized with his circumstances.[46]

Not all Americans were unsympathetic to the Latin plight. Scouts, like the Dodgers' Al Campanis, often did what they could to soothe the un-certainties of their young signees. In 1954, the scout visited Roberto Clemente in Montreal when the young Puerto Rican was seemingly a confused, discouraged, and lonely player. Campanis's appreciation for Latins, their heritage, and knowledge of the language fortified his trusting words and curtailed Clemente's plans to return to Puerto Rico, thus preserving what later became a Hall of Fame career. Bill Veeck also carefully observed the circumstances of the Spanish-speaking players. His sensitivity was rare and thoughtfully stated in his autobiography:

> Take any white [American] ballplayer away from his home and family, put him down in a Caribbean village where nobody speaks his language, have him eat strange foods which emphasize his foreignness and also upset his stomach. Have him faced, socially, in this imaginary village with completely new—and bewil-dering—customs which discriminate against him. Make it perfectly clear to him that he is not considered quite the equal of the natives and that while no offense is intended it would be greatly appreciated if he would be a good fellow and keep his distance. He just might feel that he is an outsider.[47]

Tony Oliva's first days in the United States exemplified the extent to which some Latins could be isolated. The black Cuban arrived in April 1961 after signing to play with the Minnesota Twins. The contract, however, was con-tingent on his making one of the Twins' affiliates. He did not. In addition, his disappointing release was ill-timed. Just weeks after his tryout, anti-Castro Cuban exiles trained by the Central Intelligence Agency tried to invade the island at a beachhead called the Bay of Pigs. Their attempt ended in military catastrophe and diplomatic embarrassment for the United States. The event proved traumatic for Cuban players because the ensu-ing turmoil led to restrictions on property and financial revenue—partic-ularly for those who could flee the island. Observers believed that severe travel limitations were not far off.[48] Hence, Oliva found himself unem-ployed in a foreign country, struggling with racial integration, and unable to speak English. "I didn't have any idea that I would have to stay here," he reminisced years later.[49] Virtually cut off from his home, Oliva, fortu-nately, was not abandoned. "Even though I didn't speak English everyone tried to help me—the white ballplayer, the black ballplayer, the fans," he recalled. "I live with families and they all adopted me as if I was their own son."[50]

Despite such friendliness, Oliva's early years were far from easy. Oliva hailed from the province of Pinar del Río in Cuba. Christened Pedro at birth in July 1940, Oliva borrowed his brother's passport—issued to "Tony"— in his haste to enter the United States. Brimming with confidence and an adopted name, "Tony" Oliva measured his abilities against professionals he had already competed against in Cuba. "I'd think if they could play professional, I think I can play professional too."[51] Following his signing, the future star was confident that life in the United States would not be that difficult. "I wasn't worried about the fact that I couldn't speak English," he thought at the time of his departure. "There were twenty-one other Cubans going with me, and I would be able to sit to talk to them."[52] Although he had limited transportation funds from the Minnesota Twins for the trip, Oliva brought with him dreams of the wealth he might have from a professional contract. "In Latin America, if you come from a poor family it's tough to make any money," he said. "So when I signed my first contract for $250 per month, to all my friends that was big money," especially because "alot of people over there didn't make $250 the entire year."[53]

Complications at the outset of his arrival, however, clouded his plans. Reporting late to the Minnesota spring training camp, he participated in only a few games and practices. As a result, the Twins' coaches were not able to assess his talents accurately. Also, by the time he arrived, all the organizational affiliates had filled their rosters. On the final day of camp, club officials presented Oliva and several other Cubans with documents to be signed. "I didn't know what I was signing, since I couldn't read." With this disadvantage, Oliva "thought I was joining a ballclub. . . . I was excited and happy, wondering what team had picked me." To his astonishment, Oliva had signed his own release.[54] Upon looking back, he recalled, "I didn't have any idea what it meant to be a professional."[55]

Misunderstanding official documents and contracts was easy if you could not speak the language. For instance, when Dominican outfielder Rico Carty drew the attention of professional scouts, each approached him with a contract. Carty signed all of them: "Everybody say 'Rico sign the contract.' So I sign," believing that "the more you sign, the more you play. The more you get paid, too." As a consequence, Carty simultaneously belonged to twelve professional teams. For this, the Dominican received a one-year suspension from American professional baseball. "I cried," Carty remembered. "I felt like they were making me a fool, tricking me and I had only signed my name because they all wanted me to." Baseball officials lifted Carty's suspension once they understood the circumstances of his actions.[56] In another case, Minnie Miñoso endorsed baseball glove firms in both St. Louis and Chicago. Each contract was supposed to be exclusive. White Sox general manager Frank Lane recalled, "I tried to explain the word 'exclusive' to Minnie and all he told me was one was exclusive in St. Louis and the other was exclusive in Chicago."[57]

The Twins, to their credit, did find "part time" work for Oliva with the Class D Charlotte team operated by Phil Howser. George Brophy, then Twins assistant farm director, saw "Tony when he first came to camp. He was scared to death—a tall, skinny kid who couldn't speak a word of English. He looked awful at the plate and worse in the field. But we couldn't send those boys back to Cuba because of the conditions over there."[58]

At Charlotte, Oliva joined Minnie Mendoza, another Cuban. Mendoza not only provided companionship but, most importantly, was also bilingual. Oliva's tenure with the Charlotte team, however, was both unofficial and temporary: practice with the team during home stands and maintenance work on the stadium while the club traveled. In the meantime, Howser searched for a team that might take him in.[59]

Difficulties arose when there was no Mendoza around to translate. Daily routines became a struggle for Oliva and the inability to communicate haunted his every move. Even though he lived five miles from the ballpark, Oliva opted to walk instead of taking the bus: "I could have afforded a bus, but I couldn't take one because I couldn't speak English. I didn't know which bus was the right one to take to the ballpark, and I couldn't ask anyone for directions."[60]

Loneliness was a constant companion. With the team on the road, Oliva found "there was no one for me to talk with, and I would go to the park, go back to the hotel, eat in a restaurant, walk around, and return to my room. I used to think a lot about Cuba and my family then. I missed my mother, my father, my friends, everyone."[61] Like other Cuban ballplayers, Oliva was able to pursue his career because of preferential treatment by the Castro regime. The Bay of Pigs crisis earlier that year, however, had hardened Cuba's travel policies and baseball insiders believed that Castro's benevolence toward Cuban ballplayers in America would end at the conclusion of the season. Determined to succeed, Oliva remained in the United States and became a permanent exile. "I came here with the idea that I would play baseball for five months and then go back home."[62] Finally Howser found a position for him in the Appalachian League. The Cuban then proceeded to bat well over .300 during the next three years.

At the end of the 1962 and 1963 seasons, the Twins brought Oliva up to the majors, where in sixteen total at-bats he finished with a better-than .400 average. In 1964, given the opportunity to play a full season in the big leagues, Oliva enjoyed a banner year, finishing with a league-leading .323 average. But this was only part of the story. His batting championship also included the American League leadership in hits (217), doubles

Tony Oliva. (Courtesy of the National Baseball Hall of Fame Library, Cooperstown, N.Y.)

(43), runs scored (109), total bases (374), and times at bat (672). More-over, he also belted 32 home runs. Only three years removed from his part-time job as a maintenance man for the Charlotte minor league club, the jovial Cuban not only became the second Latin to win the American League Rookie of the Year Award but also the first black player to do so. Further-more, no other rookie in that league before him had ever won a batting title. In 1965, Oliva again made major league history when, after he hit for a .321 average, he claimed a second consecutive batting championship. But Oliva also concluded his fourth year away from home, which tempered his success. "I think about my family a whole lot," he was prone to re-peat.[63] Even then he was still not completely acculturated. Responding to reporters about his prospects as a second-year player with the Twins, the perplexed Cuban asked, "Jinx? What is this sophomore jinx? I do not understand this jinx."[64]

—————

While Latins from other countries were spared the political trauma faced by the Cubans, the communication gap was a blanket concern that almost always led to awkward circumstances. Roberto Clemente, for instance, was called a "son-of-a-bitch" after making a marvelous play on an opponent. Clemente misinterpreted the phrase and cordially thanked the source.[65] Cuban Angel Scull commonly confused his teammates in the field by yell-ing, "I got it! You take it!"[66] Minnesota Twins veteran Frank Quilici failed in his attempt to teach Tony Oliva to yell "You take it" at the appropriate moment. According to Quilici, "It didn't work out, so we just tried to stay out of each other's way."[67] Freddie Frederico, trainer for the California Angels, recalled the time when infielder Félix Torres complained of a sore arm: "I worked on his left arm for a couple of days before I discovered he was right-handed."[68]

Not all such misunderstandings were minor inconveniences. In 1961, Cuban catcher Paul Casanova traveled through Charlotte, North Caroli-na, on his way to a minor league affiliate in Newton, North Carolina. "Not knowing much English or anything," he reminisced, "I didn't know how to get to Newton, 19 miles away, except by cab. I had no money—only a catcher's mitt and my clothes. When I got to Newton, I couldn't pay him." For Casanova, the journey quickly became a nightmare. "I was trying to tell him that somebody on the ball club would pay him. But he turned me over to the police and I spent the night in jail until I was bailed out and my fare paid."[69]

Zoilo Versalles's first experience in the United States in 1956 characterized the Latin pride that sometimes impeded acculturation. While driving
to a Miami bus depot, a team official explained Versalles's itinerary. According to Jerry Izenberg, the young Cuban indicated that he clearly understood his travel instructions. In Izenberg's words, however, "He did not
want to appear stupid. He didn't understand a word. He got off at the
wrong town."[70] Washington Senators owner Calvin Griffith had a straight-
forward way of preventing his Latin players from disembarking at the
wrong place. After escorting them to the bus terminals, Griffith simply hung
signs around their necks indicating their destinations.[71]

While the inability to communicate in English could be "a curse" for
Latins, "being able to speak Spanish [was] a blessing" at times according
to Felipe Alou. "When shortstop Julio Gotay, a Puerto Rican, teamed up
with second baseman Julián Javier, a Dominican, for the St. Louis Cardinals . . . they were able to conduct strategy conferences right on the field
in front of the opposing runners."[72] In another instance, New York Yankees manager Casey Stengel, in an effort to annoy Minnie Miñoso, ordered
his own player, Cuban Willie Miranda, to shout insults in Spanish whenever Miñoso came to bat. Stengel, however, was unaware that Miñoso and
Miranda were good friends. Miñoso recalled that "Willie hollered out that
Casey wanted him to shout insults at me and get me so riled up I couldn't
see the ball, much less hit it. [Instead Miranda] asked me to meet him at a
local restaurant for dinner." Miñoso then took the scenario one step further: "Well, I decided to go for an 'Oscar.' I stepped out of the box and
shook my fist at Miranda and shouted that I understood and I'd see him
at dinner." Seeing this, a happy Stengel congratulated Miranda for "up-
setting" Miñoso. Then, after Miñoso launched a game-winning triple,
Stengel blamed himself for getting the Cuban "angry."[73]

Miñoso, like other Latins who thought instinctively in Spanish, also made
public gatherings interesting affairs. While accepting the 1951 *Sporting
News* Rookie of the Year trophy, Miñoso "launched at once into a rapid
fire speech in Spanish, as the startled crowd wondered what this was all
about." Then, in an instant, Miñoso came to a full stop, turned to editor
J. G. Taylor Spink, and quipped, "Well, anyhow, Mr. Spink, thanks."
Miñoso, a very popular player, received the largest ovation of the evening.[74]

But not all were amused with such antics. Indeed, at times Spanish use
unnerved opponents. In Cincinnati one evening, the San Francisco Giants
were clubbing pitches thrown by Joey Jay. As the game wore on, so did
Jay's impatience. He finally exploded after listening to the Spanish discussion that took place between baserunner Orlando Cepeda and another

Latin at home plate. "Don't you know how to talk English?" queried the
angry pitcher. Cepeda, according to Charles Einstein, shot back, "Kiss my
ass you cocksucker. Is that enough English for you?"[75]

As the reality of their plight set in, some Latins tried formal instruction.
Felipe Alou was among those who selected this route. "About the first thing
I had done after signing to play ball in the United States was to invest
around $75 in a Hollywood [Florida] course that was going to teach me
how to speak, read and write English almost instantly," he remembered.
But his efforts proved futile because "nowhere on the records or in the
textbooks . . . was there anything similar to 'Y'all come'n back tumarrah,
heah?'"[76] Regional dialects also affected the way some Latins interpreted
the English language. "I played in the South, I played in California, I played
in New York, I played in Boston, and they all speak different. And everywhere I went I had to change. [So] what you hear from me is what I got
from listening to people" from different areas, remarked Tony Pérez.[77]
Others, like Alou, sought literature in hopes of closing the communication gap. Cincinnati infielder Elio Chacón "carried those *Little Golden
Books* that preschoolers read with him on road trips because he was proud
enough to try to teach himself the language of the country in which he had
to make his living."[78] Pedro Ramos, a Cuban pitcher with a passion for
American westerns, used the movies as a method of learning English.[79] And,
years later, Manny Sanguillen turned to children's television shows for
guidance. "I watched Captain Kangaroo on TV alot," he claimed. "I used
to watch 'Sesame Street,' too. I would get up at four in the morning and
watch them do the A-B-C's."[80]

At the outset of their careers when they were most vulnerable to the trauma of acculturation, few players could afford personal tutors or special
courses. Unless a player found a peer who spoke Spanish or a sympathetic bilingual coach or administrator, there was little recourse but to remain
silent. Scouts often provided the best advice, encouragement, and orientation, but with hectic schedules, they could offer only minimal support.
Baseball management, instead of instituting training, often merely advised
Latins to attend American movies as a way to learn the language.[81]

In an era of few accommodations, baseball's approach was commonplace. Not until the 1970s was there any movement in the United States
toward bilingual programs in public education. And prior to that, no public
officials addressed Hispanic issues on a large scale. For its part, baseball
management was interested only in fielding players who could contribute
to victories. In doing so, however, it too often failed to recognize the burden Spanish-speaking employees carried. Left to form their own adapta-

tion programs, many players chose to withdraw, often to avoid awkward and potentially embarrassing situations. And in some cases, the decision to conduct themselves solely in their language was viewed with suspicion.

Puerto Rican Juan Pizarro, temperamental at times, often refused to deal with anyone who did not speak Spanish. One irritated writer said Pizarro "either can't or won't talk English." Another reporter for *Sport* magazine complained, "He buys Spanish magazines wherever he can find them. He seldom reads English. He'd rather talk Spanish, read Spanish, see Spanish-speaking people, date Spanish-speaking girls and even treat his ailments with his special Spanish cure alls."[82] Alfonso "Chico" Carrasquel, from Venezuela, appeared equally as militant. When, in 1950, some of his Chicago White Sox teammates suggested he learn English to communicate better with his coaches, Carrasquel shot back, "Let the coaches learn Spanish so I can understand them."[83]

While clubs did not provide formal programs for orientation, they occasionally funded off-season language tutorials. Learning English while residing in their Latin homes, however, proved too difficult for some. In 1953 Dodgers outfielder Sandy Amoros arrived late for spring training in Vero Beach, Florida. The club, it appeared, had allocated funds to the Cuban outfielder for instruction in English during the winter and was confident that he would return with a working knowledge of it. But when team administrator Fresco Thompson understandably queried why he was tardy, Amoros responded, "Hokay," to every question that he posed. Thompson persisted, "Look, you must know more English than that after taking lessons. Now tell me—why are you late reporting?" "Hokay," Amoros again replied. A frustrated Thompson later said, "I won't say that Sandy didn't take English lessons that winter, but I have reasonable doubt."[84] Ironically, after the Dodgers had optioned Amoros to their farm team in Montreal, the Cuban complained, "I just getting speak English. Then they say: 'You go to Montreal.' I say: 'Hokay,' but I try to speak French, not English, up there. How I learn English, I talk French?"[85]

Several coaches and managers did speak Spanish fluently. Al López was a native of Tampa, Florida, whose parents had emigrated from Cuba. His command of both languages contributed to his managerial success in Cleveland and Chicago during the 1950s. In his earlier days as a player, López often helped incoming Latin players adjust to American life. He recalled that "at Pittsburgh during the war we brought one kid up, a Cuban boy who couldn't speak English at all. He was shortstop." According to López, "The poor guy couldn't speak English, and I had to room with him for a while and had breakfast with him, because I had to order for him and had dinner with him all through spring training at Muncie, Indiana."[86]

López's bilingual capabilities enabled him to communicate freely with such standout players as Bobby Avila and Minnie Miñoso. In addition, withdrawn or troubled Latin players sometimes sought out López for counsel. Juan Pizarro, for instance, benefited from López's tutelage. *Sport* magazine speculated that "with López, [Pizarro] couldn't hide behind a language barrier." The manager's ability to relate to the young pitcher was evident. "López handled Pizarro as a virtuoso handles a violin. He kidded him one minute, scolded him the next. He patted him on the back one minute, punched him in the ego the next. López reached Pizarro in Spanish."[87] Pizarro's potential also emerged. Between 1957 and 1960, as a member of the Milwaukee Braves, the Puerto Rican finished his tenure with twenty-three wins and nineteen losses. During the next four years with the Chicago White Sox, however, Pizarro won sixty-one games and lost thirty-eight. While many factors may have played a role, López, who had also managed the soft-spoken Beto Avila, the 1954 American League batting champion, proved to be not only an invaluable sage to Pizarro but also a cultural sanctuary.

Manager Preston Gómez's primary language was Spanish. Born Pedro in Preston, Cuba (from which he acquired his nickname), Gómez learned the game from fieldhands at the local United Fruit Company near his home. As his skills developed, Joe Cambria recruited Gómez to play for the Washington Senators for the 1944 season. The Cuban's playing career lasted only one year, but he stayed in touch with the game. His managing career commenced in 1955 when he guided clubs in Zacatecas, Mexico, and Havana, Cuba. In 1960, he led the Spokane, Washington, club to the Pacific Coast League championship. Managing a team that boasted the likes of Willie Davis, Ron Fairly, Frank Howard, and other future Dodger stars, Gómez and the Indians led the Pacific Coast League from start to finish and took the pennant by almost twelve games. His eventual popularity, however, overshadowed his earlier difficulties.

Tucked away in the far eastern part of the state, Spokane had virtually no Latin community. But baseball was no stranger to the town and its sports aficionados enthusiastically supported its Pacific Coast League entry. Spencer Harris, the team's flamboyant general manager, welcomed Gómez upon his arrival and promoted the Cuban as the "world's greatest manager." Later in the year, one local writer responded that Gómez "might have been the greatest manager in all of baseball—if he could only speak English."[88] Limited in his ability to communicate clearly, the Spokane manager, nonetheless, recognized the impact the local media often had on bewildered youthful Latins who faced the difficulties of acculturation. "Gómez really did a lot to help us with our interviews and understanding these players," claimed Chuck Stewart, a writer for the *Spokane Chronicle*. "My colleagues and I learned a great deal from him."[89] Indeed, Gómez provided the Washingtonian with firsthand experience as to the scenarios that Spanish-speaking players faced on a routine basis. During one eventful spring training in Florida, Stewart accompanied Gómez to a reunion of the Cuban's family members in Dade County. "The only Spanish I knew was 'no comprendo [I do not understand],'" recalled the journalist, who "got a taste of what Latin players endured while in the United States."[90]

Gómez worked especially hard to improve his bilingual skills. "If you do not understand me," he often reminded his players, "tell me. Besides, I'll be able to learn English quicker."[91] Furthermore, the manager encouraged Latins on his club to socialize with their American teammates. To that end, he often assigned his Spanish-speaking players to room with their American counterparts while on road trips. Spokane in the early 1960s, of course, seemed like an ideal setting for Gómez's "experiments." Public facilities were not segregated, nor were there Jim Crow bleachers at Indian Stadium. Gómez, however, did not always have it quite so easy.

Prior to his stint at Spokane, the Cuban witnessed racial turbulence during his tenure with the Havana Sugar Kings in the International League. Often when the team toured the American South, he found himself hustling for food as restaurateurs barred his black players from their establishments. He also dealt with white players who, at times, refused to use the shower facilities with blacks. Discrimination even stung Gómez personally. In one instance he "lost a girlfriend—she was from Mississippi— who refused to see me if I continued to ride the team buses with blacks."[92]

Other trying moments came after 1961, as relations between his native country and the United States dissolved. Belligerent fans routinely called the Spokane manager the "damned Cuban Communist." However, he never doubted his resolve to remain in the United States and pursue a career in baseball. "Baseball was my job, my life," he declared. "I don't know what else I would do."[93] Through his own experiences, the Cuban proved to be an important component in the development of young Latins in the Dodger chain. With Gómez at the helm, Latin players shipped to the eastern Washington town could count their blessings.

Puerto Rican René Friol arrived in Spokane in 1961. In his years in the minors, "I didn't know a word of English and there wasn't anyone on those ballclubs who talked Spanish." Players and others communicated with Friol solely with hand signals, a system that often proved frustrating for all. "It was rough on the managers as it was on me."[94] With Gómez's help, Friol's transfer to Spokane eased both his professional and social skills. The Spanish-speaking infielder could now "'hablo el español' to his heart's content," reported the *Spokane Chronicle*.[95] The paper later pointed out that the Puerto Rican developed into one of the most congenial members of the squad.[96]

Not all Spanish-speaking coaches, however, were Latin. George Genovese, for instance, was a native New Yorker and had played baseball during the 1940s in Mexico, South America, and Puerto Rico. His ability to speak Spanish and his familiarity with Latin America helped him land a scouting job with Branch Rickey. One of his first assignments, in fact, was to manage a Mexico City team during the mid-1950s. Through Genovese's prodding, Rickey expanded his recruitment boundaries into Mexico. "I had told him of the many good ballplayers that were down there and weren't getting the chance to play in the states because no one would see them," recalled Genovese.[97]

In the late 1950s Genovese joined the Giants organization as manager of the El Paso, Texas, farm team. There he coached such future major league stars as Tito Fuentes and José Cardenal. Genovese's linguistic skills helped temper the homesickness felt by his Latin players. Fuentes, Cardenal, and other Latin athletes felt less isolated. "These kids went through a great deal of difficulty. I was able to make these kids feel at home through my ability to speak Spanish."[98]

While not all managers possessed bilingual abilities, some attempted to learn. George "Birdie" Tebbetts, hired to manage the 1963 Cleveland Indians, inherited a number of Latin players. In an attempt to unify his club, he took Spanish lessons: "I want to know what these kids are talking about and I want to be able to talk to them." Tebbetts even ordered his staff to learn some Spanish and carry Spanish-English dictionaries. "This course," claimed the determined Cleveland manager, "has cost me $700 and I'm not going to waste it."[99] He dutifully carried his lesson books on all road trips. One of Tebbetts's coaches, Czechoslovakian-born Elmer Valo, attempted to teach English to player Vic Davallio; the *Sporting News* chid-

ed that "Vic's teammates are beginning to detect a Slavic flavor in his broken English."[100]

Cookie Lavagetto, however, while manager of the Washington Senators
during the 1960s, bypassed Spanish lessons and relied instead on selected
phrases taught to him by several of his Latin players. Sometimes, as he
discovered, this approach backfired. In one instance, as he attempted to
remind his runner at first base—José Valdivielso—to break up a potential
double play, he mistakenly instructed the surprised Cuban to "walk nicely to the man at second base," which Valdivielso proceeded to do.[101]

The language barrier also created social problems for Latin players. Their
inability to read English menus and unfamiliarity with American foods
often left Latins with few selections. Tony Oliva recollected, "I ate my meals
in a restaurant for colored and I would always order one of two things."
General Manager Howser had given him "two pieces of paper; on one piece
he had written 'ham and eggs,' and on the other 'fried chicken.'"[102] "I didn't
have any idea how to order food," Oliva added. "In my first three months
everything I ate was ham and eggs and fried chicken. The only time I ate
something different was when I was accompanied by other Hispanic ball
players who could order for me."[103] Occasionally Oliva felt bold enough
to order snacks unassisted. Once, the Cuban recalled, "I saw a nice choc-
olate candy bar in a drug store, and I pointed at it and bought it. I took it
back to my room to eat it that night before I went to bed. Later I un-
wrapped it and took a bite—and gagged. It was a hunk of chewing tobac-
co!"[104] Cuban pitcher Pedro Ramos remembered, "I [ate] at the Rainbow
Cafe, and everyday I [ordered] the same thing—pork chops. I haven't eat-
en a pork chop in twenty-eight years."[105] In 1953, Cuban slugger Román
Mejías claimed that he almost starved due to his inability to communicate:
"I speak no English at all and it is very hard for me. I never expec' to be
so lonely in the U.S. I couldn't eat. . . . I thought I would have to go back
to Cuba for food." After building some courage, mostly due to hunger,
Mejías found a solution. "Finally we learn to go into eating place and we
go back in kitchen and point with fingers—thees, thees, thees. After while
somebody teach me to say hom and eggs and fried chicken, and I eat that
for a long time."[106]

Early in his career, Orlando Cepeda's diet was filled with spinach, which
was served daily with his main course. He could not find the proper English phrases to refuse it.[107] Others ate hamburgers—for breakfast, lunch,
and dinner. Still another Latin devoured an entire bowl of gravy, believing it to be some type of American soup. When Felipe Alou once ordered
two "four-or-five-minute" eggs, a testy waitress insisted that the Domini-

can clarify his order. Alou responded, "Make it five." She returned with five eggs in a large bowl.[108]

━━━━━

In spite of the language problems during meals, the change to an American diet was not necessarily detrimental. On the contrary, eating regularly was a blessing. Nutritious food was a scarce commodity among Latin America's impoverished lower classes. Often Latin players had grown up mainly on beans, rice, and, in some regions, corn. Only those in the upper classes enjoyed a consistent diet of meat, milk, and vegetables.[109] "I was so poor that I never know what it meant the word 'lunch.' You wake up and maybe there is coffee and a piece of bread," recalled Zoilo Versalles of his own humble background. "For supper there is maybe rice and beans and if you are lucky a piece of meat in the beans. In between you have water. You see somebody with a piece of bread, maybe you follow him. Maybe he drops a few crumbs."[110] During his first few months as a professional, Versalles, often chided for his lack of size, poignantly queried, "How you get big with coffee for breakfast and coffee and bread for lunch and beans and rice for supper?"[111]

Felipe Alou, like Versalles, received little in terms of a balanced diet during his childhood. "For breakfast we always had strong black coffee—and bread, very dark and very filling. Even when we were two and three years old we drank coffee, mainly because it was plentiful and cheap," he remembered. A diverse and fulfilling menu was a luxury not often seen in his household. "In my country there is a saying about the type of kitchen we had," the Dominican said. "It goes like this: 'when you can see the cat sleeping between the rocks, then you know there is no food in the house.'" Alou reminisced, "I saw the cat sleeping between the rocks more times than I like to recall."[112]

Most Latins, of course, made the dietary adjustments needed to cope in the United States. Indeed, American cuisine was not unappreciated. For instance, by the time Felipe Alou and Juan Marichal reached the major leagues, the two Dominicans included hamburgers, hot dogs, and steaks in their diets. Certainly these selections contrasted with the beans and rice with which both had grown up. Marichal, in fact, was convinced that the best way for him to become adjusted to America was to eat steak regularly.[113] Another convert to American food, Tony Oliva confessed that if he could afford it, he would "eat steak three [times] a day."[114]

Neither steaks nor hot dogs alone enabled Latins to adapt to the United

States. Only time and experience could bring the cultural transition. Many players welcomed the opportunity to learn about America and worked hard toward acculturation and assimilation. A few balked. All missed their homelands, families, and friends. Also, a number of Latin ballplayers stretched their winter vacations, knowing it would be months before they could return home. As a consequence, many were chronically tardy for spring training. Willie Miranda, after showing up late, went so far as to tell his employers that he had trouble "getting his parakeet through customs."[115]

Still, as more Latins filtered into the American professional leagues their sense of isolation grew less intense. While their troubles did not cease, Latin players persevered and their baseball performances also improved. During the 1960s more Latin American ballplayers than ever before proved they were not just dependable team players but major league stars.

Notes

1. Handlin, *The Uprooted,* 105.
2. Alou, *Alou,* 26.
3. Ibid., 30.
4. Cepeda interview.
5. *Sport,* Feb. 1964, Camilo Pasqual file, National Baseball Library, Cooperstown, N.Y.
6. Theroux, *Old Patagonian Express,* 49.
7. Carleton Beals quoted in Williams, "Alternative Intellectuals."
8. Riding, *Distant Neighbors,* 316.
9. Ashby, *William Jennings Bryan,* 147.
10. Keen and Wasserman, *History of Latin America,* 530.
11. Ralph Guzmán quoted in Acuña, *Occupied America,* 293.
12. "Island communities" was coined by Robert H. Wiebe in *The Search for Order* in reference to the nineteenth-century American social milieu that he believed lacked a strong national nucleus. I find the phrase especially appropriate for the ethnic communities that, like islands in an ocean, stood apart and isolated from "mainland" culture.
13. Gann and Duignan, *Hispanics,* 40–41.
14. Mota interview.
15. Irvin interview.
16. Oliva interview.
17. Genovese interview.
18. Alou, *Alou,* 48.
19. Ibid., 102.

20. Boyle, "The Latins Storm," 26.

21. Ibid.

22. Wagenheim, *Clemente!* 57.

23. Musick, *Who Was Roberto?* 99.

24. On José Pagán, see *Sporting News,* Oct. 13, 1962; on Leo Cárdenas, see Flood, *The Way It Is,* 43.

25. *Sporting News,* May 23, 1970.

26. *Sporting News,* July 31, 1965.

27. Joe McGruff column, Mar. 1967, Bert Campaneris file, National Baseball Library.

28. Ibid.

29. McGruff column, Feb. 1, 1969, Campaneris file.

30. Ibid.

31. Ibid.

32. McGruff column, Apr. 25, 1970, Campaneris file.

33. McGruff column, May 25, 1970, Campaneris file.

34. Alou, *Alou,* 111.

35. Ed Rumill, "Javier, Rico Unsung Heroes," *Christian Science Monitor,* Oct. 13, 1967, 6.

36. *Sporting News,* Oct. 25, 1968.

37. Dick Young, *New York Daily News,* Sept. 25, 1967.

38. *New York Times,* Sept. 22, 1967.

39. Boyle, "The Latins Storm," 29.

40. Ibid.

41. Alou, *Alou,* 42–43.

42. Fowler, *Tony O!* 25.

43. Veeck, *Hustler's Handbook,* 221.

44. Alou, *Alou,* 112.

45. Ibid.

46. Craig Neff, "The Hottest Import in Japan," *Sports Illustrated,* Mar. 23, 1987, 72–76.

47. Veeck, *Hustler's Handbook,* 220.

48. Bosewell and Curtis, *Cuban-American Experience,* 43.

49. Oliva interview.

50. Ibid.

51. Ibid.

52. Oliva, *Tony O,* 8.

53. Ibid.

54. Ibid., 12.

55. Oliva interview.

56. *New York Star-Ledger,* July 19, 1970.

57. *New York World-Telegram,* Feb. 8, 1955.

58. Gordon, "Twin First by a Twin," 69.

59. Oliva, *Tony O!* 16.
60. Ibid.
61. Oliva, *Tony O!*
62. Oliva interview.
63. Falls, "Far from Pappa Pedro's Finca," 56.
64. Ibid., 57.
65. Musick, *Who Was Roberto?* 97.
66. Oliva, *Tony O!* 21.
67. Boyle, "The Latins Storm," 29.
68. *Sporting News,* Apr. 8, 1967.
69. *New York Post,* Apr. 12, 1980.
70. Jerry Izenberg quoted in Boyle, "The Latins Storm," 29.
71. Ibid.
72. Ibid., 112.
73. Miñoso, Fernández, and Kleinfelder, *Miñoso,* 89.
74. Brown, *White Sox,* 244.
75. Einstein, *Willie's Time,* 148.
76. Alou, *Alou,* 33–34.
77. Pérez interview.
78. Izenberg, *Great Latin Sports Figures,* 7.
79. Leonard Koppett, "The Brighter Yankees," *New York Times,* Sept. 29, 1964.
80. *Denver Post,* Aug. 8, 1994.
81. *New York Newsday,* Sept. 1, 1964.
82. Hirshberg, "Rough Rise," 61, 73.
83. *New York Journal American,* July 21, 1957.
84. Williams, "Amoros," 72.
85. Ibid.
86. Brandmeyer, "Baseball and the American Dream."
87. Hirshberg, "Rough Rise," 73.
88. Gómez interview.
89. Stewart interview; Gómez interview.
90. Stewart interview.
91. Gómez interview.
92. Ibid.
93. Ibid.
94. *Spokane Chronicle,* June 14, 1962.
95. Ibid.
96. Ibid.
97. Genovese interview.
98. Ibid.
99. *Sporting News,* May 11, 1963.
100. Ibid.
101. Alou, *Alou,* 109–10.

102. Ibid.

103. Oliva interview.

104. Ibid.

105. George Vecsey, "Pedro Ramos's Biggest Loss," *New York Times*, Mar. 14, 1982, 24.

106. *Sporting News,* Feb. 6, 1962.

107. *Sporting News,* Aug. 20, 1966.

108. Alou, *Alou,* 111.

109. Alex Campanis notes, author's possession.

110. Milton Gross, "Palace of Versalles," *Washington Post,* Oct. 5, 1965.

111. Izenberg, *Great Latin Figures,* 77.

112. Alou, *Alou,* 2–4.

113. Devaney, *Marichal,* 76–77.

114. Oliva, *Tony O!* 16.

115. Alou, *Alou,* 117.

•7

Nobody Cares about Us

> How could I miss him? He was the greatest natural athlete I have ever seen as a free agent.
> Al Campanis

> They say "Hey, he talks funny!" But they go to Puerto Rico and they don't talk like us. I don't have a master's degree, but I'm not a dumbhead and I don't want no bullshit from anyone.
> Roberto Clemente

*M*ajor league baseball entered America's "New Frontier" period with a new profile. By 1960, teams were integrated, clubs had relocated, and television brought games into homes on a weekly basis. Latins appeared on most big league rosters. Moreover, they did so having weathered the rough acculturation into the United States. Few American baseball followers knew of their trials. Fewer cared. But Latins' role in the upcoming decade gave notice to baseball aficionados that Latin talent had come of age. Indeed, their triumphs in the 1960s eventually eliminated some of the stereotypes that haunted their predecessors.

Outside of baseball, Spanish speakers banded together to change the status quo despite Latins' supposed passivity. As they grew in numbers, they grew in strength. With nearly six million by the middle of the decade, the Mexican American community, for instance, generated many leaders. Former boxer Rudolfo "Corky" Gonzales fought against police brutality and directed campaigns to eliminate poverty in Denver. His greatest fame, however, came from his inspiring poem "I Am Joaquín," a tale of a frustrated barrio youth. Another leader, Reies López Tijerina, rallied New Mexico's Hispanic poor. In 1966, his La Alianza Federal de Mercedes (the Federal Alliance of Land Grants) occupied a national forest campground and claimed it on behalf of the local villagers (he, at one point, captured two rangers because they "trespassed" on communal property). Entire communities soon began the move toward reform. In Crystal City, Texas, for instance, the Mexican American constituency wrested control of the school board. This success not only indicated growing Latin strength but also provided inspiration for others.[1]

César Chávez, a Mexican American field hand, was one of the most prominent. Beginning in 1965 with a strike in Delano, California, the United Farm Workers, under his leadership, successfully boycotted California's grape growing industry to gain improved working conditions for laborers. Converts to Chávez's cause included seven California bishops of the Catholic church, students, civil rights workers, Coretta Scott King, Governor Edmund G. "Pat" Brown, and Senator Robert F. Kennedy. The movement, which campaigned under the banner of the Virgin of Guadalupe (the patron of Mexico), won Chávez national acclaim and fueled the drive for further reforms. By the end of the decade the boycotts prompted ten major growers to negotiate with the United Farm Workers.[2]

Puerto Ricans also sought changes. During the 1950s, over 200,000 flocked to the mainland, most ending up in New York City in what was known as Spanish Harlem. At the outset of the sixties, the East River Rats,

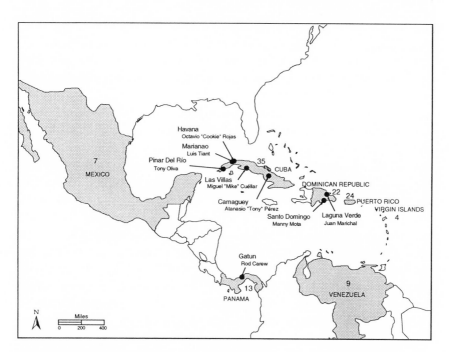

Latin American Origin of Major League Baseball Players, 1960–70. Numerals denote the total number of players from individual countries. Selected high-profile players noted.

a splinter faction from the Congress of Racial Equality, organized a series of rent strikes.[3] Other groups, like the Young Lords and the Puerto Rican Revolutionary Workers Organization, challenged the status quo that limited overall opportunities.[4] The militant approach by these second-generation Puerto Ricans sometimes proved to be effective. Their actions, largely at the university level, led to the establishment of Puerto Rican studies programs at three New York City institutions. At the core of their movement was the sense of ethnic identity based upon strength and honor.

More than any other arena, however, professional baseball diamonds provided Latins with their most high-profile forum. Once on the field they could compete equally and exhibit their special hunger. For they had survived the gauntlet of racism, the trauma of acculturation, and the burden of Latin stereotyping. And they served as the best examples of Latin tenacity and strength, for they battled alone. Although they were separated from the radical movements of the time, their participation in the national pastime exposed mainstream Americans to the Latin presence like no other faction could and helped to undercut many negative perceptions of Spanish-speaking people. Their growing success, however, magnified their frustrations as well as their skills.

Roberto Walker Clemente, perhaps more than anyone, illustrated the bittersweet story of Latin players in the sixties. Entering professional baseball in 1954 during a period of racial discord, the nineteen-year-old Puerto Rican spent his first year on the Brooklyn Dodgers' Montreal farm team. Prior to that, his only experiences away from his small town of Carolina had been occasional trips to San Juan to watch his idol, Monte Irvin, play against a local team. Born in 1934, Roberto was the youngest child of Melchor Clemente, a foreman at the local sugar mill, and his wife Luisa. As a youth he joined neighborhood teams armed with a bat "fashioned from the branch of a guava tree, a glove [that] was improvised from a coffee bean sack, and [a] ball [that] was a tight knot of rags."[5] As a teenager, his athletic skills expanded into the area of track and field. But the young Puerto Rican was obsessed with baseball and concentrated on honing his skills. "I would forget to eat because of baseball," he admitted.[6]

In the spring of his eighteenth year, Al Campanis announced a general tryout for the Dodgers at San Juan Sixto Escobar Stadium. Clemente, of course, was anxious to test his abilities. Of the seventy-two players, the youth from Carolina stood out. "How could I miss him? He was the greatest natural athlete I have ever seen as a free agent," Campanis remarked.[7] Because he was still in high school, the Dodgers opted not to sign him, but later that year the prestigious San Juan Santurce club offered him a contract. The experience proved invaluable, for the club was home to Willie Mays, who was already a star on the mainland. "The best thing that ever happened to Roberto came . . . when he played next to Willie Mays," recalled Roberto Marín, a longtime friend of Clemente's. "I think it was the inspiration of playing next to a star like Mays, and doing a good job, that was most important."[8] In 1953 the Dodgers returned with a contract. Convinced of his potential, and attempting to outbid other teams, the club offered an almost unprecedented $10,000 bonus for his signature. At most signing bonuses were usually $250–$300, but the majority of players received only a ticket for transportation. Following the formal signing, the Dodgers quickly dispatched their new employee to their minor league affiliate in Canada for the 1954 season.

Montreal was a far cry from the familiar environs of San Juan, where even in his worst moments the landscape was familiar and comforting. Thankfully, the 1954 Montreal club also had on its roster Cubans Sandy Amoros and Chico Fernández as well as Joe Black, who was bilingual. These teammates understandably became Clemente's closest companions.

His year in Montreal was not a happy one, however. Because of the bonus player rule of the time, the Dodgers risked losing Clemente to another club at the end of the season by virtue of a draft if they left him in the minor leagues. Brooklyn, against the advice of Campanis, kept Clemente in Montreal and then tried to hide him from other teams by relegating him to the bench. Clemente, unaware of the trickery, became so frustrated that he threatened to return home. Campanis convinced him to stay, but the Dodgers' ploy did not succeed. Clyde Sukeforth, who had brought Jackie Robinson to New York for his fabled meeting with Branch Rickey and still worked with Rickey in the Pittsburgh organization, spotted Clemente during a visit to Montreal. "I couldn't take my eyes off him," said the veteran scout.[9] The Pirates, who had finished last that year, made Clemente their number one pick. Clemente, however, "didn't even know where Pittsburgh was."[10]

Situated on Pennsylvania's eastern flank along the shores of the Allegheny, Monongahela, and Ohio Rivers, Pittsburgh had a distinguished professional baseball past dating back to 1882. In 1891, already part of the National League, the "Pirates," as local journalists dubbed the team, roster featured such Hall of Famers as Honus Wagner, Paul Waner, Ralph Kiner, and Pie Traynor. Pittsburgh was also home to a strong black baseball tradition. The legendary Pittsburgh Crawfords and Homestead Grays, who showcased James "Cool Papa" Bell, Josh Gibson, and Satchel Paige, thrilled fans with their daring and talented play. But by the 1950s the Pirates consistently finished last or next-to-last in the National League. Armed with his "five year plan," which became his blueprint for the club's reorganization, Branch Rickey turned the struggling franchise around. Drafting Roberto Clemente was a key factor in the plan's ultimate success.

The Pirates, of course, were thrilled with Clemente's potential, and he soon responded to their confidence by hitting .314. With Dick Groat, Bill Mazeroski, Bob Friend, and Vernon Law, the Puerto Rican vanquished the laughing-stock image that had plagued the club for a decade. By 1960, Clemente and the Pirates had arrived. His consistent hitting and spectacular defensive abilities spearheaded the club's resurgence as a pennant contender. That season the Pirates took the National League crown, and Clemente's .314 batting average and 94 RBIs contributed mightily to the Pittsburgh championship drive. Prior to the World Series, Dale Long, who had been with the Pirates, warned his Yankee teammates about the Puerto Rican: "He makes fantastic catches, he has a remarkable arm and hits .320. . . . Roberto is one of the most hungry of the hungry Pirates."[11] The Puerto Rican hit safely in each of the seven games. Joe L. Brown, general manager of the Pirates during the late 1950s and early 1960s, said that "what stood out about Roberto was that here was a tremendous athlete, a young man of unusual talent, unusual drive."[12] In fact, during that year's World Series, after Clemente almost picked off Yogi Berra, who had wandered too far off second base, Casey Stengel remarked, "We discovered then that they have a good right fielder."[13] The Pirates, in a memorable fall classic that closed with Bill Mazeroski's immortal series-ending home run, defeated the Yankees. That Clemente played a key role in the deciding game was not lost on Yankees hurler Whitey Ford. "I remember the way he ran out a routine ground ball in the last game, and when we were a little slow in covering, he beat it out," Ford reminisced. "It was something most people forget, but it made the Pirates' victory possible."[14]

Clemente excelled the following year, going into the All-Star break with a .332 average. For his efforts the National League players voted him to start at right field. "I am feeling very good," he beamed, "I will not let them down."[15] A man of his word, he collected two hits and drove in three runs, including the game winner. His hitting improved during the second half of the season and he ended with a .351 average and the National League batting championship. "There is a marvelous flamboyance in Roberto Clemente's actions," admired one journalist. "Fielding, throwing, running or hitting, he swirls with the electric grace of a flamenco dancer and castañets envelop him. He is some ball player."[16] In an exchange between Pirates batting coach George Sisler and Phillies manager Gene Mauch, Sisler bragged that Clemente "could be the next .400 hitter." "I've got news for you," Mauch replied. "He's going to get better."[17] Clemente did. Before the end of the decade, the Puerto Rican earned three more batting titles,

Roberto Clemente. (Courtesy of the National Baseball Hall of Fame Library, Cooperstown, N.Y.)

won ten Gold Gloves, and was christened Most Valuable Player in 1966. Writer Les Biederman claimed that "there isn't anything he can't do. He can hit, hit with power at times, run, throw and there just isn't a better fielder."[18]

Even as Clemente earned a reputation as one of the game's finest players, he was also becoming known as one of the game's most temperamental athletes. His adjustment to playing in the United States was not easy. Like many other Latins, the loneliness he felt, the frustration with the English language, and the racism that plagued him generated apprehension. Despite being a man of many talents and an undeniable star, Clemente often isolated himself and his humor was difficult to gauge. He was also sensitive to criticism and angered by those who suggested that he was a hypochondriac. Despite his temperamental nature, Clemente's self-confidence fueled much of his success. "It was obvious he didn't doubt his abilities to play the game," acknowledged teammate Bill Virdon. "He didn't brag, but he said things that indicated his confidence. Most people who are good know it. . . . He knew he was going to make it; he didn't even think about not making it."[19] After he became an established star, Clemente remarked, "I believe I can hit with anybody in baseball. . . . I'm a better fielder than anyone you can name. I have great respect for Mays, but I can go get a ball like Willie and I have a better arm."[20] Those who knew Clemente closely recognized the sincerity, not the arrogance, of his statements.

Journalists, however, rarely understood. "Lots of times I have the feeling people want to take advantage of me, especially writers," claimed Clemente. "They talk to me but maybe they don't like me so they write about me the way they want to write."[21] Some teammates came to his defense. "Bobby is right about some of the writers being against him," declared pitcher Bob Friend. "They hurt him more than anything, especially about that hypochondriac image. Bobby is one of the greatest players I've ever seen but he's the type who has to be encouraged by everyone."[22]

The Puerto Rican's feud with the media was well known. Journalists, particularly beat writers from visiting clubs, were wary of him. He "didn't communicate a whole lot, but I assumed it was because he didn't speak the language very well. In fact, I don't ever remember him giving any lengthy interviews to any out-of-town writers," recalled Nick Peters, who covered the Giants.[23] Writers who worked the National League circuit routinely networked information about various ballplayers to their peers. Clearly, the word on Clemente was that he was "aloof" and to "give him his space." "I never perceived him as being arrogant," added Peters. "But he wasn't that approachable."[24]

Clemente's complaints about the writers were not always so well considered. His information, for instance, was frequently not firsthand. Many times he learned about the contents of articles written about him from close friends. At one point, he chastised a journalist for supposed critical remarks about his play. Later, when he found out that the column had actually complimented his performances, Clemente apologized for his actions.[25] "Clemente was not an easy man for non-Latin sports writers to know, but he was worth the effort," declared Milton Gross of the *New York Post*.[26]

Roberto Clemente was, nonetheless, often combative. At one point, he lashed out at a group of journalists when he believed one of them questioned his team play. "Did a ball player ever come up to you and say I no team player?" he asked accusingly. "Who say that? The writers, right?"[27] Bill Mazeroski commiserated, "Some writers put words in your mouth and that's what they did to Roberto. . . . They tried to make him look like an ass by getting him to say controversial things and they wrote how the 'Puerto Rican hot dog' was 'popping off' again. He was learning to handle the language, and writers who couldn't speak Spanish tried to make him look silly."[28] The Pirates star was occasionally a victim of the "descriptive" reporting that befell his predecessors: broken English reprinted phonetically. In one interview his words were presented exceptionally cruelly: "I no play so gut yet. Me like hot weather, veree hot. I no run fast cold weather. No get warm in cold. No get warm, no play gut. You see."[29] Such quotes embarrassed and angered Clemente. He later responded, "I never talk like that; they just want to sell newspapers. Anytime a fellow comes from Puerto Rico, they want to create an image. They say 'Hey, he talks funny!' But they go to Puerto Rico and they don't talk like us. I don't have a master's degree, but I'm not a dumbhead and I don't want no bullshit from anyone."[30] Orlando Cepeda was equally bitter: "Latin ball players are labeled as being dumb," explained Cepeda. "We have to do twice as much as the American players to earn respect and a place on the team."[31] Clemente, who sometimes acted as the self-appointed spokesman for Latin players, often stood at the forefront of the battle zone between Latins and the press.

One particularly rancorous episode came during the 1960 season, when a Pittsburgh reporter admitted to Clemente that he was pressured by his peers to cast his MVP ballot for Dick Groat. "You live in a democracy," Clemente retorted, "You should not let anyone tell you how to vote." He later remembered, "I always talked about democracy when I was a kid. I got a taste of democracy then."[32] With a .314 average and 94 RBIs, Clemente was outraged when he learned of his eighth place finish for the

award. Because his pride had been damaged, Clemente's indignation lin-
gered for years. He regularly clashed with journalists. "The more I stay
away from writers, the better I am," he once screamed. "You know why?
Because they're trying to create a bad image for me. You know what they
have against me? Because I'm black and Puerto Rican." At other times,
reporters routinely heard, "You guys never give me credit."[33]

Ill will resulting from past criticisms and stereotypes remained apparent. Clemente often bristled at what he felt was a lack of attention given
to Latin players by the media. "The Latin player doesn't get the recognition he deserves," he complained. "We have self-satisfaction, yes, but after the season is over nobody cares about us."[34] Others, like Tony Oliva,
agreed. "Sometimes it seems they take the Latin players for granted. I never
let it bother me, but for at least eight years I didn't get the same recognition given some players whose records weren't as good."[35] However, Al
Campanis disagreed with some of these assessments. "I think a player like
Clemente was appreciated very much. He might have gotten more recognition had he been in New York or Los Angeles because all the press coverage is large in those cities."[36] Nick Peters added that "if Clemente had
played in New York, he'd have gotten recognition. I mean Sandy Amoros
wasn't even a good player and he got recognition because he made one
catch for Brooklyn."[37] Peters also pointed out that when Clemente played,
journalists competed less for stories because "they weren't televising the
games everyday—there was no ESPN. So the reporter, especially if he had
a tight deadline, . . . could care less about a quote."[38]

Clemente's allegations, to be sure, were not without some justification.
Kal Wagenheim, in his biography of Clemente, pointed to a 1968 study
by the U.S. Equal Employment Opportunity Commission that indicated
that although blacks and Latins constituted more than 20 percent of all
big league rosters, "they appeared in only 5 per cent of the TV commercials that featured sports figures that year."[39] "All told," claimed a *Times*
magazine report a year earlier, "Clemente has three batting titles to his
credit—but nobody has ever asked him to do a shaving-cream commer-
cial."[40] The "image-makers" themselves, Wagenheim alleged, warranted
further analysis. Although one-fifth of the five hundred players in the major
leagues were not white, "it is hard to find a single person from these ethnic groups in the press box." Of equal significance, he claimed, was that
the majority of reporters were "middle-aged; their world view was shaped
before Jackie Robinson entered baseball in 1947." White sportswriters,
however, did not fully account for the lack of recognition of Latin ballplayers. The main reason, Felipe Alou indicated, was still an obvious one.

"It would be bad business to hire speakers who cannot express themselves clearly. The same is true for endorsements and making commercials when the time comes to pick the player who will do the best job," he claimed.[41]

Writers did have specific interpretations of what they saw. The flair with which many played was viewed as exhibitionism. But to most Latin players, U.S. sportswriters could not distinguish between flash and skill. According to Tony Oliva, "Every player performs in his own way. If he's a 'hot dog,' what difference does it make [as long as] he does the job?" Oliva added that Latin Americans, but not as many Americans, appreciated Minnie Miñoso's style of play: "Minnie Miñoso was loved and recognized. Throughout Cuba Minnie is a legend as a hard competitor. He would jump to the fences with no chance of catching the ball. He made clouds of dust when he slid. They did not call him a 'hot dog.' Minnie was a hustler."[42] Stereotypes notwithstanding, the increasing number of Latin players in the major leagues reflected the confidence baseball organizations came to have in their skills.

Writers, of course, did not always belittle Latin players. The San Francisco Giants, a club with many talented Latins, provided a perfect opportunity for journalists to establish rapport with Latin players. Besides Orlando Cepeda, Giant beat writers seemed especially captivated by the spectacle of three brothers on a single roster.

By 1960, Felipe Alou was a two-year veteran with the Giants. Within a short time his career blossomed into a productive one. In 1962, as a regular, he hit 25 home runs, had 98 RBIs, and batted .316. After six seasons, the Giants sought to strengthen their pitching and traded him to the Milwaukee Braves. Following one injury-ridden season and the Braves' move to Atlanta, he collected 218 hits, 31 home runs, and 78 RBIs. Furthermore, at .327 he had the second best batting average in the National League. Only his brother, Mateo, did better.

Mateo "Matty" Alou joined his older brother in San Francisco in 1960. Considered small for an athlete (5'5" and 130 pounds), Mateo, his brother Felipe claimed, "exhibited no particular talent as a baseball player back home and the only reason he was even given a contract was because he was my brother."[43] Utilized as a part-time outfielder, he was dealt to the Pittsburgh Pirates in 1965. That year Mateo hit a feeble .231. However, Pittsburgh manager Harry Walker recognized his potential and adjusted his swing. Both Walker and Roberto Clemente, who translated for the

Pittsburgh manager, worked patiently and offered continuous encouragement to Mateo. Their efforts contributed to Mateo's .342 average and a National League batting championship in 1966. He "turned out to be an exceptional hitter, something that no one had any way of knowing when he was a scrawny teenager," recalled his slightly surprised older brother.[44] The following two years Mateo finished a close second in the batting race. Praise from his peers, however, was not always forthcoming. Indeed, Mateo's unorthodox swing sometimes brought disdain. Among the critics was pitcher Steve Carlton, who said that Alou was "the worst .300 hitter I've ever seen."[45] Gene Mauch, in defense of Alou, countered, "I admire the fellow. I tell you the fellows I don't admire. They are the .220 hitters who sit in the dugout and laugh at the way Alou bats. Maybe some of those fellows should attempt Matty's style. It certainly couldn't hurt them."[46]

Although they garnered attention the brothers did not gain notoriety until 1963 when a younger brother, Jesús, joined them on that year's Giants squad. The San Francisco sports press played up the family scenario. Harry Jupiter of the *San Francisco Chronicle* described them as "Three Alous, all of them outfielders with spectacular throwing arms, and yet totally different in appearance and style."[47] Before the end of the 1963 season, they played in the outfield simultaneously on three different occasions.[48] Never had major league fans witnessed such an event. But for Jesús, "it was no big deal, we didn't telephone home or anything. After all, we played together all the time in winter ball back in the Caribbean.[49]

What was a "big deal" was the Americanized nickname—"Jay"—given to him by American peers and writers. His real name, to his chagrin, sparked controversy among San Francisco's religious community. One rabbi said, "Jesús is ancient Greek for the Hebrew name Joshua. It means God is Salvation. As a Giants fan, I hope Jesús Alou hits .400. For baseball purposes, yes—I'd rather call him Butch."[50] A Catholic monsignor said, "A nickname would eliminate the danger of disrespect for a name sacred to Our Savior."[51] Even a local bishop agreed "it would be simpler all around to call him by a name other than the one given to our Lord."[52] Jesús bristled at the thought that his name—a popular one in Latin America—was deemed unacceptable. "My name is Jesús," he argued, "because that is what my father and mother gave me. I like the name and that is what I want people to call me."[53] As the controversy grew, so did his anger. "What is wrong with my real name, Jesús?" he asked. "It is a common name in Latin America, like Joe or Tom or Frank in the U.S. My parents named me Jesús and I am proud of my name. This 'Jay' I do not like. It is not my name."[54] Discarding "Jay," Jesús Alou stayed in the big leagues for four-teen years.

Professional writers and those in team public relations, of course, did tend to Americanize Latin names. Roberto became "Bobby," Mateo—"Matty," Luis—"Looie," Dagoberto—"Bert." To be sure, Latins had mixed emotions about these nicknames. Minnie Miñoso initially disliked being given a name ordinarily reserved for women. "In Cuba," he recalled, "everybody used to call me 'Orestes.' Now everybody in Cuba and the United States call me 'Minnie.' So I don't mind."[55] Nicknames also were *issued* by the clubs. In the early years of his career, claimed Guillermo Montañez, one team's "public relations man told me that I will be called 'Willie.'" Despite his protest, Montañez's name on the media guide was "Willie."[56] Other misunderstandings over Latin names occurred. One of the more prominent surrounded the Alou surname. "In Latin countries the mother's maiden name is tacked on to the name of all her children and comes after the husband's name," explained Felipe of his two last names—Rojas Alou. "I didn't argue [the American version] mainly because I *couldn't* argue."[57] Other nicknames, common in baseball, also appeared in place of Latin first names. "Chico," for instance—"boy" in Spanish—was routinely given to Latin players. "Dominican Dandy," however, was a nickname that all baseball observers came to respect.

Juan Marichal was among the most distinguished Latins to grace both the Giants' roster and the major league scrolls during the sixties. Born in October 1938 in Laguna Verde in the Dominican Republic, Marichal, like many of his contemporaries, grew up impoverished. When he was three, his father died and he was raised by his mother and older brother. Years later, Marichal noted his father's influence: "I don't think my father played baseball, but I know that he used to live for the gallos, for cockfighting. I think that's why I've got that in my blood."[58] Between 1955 and 1956, Marichal played for two company teams—the Bermúdez Rum Company and the Grenada Company Manzanillo team—which gave the right-hander not only a forum for his talents but also an opportunity for steady work. These teams were so poor that players occasionally traveled on horseback to face out-of-town opponents. In 1956, Marichal's pitching skills attracted the attention of Aviación, the country's air force team. "I threw a four-hitter and we beat them 2-1. That night we celebrated. The next day, I was drafted."[59] Considered a "specialist" in the service, his pay was considerably higher than that of other draftees. "That was my job in the air force," Marichal recalled. "Playing ball."[60] His "job," however, was far from lax. Indeed, the team had to win lest they face the wrath of their biggest supporter, Brigadier General Rafael Leonidas Trujillo Martínez, better known as "Rafis," son of the president. On one occasion, when the team lost a doubleheader to the Manzanillo club, the Aviación players were jailed for five days.[61] Their manager and team captain were confined for a month. "We never lost a doubleheader again while I was there," the right-hander remembered.[62]

Marichal's talent caught the eye of a number of big league scouts. In 1957, after winning approval from Rafis, he signed with the New York Giants and received a $500 bonus. The following year he flew to the spring training camp in Florida to begin his major league career. "Like other Latin players, I had problems with the food and got homesick," he recalled. To counter this isolation, he and his Latin peers often played the music of his homeland after practices. "But that made me so sad that I finally took my records and broke them one by one and stopped listening to any Dominican music at all."[63] Marichal's two-year climb to the big leagues included a brief tenure with the Giants' Class D team in Michigan City, Indiana. His stay proved profitable when he encountered a local merchant who rewarded victorious Michigan City pitchers with live chickens. That year Marichal eventually collected twenty-one of the birds.[64] Stops in Springfield, Massachusetts, and Tacoma, Washington, preceded an invitation to the big leagues. It was during his time in Springfield, while under the eye of manager Andy Gilbert, that Marichal developed his famous high kick pitching motion.[65]

The Dominican pitcher was also well-liked, particularly in Tacoma. Designated the "Laughing Boy" by the local press because of his "ever-present grin and sunny disposition," Marichal became a favorite.[66] His 11-5 record pitching for the Pacific Northwest town also had something to do with his popularity (Marichal, in fact, compiled a formidable 50-26 record during his stay in the minors). Indeed, when the right-hander departed to join the parent club in 1960, Tacoma baseball followers were in sorrow. "The blow fell Sunday when the big Giants called up Juan Marichal," reported the *Tacoma News-Tribune,* "one of the most personable and likeable of the Tacoma players. The first reaction is of disappointment. Tacoma fans might as well be philosophical about the whole thing [and] wish Juan well."[67]

Marichal's 1960 debut in a San Francisco uniform was spectacular. The rookie shut out the Philadelphia Phillies while surrendering only one hit. Moreover, Marichal's debut was the first major league contest he had ever attended.[68] And when asked if he spoke to Clay Dalrymple, the lone Phillies player to get a hit, Marichal politely responded, "I do not know him. We have not been introduced."[69] Despite their defeat the Phillies were quite impressed with the young pitcher. Manager Gene Mauch marveled, "The

Juan Marichal. (Courtesy of the National Baseball Hall of Fame Library, Cooperstown, N.Y.)

kid threw more different pitches than anyone else in the league."[70] Taco-
mans beamed at his early success. The *Tacoma News-Tribune* proudly announced that local fans were "entitled to bask in his glory."[71]

Marichal completed the 1960 season with the Giants and contributed a
6-2 record. Of his eleven starts, he completed six. More feats followed.
Before the end of the decade, the Dominican Dandy won twenty or more
games six times and his high kick windup became legendary. "If you placed
all the pitchers in history behind a transparent curtain, where only a sil-
houette was visible, Juan's high kick motion would be the easiest to identify," wrote Bob Stevens of the *San Francisco Chronicle*. "He brought to
the mound what Van Gogh and da Vinci brought to canvas—beauty, in-
dividuality, and class."[72]

Marichal's achievements, like those of his fellow Dominicans in the big
leagues, did not go unnoticed in his native country. Sports columnists in
the Dominican Republic closely monitored the activities of their countrymen in the major leagues. A typical headline read: "Mateo Alou Bats Three
Singles."[73] Juan Marichal's popularity was so great that at one point Dominican political observers believed he could have easily won the republic's presidency.[74] Dominican natives also lauded Mateo Alou, the 1966
National League batting champion. In 1968, he received a gold medal from
Dominican president Joaquin Balaguer for distinguished service to his
country.[75] Other Dominican ballplayers so honored included Felipe Alou,
Manny Mota, Rico Carty, and Juan Marichal.[76] Julián Javier, the regular
second baseman for the St. Louis Cardinals for ten years, also won praise
when he helped guide his team to three World Series. Additionally, Manny Mota became one of the game's outstanding pinch hitters. These Dominicans, to be sure, set high standards and provided inspiration for their
successors.

But these high standards also had their drawbacks. Their success led to
the pressure of satisfying two cultures. The demand for quality play in the
United States was often superseded by the insistence on appearances in the
Dominican Republic. Indeed, despite Marichal's popularity he was criticized for occasional absences from Dominican winter baseball. "After
pitching for two or three hundred innings in the States, it was hard to come
down here and be expected to play winters. There was a lot of pressure
on you to play. But there was also pressure from the Giants not to play,
because they wanted me to rest my arm," he contended. "If you don't play,
the whole country gets on you."[77]

Even the great Roberto Clemente made concessions to his Puerto Rican
supporters. Following the 1964 season he announced, "I will not play

winter ball. I look forward to a rest."[78] But his proclamation was soon watered down. After accepting the position as manager of the San Juan Santurce club, Clemente included himself in the line-up. A disturbed Pirates front office wrote, "He does not need to play. [The Puerto Ricans] put pressure on him to change his mind. The people in San Juan hounded him until he gave in to popular demand."[79] The often guarded Clemente finally admitted, "They want me to play, yes, and I want to help San Juan win the pennant."[80] Sociologist Alan Klein pointed out that "winter baseball . . . provided a strong bond between these gifted, fortunate athletes and the people they represented in the United States; it gave them a way of showing gratitude to the fans."[81] To break that bond was an invitation to intense criticism. At one point, to escape the Dominican media, Marichal purchased a home in San Francisco "and stayed there one winter so that I would not have to go home and listen to them asking on the radio as to when I was going to pitch."[82]

All of the Latin major leaguers were success stories to their compatriots. As such, they carried responsibilities and obligations their American counterparts did not have to bear. Further, their status as high-profile athletes exposed them to criticism from two different regions and cultures. This, along with the experiences that came with adaptation to a foreign land, the racial environment, and a sometimes cantankerous press corps, added strain to their success. Hence, the intensity that drove Roberto Clemente, for instance, was only in part a product of his love for the game. He also carried with him the banner of his heritage. And by the mid-1960s, as he scanned the progress of other Latins, he found many reasons to feel proud.

Notes

1. Moore and Pachon, *Hispanics*, 150–51.

2. Acuña, *Occupied America*, 324–27. For a biographical study of César Chávez, see Taylor, *Chávez*.

3. Sexion, *Spanish Harlem*, 134.

4. Moore and Pachon, *Hispanics*, 188–90.

5. Wagenheim, *Clemente!* 21.

6. Ibid., 22.

7. Ibid., 31.

8. Ibid., 27.

9. Ibid., 42.

10. Ibid.

11. *New York World-Telegram*, Sept. 19, 1960.

12. Musick, *Who Was Roberto?* 98.

13. *New York World-Telegram,* Oct. 11, 1960.

14. Musick, *Who Was Roberto?* 98.

15. Musick, *Who Was Roberto?* 160.

16. *Sporting News,* Oct. 11, 1961.

17. Ibid.

18. *Sporting News,* Apr. 20, 1968.

19. Musick, *Who Was Roberto?* 115.

20. *Sporting News,* Sept. 5, 1964.

21. Prato, "Why the Pirates Love the New Roberto Clemente," 36.

22. Ibid., 37.

23. Peters interview.

24. Ibid.

25. Wagenheim, *Clemente!* 171–72.

26. Ibid., 172.

27. Prato, "Why the Pirates Love the New Roberto Clemente," 37.

28. Wagenheim, *Clemente!* 53.

29. Ibid., 37.

30. Musick, *Who Was Roberto?* 126.

31. Cepeda interview.

32. Musick, *Who Was Roberto?* 153.

33. Ibid., 122.

34. Wagenheim, *Clemente!* 129.

35. *Chicago Tribune,* June 25, 1978.

36. Campanis interview.

37. Peters interview.

38. Ibid.

39. Wagenheim, *Clemente!* 138–39.

40. Ibid., 138.

41. Alou, *Alou,* 122.

42. *Chicago Tribune,* June 25, 1978.

43. Ibid., 122.

44. Ibid.

45. Undated clipping, *Sporting News,* Matty Alou file, National Baseball Library, Cooperstown, N.Y.

46. Ibid.

47. Harry Jupiter quoted in *San Francisco Giants Yearbook,* 14–15.

48. Ibid., 15; *San Francisco Chronicle,* Sept. 10, 1963.

49. Joseph Durso, "We Band as Brothers," *New York Times,* Aug. 14, 1975.

50. Sullivan, "The Newest Alou," 10.

51. Ibid.

52. Ibid.

53. Ibid.

54. *Sporting News, July 3, 1965,* Jesús Alou file, National Baseball Library.

55. Furlong, "The White Sox Katzenjammer Kid," 78.

56. *Eugene Oregon Register-Guard,* May 1, 1979.

57. Alou, *Alou,* 56.

58. Ruck, *Tropic of Baseball,* 63.

59. Ibid., 67.

60. Ibid., 71.

61. Ibid., 73.

62. Ibid.

63. Ibid., 75.

64. Marichal, *A Pitcher's Story,* 98.

65. Ibid.

66. *Tacoma News-Tribune,* July 11, 1960.

67. Ibid.

68. Devaney, *Marichal,* 69.

69. Ibid., 105.

70. *San Francisco Giants Yearbook,* 32.

71. *Tacoma News-Tribune,* July 21, 1960.

72. *San Francisco Giants Yearbook,* 32.

73. Wiarda, *Dominican Republic,* 122; *Sporting News,* Jan. 12, 1966.

74. Ibid.

75. *Sporting News,* July 27, 1968.

76. *Sporting News,* Dec. 17, 1966.

77. Ruck, *Tropic of Baseball,* 79.

78. Wagenheim, *Clemente!* 110–11.

79. Ibid., 111.

80. Ibid.

81. Klein, *Sugarball,* 36.

82. Ruck, *Tropic of Baseball,* 79.

•8

Pepper Blood

Baseball in America would enjoy the status of cockfighting if its players descended to Marichal's style of fighting.
Sporting News

I wonder if "the mob" would be shouting if his name weren't Marichal.
Dick Young, *New York Daily News*

*L*atin players dominated the big leagues in the sixties. Zoilo Versalles won the American League's Most Valuable Player Award in 1965 (his teammate and fellow Cuban, Tony Oliva, came in second in the voting); Roberto Clemente took the National League's top honor in 1966. Tony Oliva's 1964 Rookie of the Year trophy, in addition to his 1964 and 1965 American League batting titles, was followed by Clemente's third such award (he also won the 1961 and 1964 National League batting championships). Mateo Alou earned his own title in 1966. And their success preceded Orlando Cepeda's return to prominence. In 1966 he won the National League's Comeback Player of the Year Award; the next season he became the first major league player to win a Most Valuable Player trophy with a unanimous vote. Latin fielding also continued to be exceptional. Vic Power won consecutive Gold Glove awards at first base between 1960 and 1964. And beginning in 1961, Roberto Clemente won the first of twelve Gold Gloves in a row. Moreover, of the eleven American league Gold Glove awards handed out to shortstops, Latin players—Versalles and Luis Aparicio—captured nine of them. On the mound, Juan Marichal twice—in 1963 (25) and 1968 (26)—led the National League in wins, complete games (22 in 1964 and 30 in 1968), and innings pitched (321 in 1963 and 326 in 1968). Latin players, particularly in the American League, also exhibited their daring base-running skills. Bert Campaneris led that circuit in stolen bases six times during his career; Luis Aparicio, the heralded shortstop, won nine base-stealing crowns. In addition, Campaneris and Venezuelan César Tovar had the distinction of being the only two players ever to field all nine positions in a single game.[1]

In addition to their many awards, Latins garnered praise from their peers. Sam Mele, manager of the 1965 American League champion Minnesota Twins, declared that Versalles "inspired us to win the pennant."[2] Clemente won similar praise from Pirates management. "He won the MVP because he did so many little things," claimed manager Harry Walker. "He did the things so many stars don't: hustling on routine ground balls, breaking up double plays, taking the extra base. He has pride [and] wants people to know what he has accomplished."[3] That year, four of the top ten Most Valuable Player nominees were Latins. Even Cepeda, a victim of management criticism in San Francisco, discovered an appreciative audience in St. Louis. "It's not just his statistics," claimed third baseman Mike Shannon. "It's also what happens in the clubhouse. It's the intangibles. Orlando is a prestige player and we have him."[4] "What makes our club click," added catcher Tim Mc-Carver, "can be summed up in one word: Cepeda. He gave us a fighting chance. Cepeda's our big man."[5] According to Coach Dick Sisler, "he's a good team man. . . . When he hits, he picks up the rest of the club."[6] So popular was Cepeda in St. Louis that the *Sporting News* claimed: "You need cotton in your ears when [the St. Louis fans] applaud him."[7]

But covering Spanish-speaking players was not easy because journalists were required to make adjustments in communication. Because they received no lessons in understanding Hispanic heritage, they had to make concerted efforts to learn; some did not. Inevitably images that Latins came to hate grew from ignorance of their cultures. These players, however, did have their allies in the press corps. Stan Isaacs, for instance, carefully observed Orlando Cepeda's plight during his time on the Giants under Alvin Dark. Isaacs castigated Giants management for continually blaming Cepeda for the team's misfortunes. The reporter went on to say that "Cepeda should be ranked in the super-star class. However, he is considered [by the Giants] to be a big baby, a brooder, a dummy who does the wrong thing at the wrong time."[8] After the Giants traded Cepeda to St. Louis, Isaacs concluded that "the Giants proved incapable of giving Cepeda the tender loving care he needed—a T.L.C. no different than that lavished upon super egos like Willie Mays, Mickey Mantle and Ted Williams."[9] Divisions due to cultural gaps, of course, continued to hamper communications between the press and Latin players. "I thought a lot of that was that they were misunderstood because [many] Latins were clannish, and they stuck to themselves. [Hence] they gave the impression to some that they were arrogant, or aloof, or they could care less," remembered Nick Peters. "I mean it's a two-way street if you want to communicate. A person like Cepeda [for instance] was adored from the beginning and generally very good to the press."[10]

Their image as "hot-tempered" and "oversensitive," however, soured relations with journalists and peers. Perceptions that stemmed from earlier eras, to be sure, lurked in the minds of frustrated writers who simply cast Spanish-speaking players as "moody." In some cases, though, the image was a reality. Clemente admitted that: "We Latins get more excited than Americans. We have a lot of pepper blood. Sometimes I don't think Americans understand this."[11] Rubén Gómez, in retrospect, stated, "I could have had more press time if I had been more sociable."[12] Felipe Alou commented that "the Latin temper—that ever-burning ember—is such . . . that some hasty, angry words have been spoken at inopportune times." But Alou was quick to point out "that it is unlikely that Latin tempers are really much worse than American tempers. One fact that Latins must never forget is that as ballplayers, we were, are, and always will be, foreigners in America and we cannot hope that we will ever be totally accepted."[13] Cuban Octavio "Cookie" Rojas explained that a unique characteristic accompanied the so-called Latin temper. "There is a Latin temper and they do show it, but it is not that they are different because of who they are. What makes them different is what they are." Indeed, the "Latin personality" was, perhaps more than any other factor, a result of common upbringing. According to Rojas, "it comes from the drive and a little bit of desperation and the fear that even a simple slump will send them back to obscurity and hunger. And, of course, you have to understand the feeling of isolation."[14]

Occasional bursts of anger by Latins sometimes led to violent actions. Pitcher Rubén Gómez got into a number of scuffles with batters who felt he had thrown too close to them. And Leo Cárdenas reportedly attacked teammate Jim O'Toole with an ice pick.[15] In 1961, Twins pitcher Camilo Pascual threw a bat at teammate Bob Allison when he was chastised for not holding Minnie Miñoso close to first base.[16] While such scuffles were not foreign to any player, the "hot tempered" image remained exclusively Latin. The most infamous brawl occurred in 1965 at Candlestick Park.

Throughout the season the Los Angeles Dodgers and the San Francisco Giants battled for the National League pennant. Indeed, theirs was a traditional rivalry carried to the West Coast from New York. Furthermore, the two California cities had been rivals since the nineteenth century. The Dodgers and Giants simply magnified the divisions already established in the state. With the teams' intense badgering, by the time the Dodgers visited Candlestick Park for a three-game series in August, the atmosphere was explosive. Charles Einstein pegged it: "There was the tension of the tightest National League race in history [and] a provocative trading of beanballs, curses, and threats."[17]

Turbulence that year beyond baseball particularly affected Juan Marichal and Dodgers catcher John Roseboro. For the Giants pitcher, a devoted Dominican nationalist, the violence in his homeland was most trying. When Juan Bosch, a liberal reformer who had been elected president in 1963 but ousted by conservative generals, attempted to retake the office, President Lyndon B. Johnson dispatched 22,000 U.S. Marines to avoid "another Cuba." Order was eventually restored, but a rigid military dictatorship ruled. While Marichal did not address the disturbances of that year in his autobiography, it appears reasonable to assume that the civil unrest weighed heavily on his mind. As an indicator, Felipe Alou remembered that he "had no idea how my parents were while I was in America. Correspondence then was poor and despite three months of trying, I had not been able to get a call through to my folks."[18] Roseboro was equally torn between the pennant race and events near his home in Los Angeles. Only weeks before the Dodgers visited San Francisco a violent race riot broke out in the Los Angeles black community called Watts. Several days of chaos resulted in the deaths of thirty-four people and $200 million in property damage. Things were so intense that Los Angeles Police Department officers even arrested Roseboro's teammate, Willie Crawford, on suspicion of being a rioter. These events, coupled with the pressure of a pennant race between the two hated rivals, helped set the stage for a fiasco not soon-to-be forgotten.[19]

In a rare matchup between the two ace pitchers, Marichal started the third game of the series against Sandy Koufax, following two curse-laden, cat-calling games. As early as the first game, however, the Dominican's ire had risen. In that contest, Mateo Alou, in an effort to cause a catcher's interference call on Roseboro, attempted a fake bunt. In the course of the action, the ball missed the bat but landed squarely on the catcher's chest protector. Slightly injured, Roseboro cursed at Alou and indicated that if another such incident took place he "was going to get him."[20] Marichal, within earshot, began to bait the Dodgers catcher in defense of his countryman, just as rookie Orlando Cepeda, with bat in hand, went after Pirates manager Danny Murtaugh in the belief that the skipper ordered the beaning of Cepeda's idol, Rubén Gómez, in 1958. With such loyalties in place, by the time of the third game of that 1965 series, an explosion was imminent.

In the third inning of a close contest, the Dodgers were convinced that Marichal had already "knocked down" two of their hitters. When the Dominican came to bat, heated words passed between the Giants pitcher and the Dodgers catcher. Moments latter a scuffle ensued and Marichal, to the astonishment of the Candlestick capacity crowd, clubbed Roseboro with his bat. Roseboro, according to Marichal, had "nicked" him in the ear with a return throw to Koufax. In Los Angeles, thousands of fans witnessed the fight on television and saw Roseboro's skull deeply lacerated. Newscast after newscast flashed across the nation and by the following day Marichal was among its most prominent villains.

Warren Giles, the National League president, fined the Dominican $1,750 and issued an eight-day suspension. Others believed that Marichal had been punished too lightly. Ron Fairly of the Dodgers concluded that "he should get kicked out of the league. If he gets off that easy, what's to stop him from doing it again? And what's to stop others from doing the same thing?"[21] The *Sporting News* declared that "Baseball in America would enjoy the status of cockfighting if its players descended to Marichal's style of fighting." The paper then warned that "an attacker capable of using a bat on another man does not figure to be impressed by a penalty which costs him only one pitching turn. To us, it appears an open invitation to a Marichal type for a repeat performance."[22]

Baseball fans across the country also reacted sharply. In his first two performances in Philadelphia and Chicago following his suspension, Marichal was booed.[23] To forestall trouble, Giants officials rearranged the Dominican's scheduled starts so that he would not pitch in an upcoming series in Los Angeles. Charles Einstein later said, "It was bad enough that the Giants were coming to [Los Angeles]. You could not jam 56,000 people within the confines of four acres and expect them to tolerate Marichal too."[24]

Sports journalists hammered away at Marichal weeks after the altercation. The right-hander, many contended, lacked courage. The *Sporting News* said that any "alibis" about the pressure of a pennant race or the turmoil in the Dominican Republic could have been used in his defense "if Marichal had used his fists."[25] Another writer argued, "No matter what the Dodgers did or said to Marichal, worse has been said and done in the past. None of the victims resorted to the use of a bat."[26] The controversy seemed to transcend the incident itself, spurring comments regarding Latin traits—frequently uncomplimentary. "Orlando Cepeda, Marichal's teammate and fellow Latin, usually brings his trusty bat with him when he's leaving the dugout to join a fracas on the field, as he did this time," the *Sporting News* boldly claimed.[27] The paper later reversed its claim.[28]

Old stereotypes of "hot-tempered" Latins reemerged, however. "There are those who are quick to make this a racial incident and toss around the classic cliché about Latins and their tempers," warned Phil Pepe of the *New York World-Telegram*. "They point to Leo Cárdenas wielding an ice pick late last season in a battle with his Cincinnati teammate Jim O'Toole. They mention Rubén Gómez against Joe Adcock and Orlando Cepeda and Danny Murtaugh with a bat a few seasons ago."[29]

Marichal also had his defenders. Columnist Dick Young, for instance, tired of the continued bashing, claimed a racial bias existed in the reporting. Referring to Marichal's critics as "the mob," Young questioned "if 'the mob' would be shouting if his name weren't Marichal. What would the mob shout . . . if his name were a nice Anglo-Saxon name like Frank Thomas. . . . I seem to recall that Frank Thomas hit Richie Allen on the side of the head with a bat . . . but I didn't hear the mob screaming for Frank Thomas' head, or calling him a savage."[30] Journalist Nick Peters, whose beat then was the Giants, recognized how "very difficult" it was to cover the Giants "because we weren't objective. . . . I mean what he did was a terrible thing. [Yet] I don't think anyone in San Francisco really criticized him. I think he had the benefit of the doubt because we all knew what a good guy he was and we gave him that." Peters, however, conceded that "if I was a writer for the Dodgers, I'd have gone berserk and demanded his scalp." But the reporter added, "Maybe we could have been more objective, but he was our guy."[31] Marichal's three missed starts did enormous damage to the Giants' pennant hopes. Though he won twenty-two games that year, his team finished two games behind the Dodgers, who took the National League crown. Moreover, the incident severely hurt Marichal's reputation, haunting him and overshadowing his remarkable accomplishments.

As for the Dominicans, political problems complicated matters for the Cuban players in the United States. Fulgencio Batista had, since 1933, ruled that island with an iron fist. Backed by U.S. economic interests, which controlled many of Cuba's important resources and exports, a coalition of the military, upper-class elites, and foreign entrepreneurs provided the foundation for Batista's dictatorship. But by the 1950s nationalist sentiments emerged, spearheaded by a young lawyer named Fidel Castro, who wanted to rid the island of both Batista and North American hegemony.

Following a botched attempt in 1953, he masterminded a revolution five years later that successfully drove Batista into exile. On January 1, 1959, Castro marched victoriously into Havana. Soon thereafter, in an effort to nationalize Cuba's natural resources and lands, Castro alienated the United States and diplomatic relations ceased in 1961.

By then, the United States was deeply embroiled in anti-communist "containment" policies, largely driven by the protection of business interests abroad. The United States, which considered Latin America within its political sphere, took a dim view of any threat to its hegemony. During the 1950s, Secretary of State John Foster Dulles characterized the American position. In March 1954 Dulles, often blunt and belligerent, told a gathering of the Organization of American States that the United States was prepared to take any "measures necessary to eradicate and prevent subversive activities" in Latin America.[32] His brother Allen, director of the Central Intelligence Agency, privately suggested that he "wouldn't wait for an engraved invitation to come in and give aid" to prevent communism in Latin America.[33] President Dwight Eisenhower himself spelled out the sentiments of his administration when, in explaining the concept of the "domino theory," he warned, "you have a beginning of a disintegration that would have the most profound influences."[34]

Against this backdrop, Castro's rise to power was viewed with great apprehension, especially when his initial visit to Washington, D.C., in April 1959 did not temper American suspicions. According to the historian Charles Alexander, Eisenhower and Castro "had fundamentally differing conceptions of what kind of revolution Cuba should have."[35] The eventual break in diplomatic ties had other ramifications—it severely hampered the Cuban people in traveling freely between the two countries.

This political tension directly affected baseball. Although the Sugar Kings of the International League were based in Havana, diplomatic divisions threatened the team's home. Castro, a former college baseball player and fan, wanted to see the financially troubled franchise, which he considered "part of the Cuban people," continue even if he "had to pitch."[36] Frank Shaughnessy, president of the International League, however, was pessimistic about the Sugar Kings' future at that site. In 1960, with Shaughnessy's prodding, the International League persuaded the Havana franchise to move its operations to Jersey City, New Jersey.[37] Cuban players and coaches found themselves in a precarious position. When Nap Reyes agreed to handle the franchise, his government denounced him as a "traitor and public enemy No. 1 of Cuban baseball." Reyes responded that he had to work where he was sent.[38] Worse situations followed.

Like Eisenhower, President John F. Kennedy viewed Cuba as a "clear and present danger" and set out to undermine the Castro regime.[39] In April 1961, the ill-fated Bay of Pigs affair all but ended communications between the United States and Cuba. Cuban players again were faced with making tough choices between patriotism and profession. That year Bert Campaneris and Tito Fuentes signed with major league organizations. Their eventual success, however, did not elate all Cubans. Juan Ealo, a Cuban manager, recalled, "We were playing in Costa Rica on the day of the Bay of Pigs attack, and American scouts offered three players contracts." According to Ealo, "both Campaneris and Fuentes were young, second-string players. They knew no better and left. But our best pitcher, Joe Mitchell Pineda, understood that you do not sign yourself away to a country at the very instant when they are invading your homeland."[40]

Cuban players already in the United States were increasingly isolated from their families, friends, and homeland. The freedom to communicate appeared lost. Earlier that year, after diplomatic relations had ended, one state department official asserted, "In the past, nationals from countries with which we have broken off relations had a tough time visiting here for any reason. It is no steadfast rule, but being a ballplayer won't make any difference, I should think."[41] Travel between the United States and Cuba became a risk. In early January 1961, Cuban officials detained Camilo Pascual, Pedro Ramos, and Minnie Miñoso as they attempted to return to the United States. The players left Cuba after a few tense days.[42]

Following the Bay of Pigs fiasco, Cuban players in the United States faced what they believed was permanent isolation from their families in Cuba. "I'm worried," said Zoilo Versalles to Twins owner Calvin Griffith. "I have my father there, a brother, and my wife."[43] During that summer Versalles left the ball club in anguish when he learned that his wife could not leave Cuba. Away from the team for almost a month, Versalles rejoined after Griffith lobbied the Cuban government for her release.[44]

Versalles, like his Cuban peers in the United States, was a man without a country. This realization compounded his feeling of isolation in the United States. He sadly pointed out that "there is nothing worse to a man than to lose his home. Cuba is my country and they don't let me come home."[45] Only a year earlier he abandoned the Twins' spring training camp because of homesickness. His depression fueled his combative nature. After benching Versalles for lack of hustle, manager Sam Mele once fined him $300 for arguing the decision.[46] One teammate simply dismissed the Cuban as "nuts." Mele considered Versalles "moody, sulky, uncommunicative. He had more sulky, moody days than any other kind."[47] Though he adapted to his circumstances, his thoughts never wandered far from his homeland. Versalles exhibited his sorrow when the Twins won the 1965 American League pennant. As the team celebrated, he remembered, "I stand in front of my locker with Tony [Oliva] and Camilo [Pascual] and Sandy [Valdespino] and we don't say nothing. Tony cries. I think, this is the biggest moment I ever have in my life and I can't go home and tell about it. I have nothing to do with politics. The trouble between Castro and the United States should not cause things like this."48

Tony Oliva also carried with him the pain of separation from his family. He left Cuba just weeks prior to the Bay of Pigs incident, but opted not to return to his home so as not to jeopardize his career. Not until 1973 did he again visit Cuba. "It was hard for me not to be able to go back home," he remembered. "I thought about my family all the time."49 Neither Oliva's family nor the Cuban fans saw him perform. "I played in Mexico, Venezuela, and the Dominican Republic, but I was never able to give back to the Cuban fans my gift of playing there."50

In 1961, Pedro Ramos, who had lost his cigar store to the Cuban government, openly volunteered to join the anti-Castro rebels preparing for a Cuban invasion.51 Camilo Pascual, too, lost all of his money and property after he left the country in 1961. Even his sanctuary—the baseball field—did not shield him from the fallout of the political climate. During a 1963 game at Yankee Stadium, eight anti-Castro demonstrators rushed the field and draped Pascual with a Cuban flag. The pitcher was shocked and embarrassed.52 Some players, like Tito Fuentes, suffered quietly. During his playing days Fuentes devoted all of his free time on road trips to correspondence with family and friends. "I have no trouble getting letters out of Cuba. My mother, she write a little while ago," he noted. "I get it in eight day. I write, maybe she no get it for three, four months."53

For Cuban players, no amount of prestige or skill could change the diplomatic atmosphere that complicated their lives. Even those who were apolitical suffered because the broken diplomatic ties between Cuba and the United States rendered them homeless.

This volatile time affected all of baseball in the Caribbean. After Trujillo's assassination, Americans played winter baseball in the Dominican Republic at their own risk. Tensions were such that the 1961–62 winter league suspended play after only one month of competition. This turned out to be the least of the players' problems. In the midst of a transportation strike,

Commissioner Ford Frick ordered them to return because he feared for their safety. The decision proved to be prudent when players left the country under the protection of guards.[54]

While American players judiciously chose winter leagues during the next few years, Latin American major leaguers, save Cubans, routinely returned home. Baseball in the Caribbean was not just a year-round profession but a passion. However, under Ford Frick major league players were prevented from competing in countries other that their own during the winter season. An amendment barred players from participating in exhibitions without the commissioner's consent. Owners argued that the rule protected their "investments" from serious off-season injuries. For Cuban and Dominican players, the mandate seemed unfair.

Cuban players were especially upset.[55] Frick's ruling, in effect, prevented them from earning off-season wages as baseball players. "This [ruling] is not fair," stated an angry Pedro Ramos. "For fourteen years I play baseball. . . . It is part of my life. . . . The American boys can get jobs during the winter. They work in their hometowns. Me, I'm a stranger. I cannot get the same job an American can. My job is playing baseball in the winter."[56]

Dominican players were similarly affected. In January 1963, Ford Frick fined Felipe Alou, Julián Javier, and Juan Marichal for participating in "unauthorized" contests in Santo Domingo. Frick ruled that a Dominican exhibition was "some kind of gimmick" and that "ineligible men" had participated.[57] The "ineligibles" turned out to be Cubans Camilo Pascual, Pedro Ramos, and Joe Azcue, who had sought off-season work.[58] After Trujillo's assassination Dominican officials, hoping to curb domestic tensions, arranged a brief baseball series between Cuban and Dominican stars. Indeed, Caribbean rivalries between islands were common and had existed since the beginning of the twentieth century. Unappreciative of this history, Frick denied permission to those big leaguers scheduled to participate. Upset by the baseball commissioner's intrusion into Dominican affairs, interim president Rafael Bonelli responded, "I am the president of the Dominican Republic and I say it is alright to play."[59] The players were caught in the middle, and they knew they were in danger. "With the backing of the president and with 22,000 people in the stands for the first game, there was no way that Ford Frick could scare us out of playing," recalled Felipe Alou. "If we didn't play, there would have been a revolt right there on the spot and we would have been the prime targets."[60]

The fine infuriated him. He forcefully declared that "these are our people and we owe it to them to play. . . . Juan and I were big names. We had just played in the World Series. How could we say no?"[61] Alou's arguments also reflected his nationalism. He defiantly claimed, "It is unthinkable to many Dominicans that someone from a foreign country would tell other Dominicans who they can play ball with and who they can't."[62] Like Pedro Ramos, Alou pointed out that winter employment for Americans was plentiful in the United States: "In my country there is practically no industry and very little work. Take away baseball from us in the winter, and you take away money from us."[63]

Two years earlier, Felipe Alou had taken it upon himself to launch a campaign on behalf of Latins. Baseball policy makers, Alou believed, did not understand the problems Latins faced in the United States, nor did they understand Latin America itself. Because a statute prohibited players from fraternizing with opponents prior to games, the Dominican was fined for conversing with Cuban Orlando Peña in 1961. "Peña had only recently left his homeland and there was no going back," explained Alou. "Orlando had left behind his family, friends—everything. Here, I thought, was a man in need and I wanted to talk over things with him to see what could be done." (A few years later, the rule unchanged, the league again fined Alou for conversing with his brother, Mateo, who by then played for the Pittsburgh Pirates).[64] After this, Alou called upon the commissioner's office to create a post specifically to address the Latin ballplayers' needs and to represent them with the baseball bureaucracy.

In a decade of social and political discontent, especially among American youth, the Dominican was in concert with the times. His campaign for representation mirrored the quests of other Hispanics. No longer did they wish to be the "forgotten people" of earlier generations.[65] "We need somebody to represent us who knows what goes on in the Latin American countries," Alou told David Arnold Hano of *Sport* magazine.[66] Echoing America's own Revolutionary War sentiments, the astute Dominican said, "I could sympathize with those revolutionists, feeling as I did that Latin ballplayers were being fined, were being abused and were not being given proper audience because there was no one in the commissioner's office to represent us."[67] Almost thirty years later, Alou recognized that he "belong[ed] to a generation that overthrew a dictator in the Dominican [Republic]. To protest was a natural part of my life."[68]

Even though more Latin players competed as major leaguers during Frick's tenure than ever before, he did did not appoint a representative for Latin Americans. Frick's successor, William D. Eckert, addressed the issue

in 1965. The new commissioner appointed Bobby Maduro, former owner of the Havana Sugar Kings, to handle Latin players' affairs and represent them to the commissioner. Latins, at long last, gained some semblance
of recognition with the major league bureaucracy. Maduro's position,
however, was temporary and did little to upgrade the conditions of Latins
in the United States. By the 1970s, the office no longer existed.

Felipe Alou. (Courtesy of the National Baseball Hall of Fame Library, Cooperstown,
N.Y.)

As the 1960s closed, Latin American ballplayers, nonetheless, had clearly come into their own. American baseball followers no longer questioned their ability. Testimony of this came in 1968, when *Sport* magazine, based on the evaluation of major league general managers, named Roberto Clemente baseball's best player.[69] Little did anyone know that within a few years, full recognition would be accorded to Clemente as a result of victory and tragedy.

Notes

1. *Binghamton (New York) Press,* Sept. 9, 1965.

2. *New York World-Telegram,* Nov. 18, 1965.

3. Musick, *Who Was Roberto?* 211.

4. Mulvoy, "Cha Cha," 19.

5. *Sporting News,* Aug. 20, 1966, Orlando Cepeda file, National Baseball Library, Cooperstown, N.Y.

6. Ibid.

7. Ibid.

8. Undated clipping, *Long Island (New York) Newsday,* Cepeda file.

9. *Long Island (New York) Newsday,* Aug. 3, 1966, Cepeda file.

10. Peters interview.

11. Musick, *Who Was Roberto?* 167.

12. Wagenheim, *Clemente!* 90.

13. Alou, *Alou,* 118–19.

14. Jerry Izenberg, "Cubs' Cookie Chipping in to Crumble Ethnic Barrier," *New York Post,* Apr. 12, 1980.

15. *New York World-Telegram,* Aug. 24, 1965.

16. *New York World-Telegram,* June 19, 1961.

17. Einstein, *Willie's Time,* 242.

18. Alou, *Alou,* 134.

19. Roseboro, *Glory Days,* 24

20. Ibid.

21. *New York World-Telegram,* Aug. 24, 1965.

22. *Sporting News,* Sept. 4, 1965, Juan Marichal file, National Baseball Library.

23. *New York Times,* Sept. 3, 1965, Marichal file; Einstein, *Willie's Time,* 245.

24. Einstein, *Willie's Time,* 245.

25. *Sporting News,* Sept. 4, 1965.

26. *New York World-Telegram,* Aug. 30, 1965.

27. *Sporting News,* Sept. 4, 1965.

28. *Sporting News,* Sept. 18, 1965.

29. Phil Pepe, "Humiliation Real Punishment for Marichal," *New York World-Telegram,* Aug. 24, 1965.

30. Dick Young, *New York Daily News,* Aug. 25, 1965.

31. Peters interview.

32. Alexander, *Holding the Line,* 75.

33. Schlesinger and Kinzer, *Bitter Fruit,* 100.

34. Alexander, *Holding the Line,* 79.

35. Ibid., 259.

36. Senzel, *Baseball and the Cold War,* 73–74.

37. *Sporting News,* July 20, 1960.

38. *Sporting News,* July 27, 1960.

39. Walton, *Cold War and Counterrevolution,* 55.

40. Boswell, *How Life Imitates the World Series,* 94.

41. *New York World-Telegram,* Jan. 4, 1961.

42. *New York World-Telegram,* Jan. 6, 1961.

43. Terzain, *Kid from Cuba,* 28.

44. Ibid., 76–77.

45. Izenberg, *Great Latin Sports Figures,* 74.

46. *Sporting News,* Apr. 17, 1965.

47. Stann, "New Mark of Zorro," 41.

48. Ibid.

49. Oliva interview.

50. Ibid.

51. *New York World-Telegram,* Apr. 12, 1961.

52. *New York Daily News,* July 28, 1963.

53. *Sporting News,* July 22, 1967, Tito Fuentes file, National Baseball Library.

54. Alou, *Alou,* 80–81.

55. Brown, "Cuban Baseball," 112.

56. George Vecsey, "Pvt. Ramos Asks General for a Winter Pass," *New York Times,* Apr. 5, 1966.

57. *Sporting News,* Feb. 16, 1963.

58. Ibid.

59. Alou, *Alou,* 119.

60. Ibid.

61. *Sporting News,* Mar. 16, 1963.

62. Alou, "Latin American Ballplayers," 76.

63. Ibid.

64. Alou, *Alou,* 59–69.

65. McWilliams, *Brothers under the Skin,* 113.

66. Alou, "Latin American Ballplayers," 76.

67. Alou, *Alou,* 120.

68. Alou interview.

69. Falls, "It's Roberto Clemente," 19.

•9

Adios Amigo Roberto

Only one thing could ever really stop Roberto Clemente, and it did.
Milton Richman, *Springfield (Massachusetts) Daily News*

Greater love hath no man than this, that a man lay down his life for his friends.
John 15:13

Vera Clemente sat quietly at home as hope faded away. Manny Sanguillen was inconsolable and assisted in a desperate search for his friend. Indeed, Puerto Rico's first day of 1973 was an anxious one as crowds gathered on the beaches of San Juan offering prayers that Roberto Clemente might still be alive. Only twenty-four hours earlier, the great outfielder had been gathering food and supplies to be flown to Nicaragua where a devastating earthquake had killed thousands of citizens and rendered many others homeless. Clemente, who headed a relief program, had worked tirelessly to aid his fellow Latins. His interest in Nicaragua stemmed from a visit in November when he took a Puerto Rican amateur team there for a tournament. Warmly greeted, he befriended a young boy who had lost his legs in an accident. Through Clemente's efforts, funds were raised to supply his newfound friend with artificial limbs. His long-time comrades were not surprised by Clemente's sensitivity in these matters. Because of his efforts, he was dismayed to learn after the Nicaraguan earthquake that National Guardsmen had stolen many of the supplies intended for the afflicted. Clemente thus decided to accompany the December 31 relief flight to assure that all goods reached their intended destinations. With only a skeleton crew, the Pittsburgh outfielder boarded the weathered DC-7 on New Year's Eve bound for Managua.[1]

Within minutes of taking off the plane crashed into the sea, taking Clemente and four others with it. "It's not possible," repeated a shocked Vera

Clemente after learning of the accident shortly past midnight.[2] As Coast Guard crews panned the rough waters off San Juan for survivors, islanders prayed that their hero and his colleagues were safe. In Pittsburgh, many of Clemente's teammates were informed of the accident as New Year's Eve parties wound down. Steve Blass and Dave Guisti "kept pacing in and out of our rooms, past each other."[3] In another part of Pittsburgh, Al Oliver sat, trembling in his recliner as he listened to the news on the radio.[4] By midmorning the world realized that Clemente was gone.

Puerto Ricans were devastated. Inaugural day ceremonies for incoming governor Rafael Hernández Colón were canceled. In his first speech, the governor-elect lamented, "Our people have lost one of their glories. All our hearts are saddened."[5] By the second day of the new year eulogies poured in. "I don't think we as teammates knew him as well as we could have," said pitcher Steve Blass. "He was so much more than a great baseball player."[6] Commissioner Bowie Kuhn saw in Clemente "the touch of royalty."[7]

Pittsburgh's citizens also mourned their fallen hero. News of Clemente's death brought disbelief. "All of a sudden the New Year seems kind of

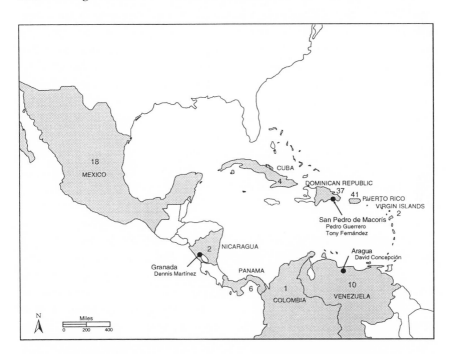

Latin American Origin of Major League Baseball Players, 1970–80. Numerals denote the total number of players from individual countries. Selected high-profile players noted.

hollow," announced Allegheny County Commissioner Leonard Staisey. "Greetings just don't ring quite right."[8] Another grieving baseball fan claimed that "nobody will ever replace that guy. When I first heard about it I was in a daze. It brought a tear to my eye."[9] The Puerto Rican community in New York City was equally stunned. "Roberto was proud to be a Puerto Rican," said one resident. "He never forgot his people."[10] Another claimed, "We have lost a man who was a glory to Puerto Rico."[11] Among the finest eulogies came from a child who viewed Clemente as a personification of all Latins. In honor of the Puerto Rican, the five-year-old wrote that he named his dog "'Puerto Rico' because nice people live there. . . . Clemente lived there."[12] The *Washington Post* added its condolences by suggesting that the scoreboard at Three Rivers Stadium change its message from "Roberto Clemente, 1934–1972" to "a man of honor played baseball here."[13] Looming high above Pittsburgh, a neon sign that usually advertised a local beer product simply read "Adios Amigo Roberto."[14]

Roberto Clemente's relief aid program for the people of Managua continued as a memorial fund in his honor. President Richard Nixon was among the contributors. Indeed, in addition to writing a personal check of $1,000, the president met with some Pirates officials and players to help organize the campaign.[15] Donations continued in the ensuing weeks accompanied by letters eulogizing the Pirate star. "I only wish this check could reflect the many thrilling moments Roberto has given me," wrote one Pittsburgh fan. An eighteen-year-old Pennsylvanian penned, "He'll never lift his cap or even smile. Oh, we'll miss him for a long, long while."[16]

Only fifteen months earlier, Roberto Clemente's career was at its peak. A self-proclaimed "old man" at thirty-seven, he led the 1971 Pittsburgh Pirates to a division title and then past San Francisco in the National League championship series. Their World Series opponents, the Baltimore Orioles, however, were a powerfully balanced club led by sluggers Frank Robinson and Boog Powell. The Orioles pitching staff was an even more impressive lot. The starting rotation of Jim Palmer, Miguel "Mike" Cuéllar, Dave McNally, and Pat Dobson had won twenty games each that year. Furthermore, the Orioles compiled 101 wins and were making their third successive trip to the series. Understandably, they were favored to take the fall classic, but few observers recognized the depth of the Pittsburgh right fielder's passion to win.

By then Clemente carried outstanding credentials. The winner of four batting crowns and the 1966 Most Valuable Player Award, he was well on his way toward collecting his 3,000th hit (which turned out to be the final hit of his career the following year). In addition, he owned a bevy of Golden Glove awards and had been named to the National League All-Star squad eleven times. In his only World Series appearance, eleven years earlier, he batted .310. Yet, Clemente remained frustrated because the lime-light still eluded him. The 1971 World Series changed that.

Always fiery, he used the fall classic as a public forum. "Nobody in this game does anything better than me," he proclaimed—and he set out to prove it.[17] The entire series was one of shifting momentum. Pittsburgh, after dropping the first two games, rebounded to take the next three. Baltimore evened the series in game six to force a climactic finale. Roberto Clemente was already the big story. Playing like a man possessed, he carried a .440 average that included a home run, a triple, and two doubles. In addition, his defense sparkled and he used every opportunity to exhibit his fielding prowess. At one point, when there appeared to be no Baltimore scoring threat, he launched a powerful throw from the right-field corner to home plate. Players from the Baltimore dugout gasped. "It's got to be the great-est throw I ever saw," remembered second baseman Davey Johnson. "One second he's got his back to the field at the 390 mark, the next instant here comes the throw, on the chalk line."[18] Clemente's actions also inspired his teammates. "You watch Roberto and you can't help getting all psyched," claimed outfielder Gene Clines. "There's the old man out there busting his ass off on every play and every game. Look, I'm twenty-five. If he can play like that, shouldn't I?"[19]

By game seven, all eyes were on Clemente. Indeed, for the Pittsburgh star, the contest was truly symbolic. For years he had fought against stereotypes that cast him and other Latins as absurd, hypochondriacal, and unintelli-gent. Similarly, he battled social habits and restrictions that he believed belittled not just Puerto Ricans but all people of color. Finally, he sought to win what he felt he earned but had been denied—recognition. Clemen-te did not fail his supporters. In the fourth inning he broke the scoreless duel by pummeling a home run. Behind Steve Blass's four-hitter, the Pirates won the deciding contest and Clemente ended a remarkable series perfor-mance with a .414 batting average. His selection as the World Series Most Valuable Player was obvious.

However, Clemente's greatest satisfaction appeared to come in the locker room as the Pirates celebrated. "I want everyone in the world to know that this is the way I play all the time," shouted Clemente. He then shared his reflections on the past. "All season, every season, I gave everything I had to this game. The press call me a crybaby, a hypochondriac . . . they say I'm not a team player. Now everyone knows the way Roberto Clemente plays."[20] As he paused for questions, one journalist queried if the series victory was his greatest moment. "The greatest moment in my career is now, this precise instant, when I'm going to answer your question." he responded. "This is the first time I've ever been able to have all of you together in one room, and I want to tell all of you that you're a bunch of good-for-nothing bums! Now that I've got that off my chest, you'll see a different Roberto Clemente. I won't complain about anything anymore."[21]

Clemente's satisfaction was complete. Earlier on national television he addressed his parents in Spanish: "On this the proudest day of my life I ask your blessing."[22] Clemente's postgame interviews characterized his career. He was both proud and humble, angry and happy, unreasonable and understanding. Most of all, he demonstrated his contribution as a pioneer in the emergence of Latin players, seeking equality and recognition for them when it was not popular to do so. Moreover, his dreams did not end there.

For years Roberto Clemente had sought to create a sports complex to serve as a training ground for young Puerto Rican athletes whose dreams included participation in Pan-American games, the Olympics, and, of course, professional baseball.[23] "He never forgot where he came from," Vera Clemente claimed. "Roberto used to see that when he was little, that kids like him had nothing."[24] Not until the 1980s did Clemente's Ciudad Deportiva (Sports City) develop as a functional operation, but many young Puerto Ricans, such as Rubén Sierra, whose stardom lay in the future, expanded their skills at a complex that also encouraged family cohesiveness.[25] By then, many of Clemente's contemporaries, such as Orlando Cepeda, Vic Power, and Félix Millán, had contributed their time in reverence of his legacy.

The passing of Clemente marked a transitional period for Latins as the first generation of post-integration players gave way to a younger group. Felipe Alou retired in 1974, Luis Aparicio in 1973, Orlando Cepeda in 1974, and Juan Marichal in 1975. Like Clemente, these Latin players helped cushion the trauma of acculturation and built a foundation for Latin hopefuls of the future. Furthermore, Clemente's outspoken opinions and leadership brought greater notoriety to the Latin plight in North America. The Puerto Rican's recognition reached a crescendo when, shortly after his death, the Baseball Writers Association of America elected him to the Hall of Fame—the first Latin to be inducted. In 1974 Clemente also won election into the Negro Baseball Hall of Fame.[26]

Clemente's induction into the Hall of Fame in Cooperstown, however, did not come without controversy. At the center of the arguments was the process of his election. Two days following his death, the Hall of Fame Board of Directors amended their five-year eligibility rule to allow early induction for the late Pittsburgh outfielder. Criticizing the format as "steamroller" methodology, writer Dick Young chose to abstain in the voting process.[27] Bill Boerg voted against Clemente's induction on the pretense that Clemente "didn't need the special privilege of an extra election to bypass the Hall of Fame's five-year wait for selection."[28] Others, however, reacted sharply to the criticism. In his column for *Newsday,* Ed Comerford chided his colleagues; any dissenter should be "flogged, broken on the rack, and then condemned to cover croquet tournaments the rest of his unnatural life." He then pointed out that "justice demands" Clemente's enshrinement.[29] Arthur Daley of the *New York Times* agreed that "any baseball writer who fails to mark his ballot affirmatively should have his buttons snipped off while being drummed out of the regiment."[30] Larry Claflin of the *Boston Herald* was more direct. "Roberto Clemente belongs in the Baseball Hall of Fame. He belongs there now, not five years from now," he maintained. "No Latin American ball player has ever been enshrined in Cooperstown. There could be no better candidate to be the pioneer than Clemente."[31] On March 31, 1973, Roberto Clemente captured the necessary votes. Later, the commissioner's office instituted an annual trophy given to the major league player who was both an outstanding athlete and an exemplary citizen in honor of Clemente.

As the trauma surrounding Clemente's death faded, Puerto Ricans turned to other players from their island for heroes. Shockingly, only a year after his retirement, one of their most prominent stars became entangled in an episode that subsequently marred his seemingly untouchable legacy. Unable to cope with his life beyond baseball, Orlando Cepeda became depressed and turned to drugs and alcohol for relief. In December 1975, drug agents arrested the legendary slugger after discovering marijuana in his baggage. Though he maintained he had been framed, a federal judge sentenced him to five years in prison. His compatriots were unforgiving. "People were afraid to talk to me," he claimed while his lawyers exhausted appeal efforts. "They said I was Mafia and all that. They used to have pictures of me at the ballparks in Puerto Rico, but they take them away. The people say I'm a bad example to my boy and to their boys."[32]

Some, however, came to his defense. Cookie Rojas led a group of former major leaguers who sought an early release for Cepeda. In an open letter to Puerto Ricans, Rojas appealed to their sentiments. "His children don't have the same friends anymore. His wife goes to the supermarket, and nobody talks to her. The kids no longer knock at the door for autographs," he told the islanders. "How can we forget all the things this man has done for his country?"[33] Cepeda served only ten months, but the long-term effects proved devastating. In an effort to change his reputation, he set up a youth baseball program. The memories of the drug bust, however, remained vivid. In 1982, a frustrated Cepeda told a reporter, "People in Puerto Rico still think I'm an addict, they want to see me burn."[34] Two years later, Puerto Ricans continued to ignore him. "I offered to give free clinics all over the island and there was no answer. I sent a letter to the governor offering him my services and I never heard anything from him," claimed the frustrated former star. He concluded, "If there is one thing about Puerto Ricans, it's that we like to throw stones and hide our hands."[35] Defeated, he and his family moved to California.

Other Latin players emerged in his wake. The St. Louis Cardinals, for instance, fielded three Puerto Rican brothers—Cirilo, Héctor, and José Cruz—in the outfield for an entire exhibition game against the New York Yankees. "They're good ballplayers," claimed manager Red Schoendienst. "They have six brothers back home, and if they come to town I'll play them too!"[36] Other young players such as Venezuela's David Concepción, Dominicans César Cedeño, César Gerónimo, and Elías Sosa, and Mexico's Aurelio Rodríguez took their posts. Cuba's José Cardenal, Bert Campaneris, Leo Cárdenas, and Miguel "Mike" Cuéllar were already stars.

Cuéllar, in fact, was arguably the best left-handed pitching prospect to come out of Latin America. Born in Santa Clara, Las Villas, Cuba, in 1937, he joined the army at age eighteen so that he could play baseball on the weekends instead of working at the local sugar mill. Cuéllar's love for the sport was such that he even knew "how to make a baseball and stitch on a cover."[37] His progress on the military team eventually caught the attention of the owner of the local Havana Sugar Kings, Bobby Maduro. But his regiment was not at all anxious to see their star left-hander leave. "The Army captain threatened to throw our scout in jail if he talked to the boy," recalled Maduro.[38] The club owner eventually arranged for Cuéllar's discharge and put the young left-hander under the care of Nap Reyes, who coached the Almendares team. "I have coached a lot of pitchers, here in Cuba and in the U.S.A., but none so quick to learn as this boy," beamed a happy Reyes. "I know he can go all the way and become a great pitcher."[39]

Cuéllar's success in the American professional leagues, however, was not immediate. The Cincinnati Reds purchased Cuéllar's contract in 1958 but then sold his rights to the St. Louis Cardinals. He then drifted in the minor leagues until 1964, when he made a brief appearance with the parent club. Unimpressed, the Cardinals dealt the Cuban to Houston. There he exhibited signs of the stardom that Reyes had earlier predicted when he posted a 2.22 ERA. In 1966, only Sandy Koufax had better numbers. The following year Cuéllar was selected for the National League All-Star squad. However, shortly thereafter problems with the Astros surfaced when they prohibited the left-hander from participating in the Latin winter leagues. Cuéllar routinely played in the off-season for additional revenue, but more importantly, he used these games to keep his arm limber. Prevented from utilizing this program, Cuéllar developed a sore arm during spring training in 1968 and won only eight games that year. Disenchanted, the Astros traded him to the Orioles at the conclusion of the season.

At his new post, the Orioles granted him permission to resume his winter baseball activities. "You can't . . . take winter ball away from the Latins," claimed Orioles scout Frank Lane, whose experience with Latins began years earlier with Minnie Miñoso while both were part of the Chicago White Sox organization. "They've been playing [winter baseball] since they were 15 and 16 years old. Their arm muscles actually stiffen up if they lay off the winter season."[40] Though the notion that Latin arms somehow stiffened up more than others' seemed remarkable, the change of venue did pay off for the Cuban southpaw and the Baltimore franchise. In his first year with the Orioles, Cuéllar won 23 games, lost 11, and captured the American League's Cy Young Award. His second year with Baltimore was even better. In 1970 he tied with two other pitchers for the league lead in wins (24), led all pitchers in winning percentage (.750) and had the most complete games (21). Astonishingly, the Cy Young Award that year went to Minnesota's Jim Perry, who won the same number of games as Cuéllar but fell considerably short in his winning percentage. Perry led the league in no other category. More surprising, though Cuéllar's overall numbers were clearly well ahead of his opponents, he finished fourth in the balloting. In 1972, following his third consecutive 20-win season, Cuéllar, whose winning percentage was the second best that year (.690), received no votes for the Cy Young Award. Even Kansas City's Dick Drago, who won only 17 games with a winning percentage of .607, captured a vote from the sportswriters. Though he was clearly slighted, Cuéllar said little about the controversial selections. His stunning consistency, however, continued. During his next four seasons, he twice won more than 20 games and earned no less than 18 victories the other two years. In 1974, for the second time, he led the American League pitchers in winning percentage (.688). By the time of his retirement after the 1977 season, Cuéllar had compiled 185 wins to 130 losses.

Fans also found plenty to like in Atanasio "Tony" Pérez. Born in 1942 in the province of Camaguey in Cuba, Pérez grew up near the sugar mills in his hometown of Ciego de Avila. Like his contemporaries, baseball filled his dreams. Reality for the young Pérez, however, was life as a laborer in the mills. "My mother would say, 'You're going to be like your daddy and your brother, work in the factory,'" remembered Pérez.[41] Luckily the sugar mill sponsored a baseball team. The future slugger quickly became a standout player and drew attention from professional baseball observers. In 1959, scout Tony Pacheco from the Cincinnati Reds successfully signed the seventeen year old to a contract. Sent directly to the club's Geneva, New York, minor league affiliate, Pérez, like others, faced the difficulties of adaptation to a new culture. "It wasn't easy" as players struggled to communicate with each other. "All I kept thinking about everyday was 'How am I going to do this? How am I going to handle that? How am I going to get around?' and all of this knowing that I wasn't going to see my family for a long time, that really bothered me," he said. Pérez was lucky enough to have Cuban company: "We had six guys from Cuba on that team and, at the end of the year, only three stayed on."[42]

Pérez was an immediate sensation. In his first year he hit 27 home runs, drove home 132, and batted for a .328 average. Another first-year player on that club, Pete Rose, remembered that Pérez "was just out of Cuba, didn't speak much English, but he was a good guy in the clubhouse, even then. [He] never had the big forearms power hitters have, he was just strong in the bottom."[43] The Reds, however, concentrated their efforts on developing Rose. According to Art Burke, "The Reds had given Rose a big bonus, and they couldn't afford to keep him on the bench. They had invested very little in Tony, however, so they had little to lose if he didn't make it."[44]

Pérez, nonetheless, continued to improve. By 1964, the Reds promoted him to the Triple A San Diego Padres. There he hit for a .309 average, with 34 home runs and 107 RBIs, which earned him the Pacific Coast League's Most Valuable Player Award. His credentials also gained him an invitation to join the Reds during the final weeks of the season. Once there, Pérez never again played minor league baseball.

In his first full year, 1964, the Puerto Rican served as a part-time player, but missed few opportunities to impress all who watched him. His tape measure home runs won him many admirers on the Reds. But beyond his teammates, little attention came his way. Frank Robinson was mystified: "They talk about the Dodgers' Jim Lefebvre and Astros' Joe Morgan. What about Pérez? He's a rookie, too."[45] Pérez continued as a platoon player into 1965, but by 1967 he had won a position at third base, hit 26 home runs, drove in 102, and batted .290. Elected to that year's All-Star team, Pérez rewarded the National Leaguers with a fifteenth inning home run to win the game. At his career's end, the Cuban had twelve seasons in which he drove in 90 runs or more, which led his peers to dub him "Mr. Clutch." His 379 home runs placed him twenty-seventh on the all-time list.

Tony Pérez, affectionately dubbed "Doggie" by his teammates, impressed all with his congeniality. "He's a doer, not a complainer. You didn't have any 'trade me or play me' ultimatums from Pérez when he rode the bench a few years back waiting for the chance to play regularly," wrote the *Sporting News* in 1965. "What baseball needs is more men like Tony Pérez."[46] Former teammate Johnny Bench later said of Pérez, "He got along with everybody. Everybody admired and respected him."[47] Indeed, Pérez's popularity was such that long after he had left Cincinnati and signed with the Red Sox as a free agent, letters poured into Boston from Reds fans concerning their past hero. "Count your blessings Boston, and please treat him well," stated one letter. "We love him, we still miss 'Doggie.'" Another claimed that the "Red Sox were the luckiest team in the world to have Pérez."[48] Pete Rose saw Pérez as not only a great performer but also a leader to the Reds' Latin players. "He was their spokesman," claimed Rose. "Whatever he said, they did. He raised Concepción. He taught them how to play, how to practice, how to be on time, that kind of stuff."[49] But not all was utopia for the likable Cuban.

While popular with Cincinnati fans, Pérez played in the huge shadows of Pete Rose, Johnny Bench, and Joe Morgan during the heyday of the Big Red Machine. "Tony would get shoved into the background, driving in his 100 runs every year," remembered former manager and player Pat Coralles. "You'd see it in the notes at the end of the stories in the paper, 'Oh,

Atanasio "Tony" Pérez. (Courtesy of the National Baseball Hall of Fame Library, Cooperstown, N.Y.)

by the way, Pérez hit a three-run homer to win the game.'"[50] Yet Pérez, unlike Roberto Clemente in earlier years, seemingly ignored his unassuming image. "I just try to hit. They pay me enough for what I do," said the Puerto Rican. "Some guys get publicity—some don't. I just try to do my job."[51]

While Pérez appeared content with his professional career, a personal vacuum existed. Since his departure from Cuba in 1959, he had visited his homeland only once. "I left all of my family in Cuba," the slugger recalled. "I was the only one here. I left my mother, sister, brother, and father."[52] At times, his personal instincts led him to ponder a return to Cuba. But his father dissuaded him. "My father told me, 'You stay; you want to play baseball. There's no future for you [in Cuba]. Your future is over there.'"[53]

In 1971, Pérez became a U.S. citizen and took up residence in Puerto Rico. Yet he still was prevented from visiting his parents and other relatives on a regular basis. For years the big slugger suffered silently while awaiting an opportunity for a reunion. In 1971 he attempted to gain entry through Mexico but failed. Finally, in November 1972 he was granted permission to spend twenty days in Cuba. "It was some kind of feeling," beamed Pérez. "There's no way I can describe it. You would have had to be there." His family still toiled in the sugar mills and his father was not in good health. As he prepared to leave, Pérez's father told him "he may never see me again."[54] The slugger, thankfully, did visit his father once more before the elder Pérez passed away. Yet, for all of his accomplishments, Tony Pérez was not completely satisfied. "You know I never got the chance to play professional baseball in front of my family. I didn't have the chance to do it," he lamented.[55]

Pérez was, of course, only one of many Cubans separated from their homeland who relocated to the United States. Following the first major wave of exiles in 1959 from Fidel Castro's Cuba, little if any contact was possible between the expatriates and relatives still on the island until 1966. Airlift programs in 1973 brought an additional 273,000 Cubans to the United States and by 1980 an estimated 118,000 "Marielitos"—refugees named after the port of Mariel from which they fled—arrived.[56] Their staggered migration depleted a traditional source of baseball talent for American professional teams. Gone were the days in which Cuban players led the contingency of foreigners into the major leagues. By 1980 Tony Pérez was among the few who remained. "I remember when there were a lot of Cubans; big names in the major leagues," lamented Pérez. "But I was one of the last ones signed. We just ran out. . . . It is a sad thing."[57]

Luis Tiant Jr. was, by the late 1970s, among the last of the pre-Castro Cubans in the major leagues. Born in 1940 at Nicanor del Campo, Tiant was the son of a legendary pitcher. Luis Tiant Sr. starred on the New York Cubans and had classic duels with such black stars as Smokey Joe Williams, Cannonball Jackman, and Satchel Paige. The younger Tiant often grinned at stories about his father. "It made me proud that people would say my father was a better pitcher than me," he declared.[58] Luis Tiant Sr., however, tried to discourage his son from pursuing a career in baseball. The experienced pitcher told his son tales of American segregation. "He didn't want me to be a ballplayer. He said the life was too hard," remembered the future major leaguer.[59] Young Tiant, however, decided to pursue the risky venture. Like so many of his peers in the middle 1950s, he hoped to join the popular Havana Sugar Kings of the International League.

In 1956, the Havana Triple A club, created in part by the old Washington Senators to help draw Cuban talent, was the window of opportunity for Cuban hopefuls. In fact, Pedro Ramos and Camilo Pascual, both stars of the major leagues, were Sugar King alumni by the time Tiant decided to try out. To make the Sugar Kings was deemed an honor. The elder Tiant, however, remained apprehensive. "The colored leagues never paid him much money, and the major leagues didn't want him because he was black," his son confessed. "He went through so many bad things like that. I think he was afraid I would have bad luck, too."[60] Tiant did. Twice he failed to make the roster. However, Bobby Avila, the former American League batting champion and a close friend of the Tiants, recommended Luis Jr. to his contacts on the Mexico City Tigers. Given the opportunity to play professional baseball in the Mexican League, Tiant accepted the ball club's offer. In the next few years, he pitched admirably and garnered fame around Mexico City. He also caught the attention of big league scouts, who pursued him in earnest. In 1961 he signed a contract with the Cleveland Indians.

That year the United States broke off diplomatic relations with Cuba. Tiant, largely apolitical, was traumatized. He had just married and was anxious to return to Cuba to show off his new bride. But as he prepared to leave, his father warned him, "Stay in Mexico. . . . Don't come home. There's nothing for you here now. Stay where you are and make a good life for your family."[61] Tiant, understandably distraught, instead went to Puerto Rico to prepare for the American professional leagues.

In subsequent years, those close to him recognized the emptiness behind his smile. "Sometimes I could feel there was something underneath. I knew he was happy with his career," remembered teammate and close friend Tommy Harper, "but it was always on his mind that his parents weren't able to share in his success."[62] At times, his feelings surfaced. "I see my fellow Cubans in the country and I watch them suffer. . . . I know of some whose parents have died and they couldn't even go home to bury them," he recalled. "Sometimes I think about my father dying."[63]

By the start of the 1964 season, the Cuban was a three-year minor league veteran pitching for the Triple A Portland Beavers of the Pacific Coast League. As the season reached the midpoint, his victorious ways won praise. One local writer credited Tiant's popularity with "the rebirth of baseball interest in Portland."[64] Only one month earlier, the Oregon Sports Writers and Sportscasters Association had voted Tiant Athlete of the Month.[65] In July they bid him farewell. "There goes Luis Tiant and his fabulous 15-1 pitching record," reported the *Portland Oregonian*. Yet local writers rationalized that "Cleveland played more than fair in leaving him here so long."[66] Tiant was also very much aware of his length of stay. In fact, he stewed about left-hander Sam McDowell, who had received a promotion months earlier. The Indians, however, appeared to have a logical reason for the move. Other than ace Jack Kralick, the club had no other southpaw in their rotation and, in lieu of a trade, turned to their minor league affiliate for help. However, in 1964 that mattered little to an enraged Tiant. Indeed, upon notification of his promotion, he announced to Portland manager Johnny Lipon that he intended to remain in the Pacific Northwest. "Why did they have to wait until I had fifteen wins before they liked me? Now more than half the year is gone and they tell me to come. Well, I don't want to go." Wisely, Lipon reasoned with the emotional pitcher, pointing out, "We both know you can do the job. But it's up to you to prove it to everyone else. Don't throw this opportunity away. It's too important. You've got to go."[67]

Luis Tiant Jr. debuted on July 19, 1964, against Mickey Mantle, Roger Maris, and Elston Howard. Yankee pitcher Whitey Ford, who by then had won twelve of fourteen decisions, opposed him. In a performance somewhat similar to Juan Marichal's debut four years earlier in the National League, Tiant struck out eleven Yankees and scattered four hits en route to a 3-0 victory. Whitey Ford later mused, "I was good enough to win. But not against this kid today." "He was outstanding," recalled writer Russ Schneider, "He seemed to be so far ahead of everyone else who came along at that stage."[68] By the end of the year, Tiant had compiled a 10-4 record that included 9 complete games and a 2.83 ERA. Indeed, lost in all of this was that between his tenure with the Portland Beavers and the Indians, Tiant amassed a 25-5 record for 1964.

Tiant's best year was in 1968 when he won 21 and lost 9. He also led the American League with the lowest earned run average (1.60) and established a Cleveland record in that category. Local writers later bestowed upon him the title of Cleveland's Man of the Year. Denny McLain's 31-victory season and Bob Gibson's major league record 1.17 ERA, however, overshadowed Tiant's achievements on a national scale.

Furthermore, his banner year was clouded by his stormy relationship with the club's first-year manager—Alvin Dark. Since his stint with the San Francisco Giants had ended so unceremoniously, Dark had guided the Kansas City Athletics in the 1966 and 1967 seasons. Indeed, his reputation remained suspect because he never seemed to keep his feelings about American black and Latin players to himself. This skipper's method of criticizing his players through the media was well known. The new manager's questionable diplomatic skills ultimately proved to be a formula for disaster for himself and for Tiant.

During his stellar 1968 season, the right-hander, who that year eventually completed nineteen games, developed stiffness in his arm that inevitably made it more difficult for him to finish contests. As a consequence, Dark grew increasingly critical of Tiant's unusual pitching motion, which the Cuban had copied from his legendary father, blaming the stiffness on Tiant's unwarranted flamboyance. Toward the end of the season Tiant's throbbing arm caught up with him and he informed Dark that he could not pitch. The following day Dark complained to the press that Tiant had "quit" on him. The Cuban pitcher, already a twenty-game winner, was furious and an angry confrontation, reminiscent of the Dark-Cepeda battles, followed. "You're not supposed to say those things about your players in the papers," shouted the pitcher. "I do my job for you and for this ball club, so I should be respected."[69] Hence, the 1968 season ended on an unpleasant note, a situation not helped when the Indians barred Tiant from playing winter baseball.

The 1969 season started out poorly when Tiant, using a more conventional pitching motion in part to appease Dark, dropped his first seven starts. Dark, already impatient with the Cuban, took little heed when Tiant complained that the winter lay-off led to his "stiff arm." "You take an arm that's usually active all the time and allow it to rest all winter long and you're going to have problems when you start pitching again," testified

teammate Stan Williams.[70] Tiant returned to his old unorthodox delivery
and Dark exploded. Again, the manager used the media to exhibit his anger.
"You can't throw your head up into the air, then look over at the scoreboard and then pitch a baseball."[71] By the end of May, Dark began using
Tiant to relieve games already deemed lost. That Tiant remained a jovial
character around his teammates scored few points with the intense Dark—
the same field boss who years earlier had kicked over trays of food in the
Giants clubhouse under the pretext that losing teams do not celebrate. To
make matters worse for Tiant, the Cleveland skipper, in midseason, had
gained de facto powers as general manager in the unstable Indian bureaucracy. Armed with new strength not seen in his days at San Francisco, Dark
traded the unhappy Cuban to the Minnesota Twins at the end of the 1969
season. Former Cleveland general manager Gabe Paul recalled that "Alvin
didn't like [Tiant] and that was all there was to it."[72]

Tiant spent one injury-plagued season with the Minnesota Twins before
they released him. However, the Boston Red Sox, hopeful that patient re-
habilitation would restore Tiant to top form, signed him shortly thereafter. Their gamble paid off in 1972 when the pitcher won fifteen games, had
the lowest ERA, and was voted the Comeback Player of the Year. Furthermore, "Looie" enraptured Bostonians. Sometimes seen as a "hothead" in
earlier years, he was cordial with the local media. "To the fans Tiant is the
symbol of a guy who hasn't always had it easy, but stuck with the game
and made it back big," wrote Larry Caflin of the *Boston Herald*. "The
people identify themselves with Tiant. His Fu Manchu moustache is what
the young people like. His daffy delivery, which almost seems like trickery, is what they love."[73]

Ironically, Tiant's popularity emerged during the same period that white
Bostonians, enraged by the Supreme Court's 1971 *Swann v. Charlotte-
Mecklenberg* decision to uphold a plan to desegregate schools through
crosstown busing, violently protested. The Red Sox themselves were hardly
pioneers in race relations. Indeed, that the club waited until 1959 to incorporate blacks into their roster gave them the dubious distinction of being
the last team to integrate. But Tiant's celebrity, it appeared, overshadowed
Boston's racial controversy.

Coincidentally, Tiant's resurrection came at a most opportune time for
his family. In May 1975, George McGovern traveled to Cuba in an unofficial capacity to initiate diplomatic discussions. The senator also carried
a letter given to him by his Massachusetts colleague, Edward Brooke, which
centered on the issue of Luis Tiant and his parents. Castro's reputation as
a baseball aficionado was well known and McGovern hoped to capitalize

on it. After some small talk, McGovern brought up the note. "I knew he was a baseball fan, and I thought the timing was right because he had just come from the national championship games. So I brought up the 'Tiant matter.' . . . He knew all about Tiant, of course."[74] It was Brooke's hope that Castro might allow Tiant's parents to visit their son in the United States. The following day, Castro responded, "I've checked on your request about Tiant's parents, and they've been advised that they can go to Boston and stay as long as they wish."[75]

Later that year, Luis Tiant Sr. and his wife stepped through the gate at Logan Field in Boston and into their son's arms for the first time in nearly fifteen years. Indeed, it appeared as if all of New England celebrated the arrival of the Tiant family. Covered by the local media, the Tiant reunion was a public affair. Within days, as their entourage neared Fenway Park, the Tiants encountered banners reading "Welcome Tiant Family." Luis Tiant Sr., who had mixed emotions about his son's desire to play professional baseball in the United States, threw out the evening's ceremonial first pitch. Red Sox fans, touched by the poignancy, gave the legendary Cuban star a standing ovation.

The Tiants never returned to Cuba. Both passed away the following year. Before their deaths they were able to see their son win two games in the 1975 World Series against the Cincinnati Reds. "I thank God for answering my prayers—to bring them here and share my best hours . . . and not to be away from them at the end," Tiant later asserted. "I have my faith. I accept God's will."[76]

Even in the face of Luis Tiant's popularity some Latin players demanded appropriate recognition of their achievements. "It started with people saying we couldn't speak English well enough for interviews," bristled shortstop David Concepción. "I think we speak English good enough."[77] Concepción, of course, did not go totally unnoticed. The five-time Gold Glove winner was voted to the National League All-Star team seven times. Moreover, as a major ingredient for the Cincinnati championships of the seventies he even appeared on the cover of the April 1975 issue of the *Sporting News*. He was dissatisfied, however, claiming his prominence was greater in his homeland. "Everyone knows that Bench, Morgan, Rose, and Seaver all got the publicity here. But in Venezuela, I am Número Uno. I make the people proud. When I play in the World Series it goes all over the world, and the people, they know that it is Davey Concepción from

Venezuela. It is good for my country," he proclaimed.[78] In the United States, however, fame continued to elude many of them. Mild-mannered Tony Pérez concurred, "It even happened to Roberto Clemente. He didn't get the recognition he deserved until he was dead."[79]

Pitcher Ed Figueroa, by far, voiced the loudest concerns. In his book, *Yankee Stranger,* the Puerto Rican blasted the media. "We Latins do not get what we should in baseball: not the money, recognition, publicity, or honors," he insisted. "They usually just give everything to the American players before any Latin players are considered." Figueroa had a point. In successive seasons he won nineteen, sixteen, and twenty games respectively. Yet, "my face has never been on the front page of the *Sporting News.* Many American rookie players have their pictures there, but although I have been a big winner, I have never had that honor." The Puerto Rican also pointed out that following his 1978 season, one in which he achieved a 20-9 record, "not one baseball magazine that came out in the spring of 1979 had my picture in it, nor were there any stories."[80]

Figueroa's bitterness reflected the disenchantment felt by many Latins. During the 1970s, as the Latin population increased, many of their leaders hoped this might lead to political strength and, eventually, greater opportunities. These hopes, however, were often dashed by the language barrier and the diversity of goals within Spanish-speaking communities. Their attempts at equity were also undermined by nativist cliques in political power. For instance, since 1959 Cuban Americans in Florida's Dade County had considerably improved the economic climate in the region. By 1970 they owned a third of all businesses in Miami.[81] "I can't think of any other migrating national group that's adapted any more successfully than Cubans have here in Miami," reported University of Miami sociologist David G. Cartano.[82] Their economic success, however, fueled a xenophobic reaction. First, Dade County's primarily white bureaucracy began to sharply curtail business permits to new Cuban entrepreneurs. Then, in 1980, Miami's citizens approved a referendum that prohibited the use of Spanish in government forms. Cuban Americans were outraged. "With the antibilingual vote, the Cuban community realized that their contributions to the greater community were not appreciated," accused one local leader.[83]

Mexican Americans also faced hurdles. By 1981, Los Angeles, like Miami, had virtually no Latin representation in city government. That close to 30 percent (some 2.5 million) of the city's population was Hispanic made their absence in municipal government even more stunning. Similar figures at the state level were equally discouraging. Only three Hispanics served as senators in a state with a Latin population of approximately 4.5 million out of a total population of 22 million.[84] On a national scale the numbers were even worse. By the end of the 1970s, when the magazine *Nuestro* promoted the notion of a "brown caucus" in government circles, only six Hispanics served in Congress.[85]

While the drive for equality stalled, some Hispanics remained optimistic. "Latinos are going to play an increasingly larger role," claimed a confident César Chávez with reference to his union's perceived impact. "I have been told by some international union people that their best luck in organization right now is among Latins."[86] Others viewed what *Nuestro* called "the new surge of Latinismo" an important asset in the political arena. "We're on the threshold of power," claimed House Representative Robert García of New York.[87]

Indeed, Latins did garner new power. *U.S. News and World Report* claimed that during the 1970s, the number of Latin women within the white-collar market jumped 8 percent. The number of Hispanic-owned firms rose by 53 percent in the same decade.[88] Not lost in this development was ethnic pride. As the "new mood" developed, *Nuestro* explained, "the Sixties raised political consciousness among Latinos . . . to the possibilities and need for change. At the same time, ethnic heritage ceased to be something to escape or be ashamed of."[89] Consequently, some believed the "Decade of the Hispanics" was on the horizon. As early as 1974, one sociologist predicted that "it will not be just a 'tacos-and-tamales' impact. Music, philosophy, literature and the whole approach to life will have an increasing Latin flavor."[90] In New York City alone a "number of stores, theaters, newspapers, magazines, and radio and television stations rely entirely or partly on Spanish."[91] *Nuestro* went further. "Everywhere a breeze is stirring for Latinos," it claimed. "We are moving into mainstream America, and we will not leave it as we found it."[92]

Major league baseball, to be sure, already had a Latin flavor, but in the late seventies the baseball "academy" increased Latin presence. Throughout most of the decade clubs continued to dispatch lone scouts to various regions of the Caribbean. Those on the Dominican beat included Epy Guerrero, who worked for the Toronto Blue Jays and was himself a Dominican, and Cuban Ralph Avila with the Los Angeles Dodgers. Avila's interest in the development of Dominican players, combined with the undeniable talent found in that country's players, spurred an effort to develop a baseball school. While Guerrero, who rarely missed a move, founded his own camp on behalf of the Blue Jays in 1977, Avila's dreams blossomed into the most elaborate academy on the island—Las Palmas.[93] With clubs eventually investing large sums of money into these baseball trade schools, the interest in Latin players reached new heights. Other scouts such as Pedro González of the Atlanta Braves and Julio Linares of the Houston Astros prodded their organizations to establish similar posts. The encampments in San Pedro de Macorís became a popular base to mine the region for potential stars. Ironically, major league baseball, which had only four Latin players twenty-nine years earlier, now set up shop in a region whose players had long been described as "good field, no hit." As these academies matured in the eighties, baseball had an unprecedented increase in Latin players.

The same could be said for the rest of the United States. "Look around, America," *Nuestro* announced. "The signs are there—stronger even than whispers, hints or flickers. The more than 12 million Latins in the U.S. have become the newest emerging American minority."[94] The "forgotten people" of yesteryear were on the verge of a cultural explosion. In April 1981, the fuse was lit at Dodger Stadium.

Notes

1. Musick, *Who Was Roberto?* 23–34.
2. Wagenheim, *Clemente!* 246.
3. Ibid.
4. Ibid., 246–47.
5. *New York Times*, Jan. 3, 1973; *New York Newsday*, Jan. 2, 1973.
6. Ibid.
7. Ibid.
8. *San Juan (Puerto Rico) Star,* Jan. 5, 1973.
9. Ibid.
10. *New York Times,* Jan. 3, 1973.
11. *San Juan (Puerto Rico) Star,* Jan. 2, 1973.
12. Musick, *Who Was Roberto?* 45.
13. *Washington Post,* Jan. 4, 1973.
14. Musick, *Who Was Roberto?* 45.
15. *Sporting News,* Jan. 20, 1973.
16. *Newark (New Jersey) Star Ledger,* Jan. 26, 1973.
17. Musick, *Who Was Roberto?* 271.
18. Ibid., 276.
19. Ibid.
20. Ibid., 278.
21. Wagenheim, *Clemente!* 212.
22. Musick, *Who Was Roberto?* 279.

23. Dick Young, "Clemente Complex Is Getting New Life," *New York Post,* Jan. 25, 1985.

24. "Que Viva Clemente!" 14–16.

25. Austin Murphy, "Rising to the Top of the Game," *Sports Illustrated,* Apr. 16, 1990, 60–63.

26. *New York Daily News,* Dec. 12, 1974.

27. *Binghamton (New York) Press,* Mar. 20, 1973.

28. Bill Boerg, "Quick Enshrinement Disservice to Roberto," *Sporting News,* Jan. 20, 1973.

29. Ed Comerford, "Clemente for Hall of Fame Now," undated clipping, *New York Newsday,* Roberto Clemente file, National Baseball Library, Cooperstown, N.Y.

30. Arthur Daley, "Sentimental Speed-Up for Roberto," *New York Times,* Feb. 22, 1973.

31. Larry Claflin, "Demands Clemente in Hall Now," *Boston Herald,* Jan. 3, 1973.

32. Orlando Cepeda file, *Sporting News* archive, St. Louis, Mo.

33. Octavio Rivas Rojas, "Cookie Rojas' Letter," *St. Louis Globe-Democrat,* July 10, 1978.

34. Cepeda file.

35. Ibid.

36. Wagenheim, *Clemente!* 253.

37. *Sporting News,* June 19, 1957.

38. Ibid.

39. Ibid.

40. Morris Siegel, "'Tonto Has Quiet Ride,'" *Baltimore Review,* Oct. 12, 1969.

41. Burke, *Unsung Heroes,* 137.

42. Pérez interview.

43. Oleksak and Oleksak, *Béisbol,* 126.

44. Burke, *Unsung Heroes,* 138.

45. *Sporting News,* Aug. 14, 1965.

46. *Sporting News,* May 17, 1965.

47. *Philadelphia Inquirer,* May 9, 1983.

48. *Boston Globe,* July 13, 1980.

49. *Philadelphia Inquirer,* May 9, 1983.

50. Ibid.

51. Burke, *Unsung Heroes,* 136.

52. Pérez interview.

53. Ibid.

54. *Sporting News,* Tony Pérez file, Jan. 27, 1973, National Baseball Library.

55. Pérez interview.

56. Moore and Pachon, *Hispanics,* 36.

57. Undated clipping, Pérez file.

58. Tiant, *El Tiante*, 25.

59. Ibid.

60. Ibid.

61. Ibid., 27.

62. Ibid., 28.

63. Ibid.

64. *Sporting News*, July 20, 1964; Regalado, "The Minor League Experience," 65–70.

65. *Portland Oregonian*, July 16, 1964.

66. *Portland Oregonian*, July 20, 1965.

67. Tiant, *El Tiante*, 39–40.

68. Ibid., 41.

69. Ibid., 71.

70. Ibid., 78.

71. Ibid., 79.

72. Ibid., 84.

73. Larry Caflin, "Tiant an Amazing Story," *Boston Herald*, Sept. 22, 1972.

74. Tiant, *El Tiante*, 187.

75. Ibid.

76. Luis Tiant file, National Baseball Library.

77. *Sporting News*, Nov. 20, 1976.

78. Oleksak and Oleksak, *Béisbol*, 133.

79. *Sporting News*, Nov. 20, 1976.

80. Figueroa and Harshman, *Yankee Stranger*, 134, 137.

81. Moore and Pachon, *Hispanics in the United States*, 45.

82. "The Newest Americans," 36.

83. "Hispanics Make Their Move," 60.

84. García, "Hispanic Migration," 15.

85. Ibid., 61; "Here Comes the Latino Era," 15.

86. "Here Comes the Latino Era," 15.

87. Ibid.; "Hispanics Make Their Move," 62.

88. "Hispanics Make Their Move," 62.

89. "Here Comes the Latino Era," 18.

90. "The Newest Americans," 34.

91. Ibid., 36.

92. "Here Comes the Latino Era," 19.

93. Klein, *Sugarball*, 63–65.

94. "Here Comes the Latino Era," 12.

• 10

Fernandomania

Can you imagine what it means to the whole country of Mexico and to disadvantaged people everywhere? Here's a kid from an obscure little village in Mexico. He's never had much. Now they look at him . . . and they can say "Look at Fernando—he's a hero and he's one of us."
Tommy Lasorda

The rest, señores, is right out of a dream,
For every time Fernando throws
He beats another team.
Jess Gutiérrez, "The Ballad of Fernando Valenzuela"

*O*pening Day was especially nerve-wracking for the Los Angeles Dodgers as they prepared for the 1981 season. Like most clubs, the Dodgers had planned on using a veteran pitcher, but due to a last-second injury to the scheduled starter, Jerry Reuss, the April 9 pitcher turned out to be a twenty-year-old rookie left-hander from Sonora, Mexico, named Fernando Valenzuela. He did not disappoint them. That afternoon he defeated the defending Western Division champion Houston Astros 2-0 and allowed only five hits. But those in attendance sensed the significance of the Mexican's performance was much deeper than simply the final score. "I've been playing pro ball for twenty years and I've never seen anything like him," remarked his teammate Reggie Smith.[1] Astros manager Bill Virdon concluded, "He may be twenty, but he pitches thirty."[2] The first of eight consecutive victories, the game commenced "Fernandomania."

A year earlier Raul Yzaguirre, editor of the Hispanic journal *Agenda*, pronounced that the next ten years would be the "Decade for the Hispanic." Convinced that a "golden age" was near, he envisioned in the United States an era of unprecedented Hispanic accomplishments, increased awareness, explosive creativity, and greater Latin influence.[3] Others shared the editor's optimism. In 1977, *Nuestro* writers had anticipated Yzaguirre's predictions. "Mexicans, Puerto Ricans, Cubans, and others from Latin America are starting to discover a surer sense of their common identity." To *Nuestro,* the signs clearly exhibited that "a new era for Latinos had now begun."[4]

Despite the optimism, Hispanics had no universal event or figure to rally around as they entered the eighties. Few of the leaders of the sixties remained prominent; major community organizations held only nominal appeal. Furthermore, the political spearheads of the past were handicapped by a largely apolitical constituency. And cultural heroes appeared all but absent. As early as 1974, one Latin YMCA leader in New York complained that "there are black heroes, black films, black music and black movements. [However] Spanish-speaking kids don't have an established image to look up to."[5] Hence, by January of 1980, Hispanics appeared fragmented and docile. La Raza had numbers, culture, and pride, but lacked a nucleus—a point of incentive—to ballyhoo its Latin heritage. Indeed, America's "forgotten people" remained well outside the limelight. In April 1981, this changed.

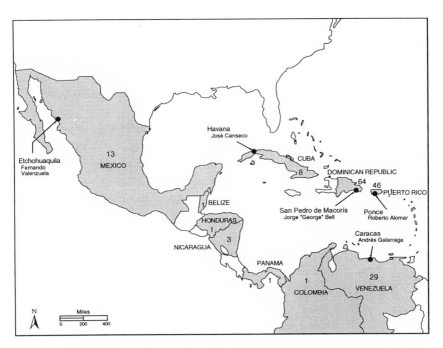

Latin American Origin of Major League Baseball Players, 1980–90. Numerals denote the total number of players from individual countries. Selected high-profile players noted.

Fernando Valenzuela's rise to stardom was a classic Horatio Alger tale. Born in 1960 and raised in Etchohuaquila, a pueblo in the northern Mexican state of Sonora, he was the youngest of eleven children. Valenzuela's hometown was not unlike so many other poverty-stricken communities seemingly bypassed by the ideals and promises of Mexico's 1910 Revolution. So poor was his community that not until 1970 did electricity reach it. The town's constituency, however, did not lack pride and much of it was stored in the community baseball team. In 1973, Valenzuela was the youngest of seven brothers listed on the Etchohuaquila roster.[6]

When Valenzuela turned sixteen, he caught the attention of Avelino Lucero, manager of the Los Mayos de Navojoa club of the Mexican League. Lucero signed the young left-hander onto his team and into the world of professional baseball. During the next two years, as he learned the ropes of his trade, the Sonoran played for different clubs within the prestigious league. Soon thereafter Mike Brito, a scout for the Dodgers, spotted him playing for Puebla. Brito had gone there to investigate another player, but seeing potential the scout acted swiftly and reported his findings to Al Campanis, the Dodgers vice president. Campanis's instincts were keen thanks to his experience with Latin American players. Furthermore, the vice president, who undoubtedly recalled his club's decision not to protect Roberto Clemente years earlier, encouraged Brito to pursue his findings. In fact, Campanis himself went to Mexico to see Valenzuela. Impressed with his pitching prowess, the Dodger representative, through a complicated deal, purchased Valenzuela's contract and dispatched him to the minor leagues. Throughout 1979 and into 1980 the southpaw developed his skills and mastered the screwball, which later proved to be the greatest weapon in his arsenal of pitches.

In 1980, Valenzuela mystified Class AA players in the Texas League while the big league Dodgers grappled with the Houston Astros for the Western Division crown. By September, the Dodgers promoted him to help bolster their waning pitching staff. He succeeded well beyond their expectations. Valenzuela pitched 17²/₃ innings, did not allow a single earned run, and struck out 16. Indeed, his brief 1980 stint in the majors came on the heels of 35 consecutive innings at San Antonio in which he gave up no earned runs. In effect, he did not allow an earned run in 52 consecutive innings that year. Hence, as the Dodgers ended their 1980 season with the frustration of falling one game short of the title, they looked optimistically to the future. In the meantime, other ingredients that created "Fernandomania" fell into place.

Valenzuela reached the majors when the United States boasted one of the largest Spanish-speaking populations in the hemisphere. While Census Bureau data placed the Hispanic population at 18.8 million, knowledgeable observers estimated the figure at 23 million—if all of the undocumented immigrants were included. Only Argentina, Colombia, and Mexico had larger Spanish-speaking populations.[7] Within the decade prior to Valenzuela's opening day appearance, the Hispanic population had increased by more than 50 percent.

Fernando Valenzuela. (Courtesy of the National Baseball Hall of Fame Library, Cooperstown, N.Y.)

Furthermore, Latins in the United States clearly desired to maintain their cultural ties. "Fewer Hispanics than ever before equate making it in America with becoming part of America's cultural mainstream," claimed Mitchell Shields, senior editor of the economic journal *Madison Avenue*.[8] To be sure, years of discrimination contributed to this outlook. Many Mexicans in the United States had tried to cope with this by accelerating their acculturation, some even raising their offspring to speak only English. These attempts to hasten their acceptance, however, often proved fruitless. One Hispanic businessman in Southern California explained that "Mexican Americans found out that they could be assimilated, [only to learn that] it didn't make any difference. They still suffered from discrimination."[9] Largely, however, Latins wanted "to be part of the national economic and social life without having to give up their ethnic identity or culture."[10] Geographic proximity to Mexico certainly made it easy to maintain cultural traits. The persistence to maintain a sense of Latin identity, carried over in each generation since the nineteenth century, fueled the drive to pursue civic ordinances on their behalf. Latins in several cities fought and won mandated bilingualism in the public schools. Clearly, by the 1980s the expansive Latin population in many urban areas fortified the use of Spanish on a routine basis. During the seventies, for example, New York housed over 2 million Hispanics; Los Angeles, 1.5 million; and San Francisco, 390,000.[11] Of these, some 5.06 million were those of Mexican heritage.[12] Interestingly, of the top ten Spanish-speaking markets, five cities— Chicago, Houston, Los Angeles, New York, and San Francisco—were the homes of National League teams.

The Spanish-language media, as a result of this Latin growth, substantially multiplied in numbers and power. Newspapers written in Spanish, for instance, increased to 65 from 40, and magazines to 65 from 25.[13] Radio stations that broadcasted in Spanish grew to 200 from 60. As an indication of the importance of these numbers, one leading magazine learned that in San Antonio, Texas, 90 percent of the Mexican American population used radios as their primary source of news and entertainment. Moreover, 85 percent of them preferred Spanish-language radio over English broadcasts.[14] Television, too, expanded. In that medium, markets sprouted to 167 from 12. Furthermore, the Spanish International Network (SIN), a chain of Spanish-language television stations and cable companies with origins in Latin America, gave Hispanic audiences in the United States the opportunity to watch regularly scheduled broadcasts and news from Mexico, Central America, and South America. "You can get all the news in Spanish—read the Spanish daily paper, watch Spanish TV, listen to Spanish radio," claimed Miami's first Latin mayor, Maurice Ferre, whose town included more than 800,000 Spanish-speaking residents. "You can go through life without having to speak English at all."[15] One Miamian of Cuban extraction proudly stated, "We buy in Spanish, sell in Spanish, marry in Spanish and make love in Spanish."[16]

Twenty years earlier, one enterprising and insightful Latin, René Cárdenas, realized the potential of a strong Latin constituency. A native of Nicaragua, Cárdenas toiled as a journalist and broadcaster in Managua before moving to the United States in 1951. While he adapted to the culture and language of his new home, he investigated opportunities in sports journalism. His exploration proved timely. In 1957, rumors of a Dodgers' exodus westward became reality when club president Walter O'Malley formally announced his intentions. "The Dodgers were coming [to Los Angeles]," remembered Cárdenas. "There were so many Spanish speaking people in L.A., I just figured it was a logical thing. They were going to broadcast Dodger games on the radio in English. Why not do it in Spanish?"[17]

There was precedence for his actions. As early as 1936, the National Broadcasting Company inaugurated shortwave broadcasts of the World Series and All-Star Games to Latin America. Elio "Buck" Canel, an American of Spanish heritage, covered the play-by-play and emerged a celebrity among his Latin fans, which numbered in the millions.[18] However, not until 1954 was his familiar "No se vayan, que esto se pone bueno!" (Don't go away, this is going to get good) catch phrase heard by Spanish-speaking listeners in the United States.[19] Moreover, Canel reported only major league baseball's two feature events. René Cárdenas, on the other hand, saw room for expansion.

Cárdenas's proposal to the Los Angeles Spanish-language station KWKW came when California's Latin community, primarily Mexican, had grown tremendously. Between 1940 and 1960 the Latin population more than tripled from 416,140 to 1,426,538. Indeed, the Hispanic population in Los Angeles alone by 1960 was 600,000. The city, however, boasted only two Spanish-language radio stations—KWKW and KACL. Moreover, only KWKW broadcasted full-time. Its listeners routinely tuned in for call-in talk shows, advice on recipes, soap operas, and, of course, news featuring stories from both Mexico and the United States. Indeed, Spanish-language radio across the country provided, according to historian Richard A. Garcia, "a sense of cultural and psychological cohesion."[20]

Cárdenas's proposal intrigued William Beaton, the station's manager. With Beaton's support, the plan reached the offices of the incoming Dodgers. Mindful that their new locale included a thriving Spanish-speaking community, the Dodgers bought into Cárdenas's idea. This pioneering move marked the first Spanish-language broadcasts of a single team throughout an entire season. And when the ball club premiered in 1958 as the Los Angeles Dodgers, a proud René Cárdenas sat in the Coliseum pressbox and, justifiably, called the play-by-play.[21]

These events were significant to Jaime Jarrín, a native of Ecuador who joined Cárdenas in the booth in 1959.[22] Like Cárdenas, Jarrín had migrated to the United States following minimal success as a broadcaster in his homeland. Still in his early twenties, Jarrín joined KWKW in 1958 and was the station's news and sports director when the Dodgers arrived on the West Coast. In 1962, Cárdenas left the station for Texas to promote baseball broadcasts in that region. With the departure of his mentor, Jarrín slowly developed his own identity among the listening audience.[23] Moreover, at every opportunity he profiled Latin players.

These attempts by Jarrín and Cárdenas were like previous efforts to develop followings for players in ethnic neighborhoods. During the 1920s, John McGraw's quest to incorporate a Jewish player to help the financially strapped New York Giants was no secret. And he was not alone in this type of promotional scheme. "McGraw's efforts to find Jewish players were no different from the Yankees' attempt to sell 'Poosh 'Em up Tony' Lazzeri as an Italian hero to New York's second-generation Italian population or attempts in St. Louis and Cincinnati to attract German audiences to the ballpark by advertising their clubs in German-language newspapers," historian Peter Levine argued.[24]

Although the Dodgers were aware of the huge number of Spanish-speaking fans, they did not appear to expand their minimal scouting forces in Latin America. Not until the early 1960s did the team attempt to cater to the Latin community by nurturing a right-handed pitcher from Arizona named Phil Ortega. Ortega, unfortunately for the Dodgers, appeared more adamant about his Yaqui Indian background than anything Hispanic. Picking up on this, the *Los Angeles Times* insensitively called Ortega "Geronimo on the Warpath."[25] Dodgers vice president Buzzie Bavasi was less than amused at the deviance from his plan: "I wish you guys would stop calling him an Indian. He's Mexican."[26] Later Bavasi complained, "There can't be more than six hundred Indian baseball fans in Southern California, but there are at least four thousand Mexicans." Ortega's strong association with his Indian heritage continued to undermine Bavasi's promotional desires. Following one interview Bavasi lashed out, "I could have scalped [Ortega] the other day when he told Vin Scully on the pre-game show that he is an Indian."[27] That Ortega spoke no Spanish created a huge drawback. The attempts to "Mexicanize" Ortega, of course, failed on all fronts. In addition, he never matured into a top-flight pitcher. Other Dodger Mexican signees, such as José Peña and Vicente Romo, also fell short of their expectations.

In the meantime, Jarrín's expanding audience coincided with the growth of the Spanish-language media. Jarrín himself became a celebrity and earned achievement awards in broadcasting.[28] Much to Jarrín's frustration, however, most of the Latin stars played in cities outside of the major media centers. Hence, his focus on Roberto Clemente, Juan Marichal, Orlando Cepeda, and other Latin stars could be only minimal.[29]

Jarrín's awareness of baseball's popularity within the Los Angeles Mexican American enclave compounded his frustration. Baseball had been well-rooted in Mexican American communities long before the Dodgers arrived. Sunday afternoon family gatherings often took place near baseball diamonds, where friends and relatives participated in municipal city contests. On special occasions local parish priests sometimes blessed the players and fields prior to the games. Mexican and Mexican American fans also appreciated professional play, especially when a compatriot graced the field. During the early 1950s, the aficionados bequeathed hero status upon Memo Luna, a Mexican national who pitched for the San Diego Padres in the Pacific Coast League. A few Mexican players also reached the major leagues. In the 1930s, Sonoran Mel Almada played for seven big league seasons. Cleveland's Bobby Avila, from the state of Jalisco, also gained prominence by winning the 1954 American League batting title. "It was great to get a following from our own kind," recalled Avila's teammate, Rudy Regalado, an American of Mexican heritage. In certain regions, where there was a large Latin population, the fans came out in force. For instance, when the Indians visited San Antonio, Texas, during 1955's spring training, "so many people crowded up against the door [of the bus] that the driver couldn't open it."[30]

Unfortunately, Almada, Avila, and other major leaguers played in Eastern cities far away from support they might have received in the West. Hence, Luna, though a minor leaguer, benefited from the Mexican American desire to honor their own and was a frequent guest at Mexican American functions. His big league career, however, was remarkably short-lived when an injury in 1954 ended it after just one inning.[31]

Not until 1977, when Los Angeles–born Roberto "Bobby" Castillo joined the Dodgers, did local Mexican fans have a potential big league star in their midst. Although he was used largely in relief and never gained national prominence, he did play an important role in teaching his most effective pitch, the screwball, to Valenzuela. These lessons, to be sure, were premeditated. Recollecting the success that previous Dodgers' relief stars Jim Brewer and Mike Marshall had utilizing the pitch, Al Campanis speculated that Valenzuela and the screwball would be a good combination. Indeed, the pitch had prolonged Castillo's big league career and eventually led to his resigning with the Dodgers in 1979. "We're going to teach Valenzuela the screwball," Campanis announced in 1979 and promptly dispatched Castillo to Arizona at season's end.[32] When the two pitchers encountered one another in the Arizona Instructional League, Castillo and Valenzuela "immediately became companions on and off the field. Fernando was naturally attracted to someone who might help him, who spoke the same language, and who shared some of the same experiences," relates biographer Mark Littwin.[33] As Valenzuela, under Castillo's tutelage, developed the screwball, Giants icon and Hall of Famer Carl Hubbell, who had brought the pitch into the limelight years earlier, wandered to the training camps that were close to his home to catch a glimpse of the Mexican southpaw. "Best screwball since mine. He's a natural," the legendary Hubbell told a companion.[34] With the help of this weapon, the Dodgers' long search for a true Latin star came to a surprising and delightful end.

Following Fernando Valenzuela's opening day victory over Houston, he victoriously completed a game with San Francisco. He followed that with three consecutive shutouts over San Diego, Houston, and San Francisco. By May 3, when he faced Montreal, Valenzuela was 5-0 and had allowed only one run. When Valenzuela had finally given up a run in the eighth inning of his second start, George Vecsey of the *New York Times* wrote, "The authorities should have stopped the game and sent the baseball directly to the Hall of Fame, because that run was the first allowed by Fernando Valenzuela . . . in 69 ⅓ innings, dating from the summer of 1980 in the Texas League."[35] This was actually the first *earned* run the left-hander had surrendered, but Valenzuela's dominance was already the stuff of hyperbole. The rookie was victorious in three more complete games, including another shutout, this time victimizing the New York Mets. "Unbelievable!" claimed one paper. "Fernando Koufax!" proclaimed another.[36] Across the nation, George Vecsey rhapsodized, "To watch Fernando Valenzuela at this stage in his career is probably like seeing Babe Ruth when he was just a few months out of the orphanage in Baltimore, or Joe Louis when he began fighting main events in Detroit, or Willie Mays in his first season in the Polo Grounds."[37] Valenzuela's remarkable development equally captivated his teammates. After the left-hander's win over the Giants in San Francisco's frigid Candlestick Park, pitcher Bob Welch remarked, "The wind was blowing right in our faces. I could have gone to the clubhouse for a whirlpool or something, but I wanted to watch Fernando. He is unbelievable."[38] Not until his encounter with the Philadelphia Phillies on May 18 did the rookie finally taste defeat. However, Valenzuela's popularity had already reached astronomical heights.

In Los Angeles the Spanish-language paper *La Opinión,* which had always proudly displayed the achievements of Latin big leaguers, wasted no time in promoting "el novato estrella" (the rookie star). Following his opening day victory, the paper's front page proclaimed, "VALENZUELA BLANQUEA A LOS ASTROS, 2-0" (Valenzuela blanks the Astros, 2-0). Calling him a natural talent, Jaime Jarrín told the daily that the left-hander had "the personality of an idol."[39] Sports editor Rodolfo García could scarcely contain himself, claiming that "Fernando was born to win."[40] For the next several days, *La Opinión* saturated its sports section with pictures of Valenzuela.

Los Angeles Latins—predominantly Mexican and Mexican American—euphorically turned out in force to support him. "The Mexicans, particularly in Southern California, were dying for a hero," recalled Jaime Jarrín. "The community really took Fernando in as their son." Things were such that even "older ladies would call into the station on a daily basis to tell us they were going to light a candle to Our Lady of Guadalupe on behalf of Fernando."[41] Many sent him religious relics (later an ambitious aficionado even forwarded to the left-hander water that he claimed came from Lourdes). During one community relations visit into the Mexican community in East Los Angeles—which drew two thousand—one fifty-eight-year-old grandmother told reporters, "As old as I am, I came to see him—I would like to touch him—give him a little kiss."[42] At the neighborhood park where he appeared, a stunned county recreation official proclaimed, "We've never had anything like this before. He's a phenomenon and it's a phenomenon."[43] *La Opinión,* of course, led the charge. "Arriba Sonora," it announced following "El Zurdo de Oro's" (the Golden Lefty's) third victory.[44] By the end of the month, an overly enthusiastic Rodolfo García predicted that, barring any problems, Valenzuela would be an all-star, win the Cy Young award, and enter the hall of fame.[45]

In the season's second month, the Mexican star was emblazoned across nearly every issue of *La Opinión.* Two days after the pitcher had tied a major league record for consecutive victories at the start of the season for a rookie, photos of Valenzuela, his parents, and his sister accompanied an article on the front page. Given the paper's highly religious readership, that this piece rivaled another concerning a recent assassination attempt on Pope John Paul II was ironic. The picture of the Valenzuela family was even larger than that of the pontiff.[46] The left-hander's popularity soon overran the National League map. In San Antonio, Texas, where Valenzuela played minor league baseball, only Henry Cisneros, the newly elected mayor, was featured in more articles than the pitcher.[47]

Fernando Valenzuela's importance to the Latin community in the United States mirrored that of baseball heroes of the past whose heritage bore special significance to those like themselves. Hank Greenberg, for instance, was a powerful presence within America's Jewish community during the 1930s and 1940s. Moreover, his successful baseball career, as Peter Levine notes, "allowed Jews to challenge openly, if only vicariously through him, any suggestions of Jewish weakness."[48] Jackie Robinson did the same for black Americans. "Fans here and everywhere he goes are simply idolizing him. They yell to him from the stands, want to talk to him, want to shake his hand," wrote journalist Sam Lacy.[49]

Naturally Valenzuela was equally famous in his native country. Mexican film star Cantinflas reflected on this mood when he said of Valenzuela, "He's very Mexican—this Fernando. I'm proud of him and all of Mexico is proud of him."[50] Following the regular season, Valenzuela drew record crowds while playing in Mexico's Pacific League. Twenty thousand people, including American baseball commissioner Bowie Kuhn, saw Valenzuela pitch the Orangemen of Hermosillo past the Ponce Lions of Puerto Rico for the Caribbean League championship. At one point, twenty-five thousand people gathered in Mexico City to attend a baseball clinic given by the pitcher.[51] Crowds from both Mexico and the United States visited Etchohuaquila as if they were visiting a holy site.[52] Indeed, Etchohuaquilans especially benefited from Fernandomania. The Mexican government, which had so long ignored the village, saw to the construction of long overdue public services, including a new highway, paved roads, street lamps, and a new baseball stadium.[53]

Latins of many nationalities also cheered the Mexican hero. Luis Rodríguez-Mayoral, a Puerto Rican public relations representative for Latin players and a longtime friend of the late Roberto Clemente, remarked that "Puerto Ricans were very happy" about Valenzuela's success. "Though there are differences and different levels of patriotism, when Valenzuela won, Venezuelans, Panamanians, and all Latins were happy about it."[54]

Felipe Alou concurred: "He made a great impact on baseball. And he didn't develop his skills from any big program. Most Latins come [to the United States] from zero programs, zero backgrounds, zero playing fields and compete against American players who developed under better conditions. Valenzuela's talents were God-given."[55]

Valenzuela, however, seemed undaunted by the excitement. "Yes, I am proud and happy that the people are treating me so nicely," he often told reporters. But he was also selective in his comments. "Fernando is an introvert, a nice kid," stated Tommy Lasorda. "He doesn't say much, but he understands everything."[56] An earlier experience with the language barrier may have contributed to his approach. As a student in a 1980 spring training orientation program, Valenzuela's attendance in an English class was brief. When asked to respond to a question about ordering meals in English, a peer prodded him to reply "Taco." "The room, filled mostly with veterans, broke up laughing. Valenzuela left the class and never returned."[57] He was also prone to reminding English-speaking journalists that playing professional baseball in the United States did not figure in his earlier goals—comments that were strikingly reminiscent of Mexico's nationalism in the sixties. "I liked baseball as a kid, but I never thought about playing it in the United States," he claimed.[58]

Faced with the prospects of losing out on great stories because of their inability to speak Spanish, English-speaking journalists, as they were not likely to do in previous eras, called upon their bilingual colleagues to get inside scoops on Valenzuela. "We weren't well-equipped to deal with a Spanish-speaking star," lamented one veteran reporter who spoke only English.[59] According to the *New York Times,* local Los Angeles newspapers "switched Spanish-speaking reporters from other beats to cover baseball and interview" Valenzuela "and the Los Angeles *Herald-Examiner* dispatched its executive sports editor to fly to the rural hamlet of 20 or so homes in Mexico, where Valenzuela grew up."[60] They were followed by a team of reporters from the *Los Angeles Times, Long Beach (California) Press-Telegram,* and *Dallas Times-Herald. Sports Illustrated* did three Valenzuela stories in a six-week period. And within a three-month span, the *Los Angeles Times* ran forty. Television was not far behind. In Los Angeles, three local broadcasters—KABC, KNBC, and KNXT—produced Fernando documentaries in May. Valenzuela's fame even drew a Swedish film crew into the calamity and led one of its reporters to ask, "Is this a slice of Americana?"[61] In the quest to scrutinize the Mexican further, reporters even "resurrected" Carl Hubbell for an assessment. The Hall of

Famer welcomed the fallout from Valenzuela's fame. "I think most people thought I was dead," he told reporters. "But this kid has made me more popular than ever."[62]

Valenzuela's impact was felt all across baseball. Taking note of his value and his inability to drive, Vin Scully quipped, "The way [Valenzuela's] going he ought to be delivered in a Brinks truck."[63] Indeed, at one point during the season the Federal Bureau of Investigation took seriously a kidnap threat in St. Louis.[64] Advertisers also capitalized on the euphoria. One poster company "pre-sold 50,000 posters at $3 apiece." The jubilant manufacturer claimed, "Fernando's poster is going to rank right up there in popularity with the man who wears the cape."[65] In hopes of establishing greater ties with Hispanics, the Dodgers rushed a poster of Bobby Castillo, Pepe Frías, Manny Mota, and Valenzuela for free distribution to the Latin community. Attendance figures increased during his appearances. Following the Mexican's rookie season, the *Sporting News* reported that each park averaged at least nine thousand more fans when he pitched.[66]

Most jubilant of all was Jaime Jarrín, Valenzuela's interpreter at press conferences. In the broadcast booth, Jarrín's play-by-play soon garnered an audience of gargantuan proportions. Thirty-one affiliates tied into Jarrín's KTNQ—the new Dodgers' Spanish-language station—broadcasts on the evenings that Valenzuela threw. "One of them broadcasts to Mexico City's 8.9 million people and Jarrín is now heard by a potentially larger audience than Vin Scully's 24 English-speaking networks," *Inside Sports* reported.[67] Jarrín became the most popular Latin sports announcer since Buck Canel. Indeed, millions of Latin baseball fans either listened to the voice of Jaime Jarrín call a Valenzuela-pitched game or watched him on Televisa, one of Mexico's most powerful television networks. Throughout the 1981 and 1982 seasons, Televisa carried every Valenzuela game to Mexican viewers.[68] "Latins are very sports-minded people and for far too long we have been waiting for a Dodger to call our own," claimed Jarrín. "I believe with all my heart that Fernando is the one."[69] Latins in southern California in particular desired a Mexican national because "Fernando is from the state of Sonora, a main source of immigrants to this area."[70] Valenzuela's success on the diamond, to be sure, fueled the excitement. But his tremendous popularity transcended his achievements on the field. "Fernando was a once-in-a-lifetime experience," Jarrín reasoned. "He became a culture, a pole to which many happenings gravitated. With him in the spotlight, many people who did not speak the language became interested in learning Spanish—people who did not know baseball became eager to know the game."[71] "This is the first time ever in the history of

Hispanics that any single Latino has achieved such phenomenal success," observed Renny Méndez Martín, a former state department official. "He's a phenomena. He is history."[72]

Not to be overlooked, of course, was Valenzuela's genuine pitching prowess, which helped baseball's tainted image. Following the summer strike, the season reopened with the All-Star Game in Cleveland and Valenzuela starting for the National League. He enhanced his legacy in October when, in the third game of the World Series after the Dodgers had dropped the first two, he pitched a complete game victory over the New York Yankees. With their hopes revived, the Dodgers went on to win the championship. The lefty finished the season with a 13-7 record, leading the National League in complete games (11), shutouts (8), innings pitched (192), and strikeouts (180). His remarkable—albeit strike-shortened—season was enough to earn him both the Rookie of the Year and Cy Young Awards, the only player ever to do so. In addition to his other honors, the *Sporting News* bestowed upon him the Silver Slugger Award for being the best hitting pitcher in the National League and pronounced him their choice for the Major League Player of the Year Award.

So taken was the baseball world that one writer published a biography on Valenzuela only three months into the season. Even international politics was not immune to Fernandomania. In June President Ronald Reagan and President José López de Portillo of Mexico invited Valenzuela to lunch with them. When the Dodgers star arrived, over fifty journalists and photographers were there to greet him when normally only twelve showed up for such functions. "I don't believe this," cried one White House official. "For the Schmidt state dinner there couldn't have been more than four press people at the entrance, and look at this."[73] Later that summer, the Mexican left-hander received the keys to Mexico City and was again invited to visit with López de Portillo.[74] The year culminated with a commemorative coin that featured Valenzuela's image with the phrase "A Mexican Hero. An American Pastime" engraved on one side. Organizers immediately received 3,000 orders in two weeks.[75]

In some circles, however, Fernandomania caused apprehension. Mexican critics argued that Televisa exaggerated Valenzuela's image and thus made him appear invincible and a "gringo-killer." Furthermore, those in the political arena lashed out at the Partido Revolucionario Institucional (Institutional Revolutionary Party) for politically exploiting the rookie. Likewise, some commentators criticized Mexican sportswriters and baseball fans for not having the insight to spot Valenzuela's talent before Americans could exploit him.[76]

During the spring of 1982 criticism of Valenzuela reached a crescendo on both sides of the border as he negotiated with the Dodgers for a higher salary. Valenzuela's worth to the Dodgers was considerably higher than the $42,000 he received during his rookie year. As the two parties jockeyed for an agreement, negative comments were fired from all fronts. The most prevalent target was Valenzuela's agent, Tony DeMarco, who, according to the pitcher's supporters, "misguided" the young star.[77] "We in the Hispanic community feel that Fernando has been misled by his so-called agent," claimed the vice president of the Mexican Chamber of Commerce of Los Angeles. "The response of the community has been, 'Well, you know if this kid only cares about money, why should we care about him?'"[78] Similarly, informal polls conducted in Mexican American communities revealed support for the Dodgers' position. *La Opinión* echoed these sentiments: "We're not against Fernando, but he's asking for too much money."[79]

However, the roots of disenchantment during Valenzuela's eventual holdout went much deeper than the criticism of DeMarco. After the Dodgers, frustrated in their desire to sign the star pitcher, warned that the rescinding of his work visa could lead to his expulsion from the United States, the League of United Latin American Citizens (LULAC) sent a stinging "Leave Fernando Alone" telegram to both the Department of Labor and Immigration and Naturalization Services.[80] League members also made plans to initiate a boycott of Dodger games that year in support of Valenzuela.[81]

Interestingly, LULAC's support of Valenzuela characterized the newfound bond between Mexican Americans and Mexican nationals. Since the 1930s and 1940s, organizations like LULAC and the American G.I. Forum were created to support only Americans of Mexican descent. Their positions, moreover, highlighted the schism between Mexican Americans and Mexican nationals that was rooted in the nineteenth century. This division softened during the 1970s with a resurgence of cultural awareness and rigid immigration policies. "We should show the world," Edwin Morgan, LULAC's national director, said in 1977, "that we are aware of the continuing political repression, the repression of human rights that is ongoing not only against Blacks, but certainly against Chicanos, against Mexicanos, and other brother Latins."[82] The support for Valenzuela, five years later, helped to cement this bond. One Mexican American businessman anticipated that "there could be a mobilization of Hispanics [against the Dodgers] like you've never seen before."[83] To him, the Dodgers' role in the negotiations reflected a traditional attitude toward Latins in the United States. He announced, "We want to show the public [that] here is another example of Hispanics being kicked around."[84]

Some Mexican observers saw American arrogance toward its Latin neighbors in the negotiations. In his study of Mexican perceptions of the United States through the Valenzuela phenomenon, historian David LaFrance discovered that "the Dodgers and the United States press were . . . accused of making Valenzuela look like a cunning Mexican who was trying to take advantage of the situation to demand more than he legally deserved."[85] Mexicans fumed at depictions of Valenzuela as a "roly-poly, beer-drinking, taco-eating, dumb and poor Indian from some god-forsaken Mexican pueblo where people still sleep against cantina walls with sombreros pulled down over their eyes."[86] Some writers did link the pitcher with burritos and beer, even during the euphoria of Fernandomania. "I wrote a burrito line on opening day," admitted Mark Heisler of the *Los Angeles Times*. "All of us knew better than to have used a watermelon reference in a story concerning blacks, but we were less prepared to deal with Latin sensibilities."[87] The press was so insensitive that only weeks after Valenzuela's opening day victory over the Houston Astros, George Vecsey felt relief at the rookie's inability to read English: "As long as reporters and editors permit phrases like 'Valenzuela had flicked aside the Houston Astros like so many flies on his plate of tortillas' . . . it is just as well that [he] does not read English. Otherwise," he warned," he might get the idea some North Americans carry around unpleasant stereotypes of Mexicans."[88] Still, Jim Murray, during the Valenzuela 1982 holdout, titled his column "Is Fernando a Bandito?" He followed up by suggesting that Valenzuela was a fellow "who's probably got no shot in real life" and advised the pitcher that "he should get on his knees and thank Our Lady of Guadalupe he's got a job."[89] Throughout the entire episode, Valenzuela himself lashed out in frustration: "I am only twenty-one years old, but I am not a boy. I am a man, and I have the same need to be considered with dignity and respect as does every other man."[90]

Valenzuela eventually capitulated and agreed to the Dodgers' offer of $350,000—the highest amount ever given to a second-year player. The following year, after negotiations between the two parties had again stalled, an arbitrator ruled in Valenzuela's favor, awarding him a $1 million contract for a single season. Valenzuela was, indeed, a bona fide star. This was not just hype because throughout most of the decade he was among the top pitchers in baseball. He proved to be a dependable starter for the Dodgers and not until August 1988 did he miss his turn in the starting rotation—after 255 consecutive starts.

By the end of the 1990 season he had accumulated 144 wins against 116 losses for the Dodgers. Moreover, in postseason play, Valenzuela earned a 5-1 record, which included a World Series victory. During the 1980s, he led the National League in complete games three times (1981, 1986, 1987) and twice in innings pitched (1981, 1984). From 1981 to 1988, he averaged 15 wins, with 21 in 1986. In that span, he averaged 255 innings per year. Four of those seven years he was a top five contender for the Cy Young Award and was named to the National League All-Star team for six consecutive years (1981–86).

Fernando Valenzuela did not finish his career with the Dodgers. An arm injury kept him out for the bulk of the 1989 season, and the following year proved to be unproductive. In March 1991, the club released the Mexican pitcher and the unceremonious nature of that action led to bitterness. "Nobody said anything. Nobody explained to me why I was being released," he asserted.[91] He filed a grievance against the club that he later dropped. But from the Dodgers' point of view, he had pitched poorly throughout the spring and exhibited little in the way of improvement. An uncomfortable Peter O'Malley, in a rare interview concerning team personnel, told journalists, "We gave Fernando a good faith opportunity to win a job and he did not."[92] In a solemn press conference following his release, Valenzuela, whose English by then was much improved, appeared alongside Jaime Jarrín, who had, years earlier, interpreted many interviews for the star. "This is how it began, and this is how it will end," Valenzuela told reporters. "Baseball is fun for me. But today, it is not fun."[93] Others were more expressive. "Who among his people—not Cuban, not Dominican, not Puerto Rican, but Mexican—had ever represented an entire nation in American baseball more nobly?" Mike Downey asked his readers. "We don't mean to speak about him as though he died. But a little life did just ooze from the Dodgers."[94] The *Los Angeles Times* reminded Dodgers fans of "the pudgy kid from a village in Mexico, who at the age of 20, became a role model for the American work ethic." And in a fitting conclusion, it proclaimed, "He gave us joy, the greatest of baseball's gifts. Adios to a special Dodger."[95]

After time with the California Angels, the Mexican League, and the Baltimore Orioles, Valenzuela returned to Dodger Stadium in July 1994 as a member of the Philadelphia Phillies. Thirteen years after he captured all of baseball, and just three years after his unassuming exit from the Dodgers, traces of the old magic still remained. The local press greeted him warmly. His appearance, wrote Michael Ventre of the *Los Angeles Daily News,* was like "welcoming an old friend who has changed only a bit."[96] "Seeing Fernando Valenzuela in red was like seeing a green robin," added Mike Downey of the *Los Angeles Times.*[97] The Dodgers hastily arranged a ceremony to honor him on the evening of the first game of the series. "I thank the fans. They still remember those moments from the 80s," he calmly told reporters.[98] The sparks of yesteryear, however, again ignited when Valenzuela pitched in the series finale, "with the crowd chanting 'Meh-ee-co, Meh-ee-co,' and applauding Valenzuela's every wink and shrug, it felt like a festival." Orel Hershiser, his pitching opponent and former teammate, was moved by the affection. "I was glad they were cheering him," claimed Hershiser. "That's what you want the home crowd to do when they see a returning champion."[99] Though he lost, the game appropriately featured another Valenzuela characteristic: a sold-out house. Panning the stadium and witnessing the adulation bestowed upon his former star pitcher, Tommy Lasorda concluded, "They appreciated all that he did for them."[100]

———

Rodolfo Acuña was disappointed in the so-called Decade for the Hispanics. "For the poor, as well as the working class, the first half of the 1980s was a nightmare."[101] He went on to point out that the Chicano heroism "of the late 1960s by the second half of the 1980s was part of the nostalgic past."[102] Moreover, he argued that the activist of yesteryear had given way to the "broker" Hispanic. His case was not unfounded. As "baby boom" Latins approached middle age, many saw themselves in a new light. "We are the 'new wave' Hispanic," said one Orange County, California, lawyer. "Instead of entering the system uneducated, we're coming in with a stronger profile and with a greater economic foundation than our predecessors."[103] But not all Latins could, with justification, profess this optimism. "Government policy worsened for the poor," according to Acuña.[104] For many Latins, the Ronald Reagan era was a setback. In 1984, for example, a presidential Task Force on Food Assistance concluded that "there is no evidence that widespread undernourishment is a major health problem."[105] The statement seemed incredible in that census data revealed that 42 percent of all Latin children under the age of six lived in poverty. To be sure, the Reagan administration, despite the enormous growth of Spanish-speaking Americans, did little to foment equity for those whose finances and opportunities were, at best, marginal.

Hence, by Acuña's gauge, heroism and leadership, as applied only to social activism, was a scarce commodity within Latin communities. But this yardstick had its limitations. Inspiration came in other circles. Many Latins, particularly those who faced limited opportunities, looked for symbols of hope. Others concerned themselves with identity and cultural cohesion. Though he never lifted a banner in the name of civil protest, Fernando Valenzuela during the early eighties filled this vacuum; he was the centerpiece of the Latin community—particularly in the Mexican American enclave. Few personified the battle-cry of César Chávez and his followers, "sí se puede" (it can be done), better than Valenzuela. Many Latins identified with his humble origins, inability to speak English, and work ethic. And many more looked at him with pride as he captured the limelight by virtue of his skill as a professional in the United States. Moreover, he was not just a member of the Dodgers, he was their ace and, more unusual, a pitcher who could hit. His emergence did more to stimulate Latin cultural cohesion than any prior event of recent history. And his success—magnified by the national and international media—drew the attention of mainstream Americans to America's "forgotten people" in a manner not seen in the past.

In addition, Valenzuela's fame held deep meaning for his compatriots. Traditionally apprehensive of their neighbors to the north, Mexicans watched the euphoria over their countryman with raised eyebrows. Never before had one of their own so captivated an American audience. Furthermore, as his prominence grew, Valenzuela not only became a symbolic link between mainstream American and Latin cultures but also helped to strengthen ties between Mexican nationals and Mexican Americans.

Fernandomania, more importantly, helped to bridge domestic gaps between American Latins and society at large. "Indeed, it often seems that there are two separate communities [in Los Angeles], isolated from each other—the English-speaking white and black residents, and those who speak Spanish," observed Robert Lindsey of the *New York Times* during the height of the Valenzuela craze. "Until now, the two have not had much in common. But Valenzuela has changed that."[106] Five years after the euphoria, one local television personality claimed that "Valenzuela filled a void that has long existed for a Mexican or Mexican-American sports hero in Los Angeles. What's also so important is that there is the feeling among Hispanics that Valenzuela has succeeded without selling out." His reluctance to use English in a public forum "seems to be appreciated by Hispanics, for whom the Spanish language has been a historic cornerstone of both pride and discrimination."[107] This point was

not lost on a Latin community that had traditionally resisted assimila-
tionist forces in the United States. Valenzuela epitomized, to many, Latin success without having abandoned his culture. American reporters,
players, and management, in effect, had to deal in his terms, his language.
Perhaps most importantly, for many in the Mexican American community, Valenzuela's fame catapulted their identity into the national limelight as never before and in a manner that captured the essence of their
culture. "He makes me feel proud," claimed one fan of Mexican heritage. "When he looks good we all look good."[108]

Notes

1. Littwin, *Fernando!* 7.
2. Ibid., 42.
3. Yzaguirre, "Decade for the Hispanic," 2.
4. "Here Comes the Latino Era," 12–19.
5. "Newest Americans," 36.
6. Littwin, *Fernando!* 19–20.
7. Skidmore and Smith, *Modern Latin America,* 355–56.
8. Shields, "Hispanics Step Out of the Melting Pot," 67–72.
9. Frank Sotomayor, "Latinos: Diverse Group Tied by Ethnicity," *Los Angeles Times,* July 25, 1983. One is reminded of the Nisei efforts to win acceptance by the Western mainstream population. Though, through organizations like the Japanese American Citizen's League, they promoted themselves as "super patriots," the prejudice against them and their heritage proved to be too deep for them to overcome. For a comparative study of this analogy see Daniels, *Concentration Camps.*
10. Sotomayor, "Latinos."
11. Rustin, "Spanish Market," 20–52.
12. Ibid., 20.
13. Moore and Pachon, *Hispanics,* 121–22; Grebler, Moore, and Guzman, *Mexican-American People,* 429–32; Guernica, "The Hispanic Market," 4–7.
14. Ibid.
15. Shields, "Hispanics Step Out of the Melting Pot," 70.
16. "Newest Americans," 36.
17. Johnson, "Rene Cardenas," 50–55.
18. Boyle, "'El As,'" 33–40.
19. Press release, Eli "Buck" Canel file, National Baseball Library, Cooperstown, N.Y.
20. Garcia, *Rise of the Mexican American Middle Class,* 106.
21. For more on the Dodgers' Spanish-language broadcasts, see Regalado, "'Dodgers Béisbol Is on the Air.'"

22. Rustin, "Spanish Market," 20–52; Garcia, "Hispanic Migration," 14–17; Weisberg, "In Any Language," 16–18.

23. René Cárdenas, it should be noted, ventured to Houston and eventually helped to develop the Astros' Spanish-language broadcast network. He rejoined Jaime Jarrín in 1982 to broadcast Dodgers games.

24. Levine, *Ellis Island,* 109.

25. *Los Angeles Times,* 1964, Phil Ortega file, National Baseball Library.

26. Ibid.

27. Ibid.

28. Páramo, "Jaime Jarrin," 6–9.

29. For a deeper analysis of the development of Spanish-language sportscasting in Los Angeles, see Regalado, "'Dodgers Béisbol Is on the Air.'"

30. Regalado, "Minor League Experience," 65–70.

31. Regalado, "Baseball in the Barrios," 47–59.

32. Littwin, *Fernando!* 33.

33. Ibid., 33.

34. Ibid., 32.

35. George Vecsey, "Valenzuela Shows Gifts of a Natural," *New York Times,* Apr. 25, 1981.

36. Fernando Valenzuela file, National Baseball Library.

37. Ibid.

38. Ibid.

39. *La Opinión,* Apr. 10, 1981. To its credit, the paper continued to run features on other Latins players, most notably Luis Tiant, who was attempting a comeback with the Portland, Oregon, minor league franchise. Additionally, each month *La Opinión* posted the progress of all major league players from Latin America.

40. Rodolfo García, *La Opinión,* Apr. 10, 1981.

41. Jarrín interview.

42. *Sporting News,* May 19, 1981.

43. Untitled clipping, May 24, 1981, National Baseball Library.

44. *La Opinión,* Apr. 19, 1981. The paper, in its April 23 issue, also devoted an entire page to photographs of the pitcher's visit to the presses of *La Opinión.*

45. Rodolfo García, *La Opinión,* Apr. 24, 1981.

46. *La Opinión,* May 16, 1981.

47. Between May 1 and May 10, 1981, the *San Antonio Light* and the *San Antonio Express* ran a total of three major features on Valenzuela.

48. Levine, *Ellis Island,* 138.

49. Tygiel, *Baseball's Great Experiment,* 130–31.

50. Untitled clipping, May 24, 1981, Valenzuela file.

51. LaFrance, "A Mexican Popular Image," 16.

52. Heisler, "Fernando's Path of Glory," 13–14.

53. LaFrance, "A Mexican Popular Image," 14–23.

54. Rodríguez-Mayoral interview.

55. Alou interview.

56. Vecsey, "Valenzuela Shows Gifts of a Natural."

57. Castro, "Something Screwy Going on Here," 34.

58. *Sporting News,* May 9, 1981.

59. Heisler, "Fernando's Path of Glory," 13.

60. *New York Times,* Apr. 29, 1981.

61. Heisler, "Fernando's Path of Glory," 14.

62. Ibid.

63. Rivera, "Only Land," 54.

64. *Sporting News,* June 27, 1981.

65. *Los Angeles Daily News,* May 31, 1981.

66. *Sporting News,* Dec. 19, 1981.

67. Heisler, "Fernando's Path of Glory," 13; Weisberg, "In Any Language," 16–18.

68. LaFrance, "A Mexican Popular Image," 16.

69. Rivera, "Only Land," 47.

70. Jim Kaplan, "Epidemic of Fernando Fever," undated clipping, Valenzuela file.

71. Páramo, "Jaime Jarrin," 6.

72. *Los Angeles Daily News,* Oct. 30, 1981.

73. *Washington Star,* June 10, 1981.

74. LaFrance, "A Mexican Popular Image," 17.

75. Jeff Snyder, "Commemorative Coin Is Struck for Valenzuela," *Los Angeles Daily News,* Oct. 30, 1981.

76. Ibid.

77. *New York Daily News,* Mar. 14, 1982.

78. Bill Brubaker, "Fernando's Wild Pitch," *Los Angeles Daily News,* Mar. 21, 1982.

79. Ibid.

80. *Sporting News,* Mar. 27, 1982.

81. LaFrance, "A Mexican Popular Image," 19.

82. Gutiérrez, *Walls and Mirrors,* 202.

83. Brubaker, "Fernando's Wild Pitch."

84. Ibid.

85. LaFrance, "A Mexican Popular Image," 19.

86. Ibid., 20.

87. Heisler, "Fernando's Path to Glory," 14.

88. Vecsey, "Valenzuela Shows Gifts of a Natural."

89. Jim Murray, "Is Fernando a Bandito?" undated article, Valenzuela file.

90. LaFrance, "A Mexican Popular Image," 19.

91. *Los Angeles Daily News,* June 30, 1994.

92. *Los Angeles Times,* Mar. 30, 1991.

93. Mike Downey, *Los Angeles Times,* Mar. 29, 1991.

94. Ibid.

95. *Los Angeles Times,* Mar. 30, 1991.

96. Michael Ventre, *Los Angeles Daily News,* July 1, 1994.

97. Mike Downey, "He'll Always Be a Familiar Face," *Los Angeles Times,* July 4, 1994.

98. Ibid.

99. Ibid.

100. Ibid.

101. Acuña, *Occupied America,* 413.

102. Ibid., 448–49.

103. *Los Angeles Times,* July 24, 1983.

104. Acuña, *Occupied America,* 449.

105. Ibid.

106. Robert Lindsey, "Los Angeles Is Wild over 5-0 Valenzuela," *New York Times,* Apr. 29, 1981.

107. Castro, "Something Screwy Going on Here," 34.

108. Rivera, "Only Land," 54.

The Spirit of the Latin

It doesn't look like the chance to manage in the big leagues is going to happen.
Felipe Alou

Felipe Alou . . . was a near unanimous choice as the National League's "Manager of the Year."
San Francisco Chronicle

At the start of the eighties, Latins had been part of major league baseball for the better part of one hundred years. The roots of baseball in Latin America extended even further. Yet, only two players from that region had been inducted into the Baseball Hall of Fame in Cooperstown. Roberto Clemente's untimely death assured him quick admission in 1973, while in 1977 Martín Dihigo, the famed star of the black leagues, was also voted in posthumously. Not until 1983 did Juan Marichal became the first living Latin player to gain entry. His election, understandably, received tremendous applause in his homeland. The Dominican Republic press corps "hailed this recognition by U.S. sportswriters as one of the greatest sporting events in the island nation's history."[1] One of many Latins to endure the hardships of American racism and acculturation, Marichal viewed his induction in nationalistic terms. Indeed, half of his acceptance speech was given in Spanish. "The triumph of getting in the Hall of Fame wasn't just for me, " he told the audience. "It was for all the people of the Dominican Republic."[2] That the legendary right-hander's triumph at Cooperstown came after he had been denied entrance the two previous years was not lost on some observers, however. After Marichal fell just short of the number of votes needed for entry in 1982, Art Rosenbaum of the *San Francisco Chronicle* divulged that "at least two baseball writers of my acquaintance indicated, without confessing, that the Marichal-Roseboro incident is not forgotten."[3] With induction secured a year later, he concluded, "It was good to see the Hall of Fame voters come to their senses on Juan Marichal."[4]

In the following year, Luis Aparicio won entrance into the Hall of Fame. Like Marichal, he voiced his nationalistic sentiments during the induction ceremonies. His distinction, declared Aparicio, was not simply for him and his family, but "for all of the people of Venezuela who lived this experience as if it were one of their own."[5] When the announcement of his election was delivered during a winter league game in Caracas, the crowd followed its cheer by singing the Venezuelan national anthem. President Jaime Luchinchi, in a congratulatory note to Aparicio, declared him to be the "ideal" Venezuelan athlete, "persevering, strong and full of the courage needed to continually excel."[6]

Rod Carew collected his 3,000th hit—only the second Latin player to do so—a year after Aparicio's induction. Born in Gatún within the Canal Zone but raised in New York, Carew had by then built a remarkable résumé that included seven batting titles. "Rod Carew is Picasso at the plate. An artist at work," praised columnist Jim Murray. "He wields a bat the way Pablo wielded a brush. He is a portrait. The game, the score, the league pale into significance. People come to see the artist, not the contest."[7]

Murray's eloquent description, however, masked the reality of Carew's recognition. It was nil. As early as 1977, *Time* magazine, which featured Carew on its July cover with the headline "Baseball's Best Hitter," took issue with its colleagues. "Carew's feats have gone virtually unnoticed by the national press," claimed *Time*. Moreover, the slugger lost endorsements in the process. "In an era of jocks selling everything from perfume to pantyhose, Carew has made no commercials despite handsome looks and a charming magnetic personality." In subsequent years, things changed little for the talented player despite his continued powerful hitting, with batting titles and a serious challenge to the .400 mark through much of 1977.[8]

Granted, in that period he at times lacked congeniality. "When I first came up to the Twins, I sulked a lot," he once admitted.[9] Mike Downey pointed out that had Carew "been a more ostentatious personality, had he courted the media or dazzled them with flamboyant actions on the field, chances are he would not have been short-changed in the recognition department." The *Los Angeles Times* reporter, however, added that "as horsehide hitters go—as baseball players go—there is only one thing that he has been: one of the best."[10] His lack of attention became abundantly clear when, on the anticipated day of his milestone 3,000th hit, the Angels received no out-of-town press credential requests, while the Yankees issued two hundred to reporters who wanted to cover Tom Seaver's 300th victory. Furthermore, Carew was not resigned by the Angels following the 1985 season and, according to an arbitrator, was victimized by collusion on the part of the owners when no one picked up his contract. "Sadly, Carew's career was aborted by an unfair act by baseball's owners, and not by his

Rod Carew. (Courtesy of the National Baseball Hall of Fame Library, Cooperstown, N.Y.)

own decision," claimed Michael Oleksak and Mary Oleksak in their study of Latin players.[11]

But Carew's numbers were indisputable. By the time of his forced retirement, he had won seven American League batting titles, collected 3,053 hits, been named the 1977 American League's most valuable player, and finished his career with a .328 batting average. In 1991, he became the fifth Latin player to be elected into the Hall of Fame.

————————

During the 1980s, many of the Latin baseball pioneers strove to attain instructional positions within big league organizations. By the end of the decade, four out of the fourteen American League teams employed Latin coaches, while half of the National League's twelve clubs carried them.[12] In addition, most teams hired former Latin players to serve as scouts and, in some cases, tutors to help upcoming players. Many also made special efforts, not seen in past years, to help orient their players to American customs and language. "We set up classes for them all summer long," explained Al Harazin, the Mets' senior vice president in 1987. "We're trying to help them relax, give them every opportunity to succeed. It's a common sense thing. It should have been done a long time ago."[13]

Ironically, attention given to the lack of ethnics in baseball's echelons came at the expense of Al Campanis, a vice president with the Dodgers. On April 6, 1987, during an interview on ABC's "Nightline," which aired a program commemorating Jackie Robinson's entrance into the major leagues forty years earlier, Campanis blundered in response to interviewer Ted Koppel's question about why so few blacks held management positions in baseball. The former scout responded, in part, that they lacked the "necessities"—a statement that unleashed an uproar of condemnation of hiring inequalities in bureaucratic and supervisory jobs in sports.[14] Campanis, who during his scouting career had encouraged, promoted, and befriended many Latins, surprised many with his sentiments.[15] Depicted as a symbol of the old guard that stood in the way of ethnic advancement in major league baseball, Campanis was fired. His statements, however, spurred the creation of opportunities many former Latin players needed to win management positions in professional baseball.

At the time of the Campanis uproar, forty-seven years had passed since Mike González—the first Latin manager—had guided the St. Louis Cardinals for six games. And not until 1969 did another Latin, Preston Gómez—who eventually managed for seven years—win a post as a club skipper. In 1988, the California Angels named Octavio "Cookie" Rojas manager. But his was only an interim position and he was not rehired for the subsequent season. With this track record, questions were raised about the ability of Hispanics to hold leadership roles. Opinions among Latins were mixed. "I have always felt that if you have the ability, you will get an opportunity," pointed out Preston Gómez in a somewhat idealistic manner. "But no one is going to give you a job just because you are Latin."[16] Phillies coach Tony Taylor, however, disagreed. He claimed that Latins already carried the appropriate managerial qualifications. "To be given a managing position would be the ultimate recognition. I wish they'd give [us] some opportunities because we have Latin Americans who are very good baseball men."[17] Some Latin coaches with vast experience remained frustrated. "I think I am more qualified than some people now managing," claimed Tony Oliva. "But I will not apply for the job. I don't want to be embarrassed."[18] Likewise, Dominican Ozzie Virgil, confident of his abilities, was disappointed with the lack of opportunity. "I had one intention when I became a coach, and that was to get a chance to manage. . . . I think blacks and Latins are in the same boat about this."[19]

As the controversy raged, Felipe Alou quietly manned his post as manager of the Expos' single A club in West Palm Beach, Florida. By then, it appeared that his career had come full circle. His more than thirty years in professional baseball, when integration was barred in some states, had begun in Melbourne, only fifty miles to the north. Alou's ability to overcome racial and cultural barriers led to a successful seventeen-year major league playing career. By his retirement in 1972, his reputation as a congenial hard-working professional remained intact. In 1975, the Montreal Expos hired Alou to coach one of their minor league affiliates. For the next twelve years, he drifted within the Expos organization, compiled a record of 844-751, and won two minor league championships. In the meantime, as big league clubs went through the usual array of managerial changes, Alou, always overlooked, remained in the minor leagues. By 1989, he landed in West Palm Beach at the single A level with, apparently, no promotion to the majors in sight. Reconciling his circumstances, he claimed, "I did want to manage in the big leagues at one time, but now I don't know if I want to anymore." As he thought further, however, the Dominican's frustration surfaced. "You know, I was available twelve years ago. I'm fifty-three years old now and I'm not getting any younger. As a manager you can win, win, and win. I got all kinds of rings from winning . . . but [those] didn't get me a promotion." He concluded that "it doesn't look like the chance to manage in the big leagues is going to happen."[20]

Octavio "Cookie" Rojas. (Courtesy of the National Baseball Hall of Fame Library, Cooperstown, N.Y.)

Three years later, opportunity arose. In 1992, the Expos, who indicated promise in the spring, were struggling by the season's second month. Frustration in the front office peaked in May, which led to the firing of skipper Tom Runnells. Felipe Alou, who was assigned to a coaching post on the club that year, was named to replace Runnells on an interim basis. Inheriting a club with a 17-20 mark, he took the Expos to an 87-75 record and a second place finish in the National League's Eastern Division. Remarkably, the organization hesitated before offering the Dominican a contract for the 1993 season. After strong suggestions that he might leave, the Expos rehired him. In his sophomore year, Alou and his club repeated a second place finish with a 94-68 record. His success notwithstanding, winning a managerial position was not necessarily fulfilling for all Latins.

Like Alou, Tony Pérez remained in baseball following an extraordinary twenty-three-year career that ended in 1986. The Reds immediately offered the popular Cuban a coaching position with the parent club, where he remained through the 1992 season. However, the Reds had been in chaos since the banishment of their former manager and Cincinnati icon Pete Rose in 1991 due to a gambling controversy. To further complicate matters, Marge Schott, their outspoken owner, had earned a year's suspension because of racial slurs she had directed at some of her players. These matters, compounded by the inability of the club to win a divisional title in 1992, drove team management to make a change. At the end of that season, the Reds named Tony Pérez as their skipper for the ensuing year. Unlike Alou, the Cuban had served no apprenticeship as a minor league manager. Nonetheless, the Reds, who offered him a one-year contract, appeared committed to their former star.

But the facade of loyalty crumbled after 44 games. The team, which had not played well in the first two months, had compiled a disappointing 20-24 record as summer neared. Then, following a 1-6 trip to the West Coast, Jim Bowden, the club's general manager who ran operations in Marge Schott's absence, fired Pérez and hired Davey Johnson to replace him. Incredibly, earlier in the day Bowden had told reporters who questioned his commitment to the Reds' skipper, "I support Pérez, he's my manager."[21] The news of Pérez's dismissal was met with outrage. Branded "gutless" and "indecent" by his players, Bowden offered little in the way of a direct explanation for his decision. His detractors, however, were more explicit. "My God, how in the hell can you judge someone after forty-four games?" asked Seattle and former Reds manager Lou Pinella. Ron Oester, a member of Pérez's coaching staff, resigned in protest. Angels skipper Buck Rogers was suspect of Bowden's motivations. "Unless he did some funny things, or lost the ballclub to the point of no return, something is not right. I can't believe it was based on his record."[22] The Reds, of course, did have an image problem by the end of the 1992 season and it was conceivable that the hiring of a beloved former star to manage the club was a calculated move to ease their wounded reputation.

Some observers pointed out, however, that Bowden's hiring of Johnson into the club's scouting staff during the off-season was a means of easing him into the top spot at the earliest opportunity. Pérez, of course, was heartbroken. "I don't think it's fair," he told reporters with tears in his eyes. "Was I cheated? I don't know. But I don't think it's fair. I think I did a good job."[23] The change of managers did not help the club's fortunes that year and they never challenged their opponents for the division crown. In the meantime, the longtime relationship between Pérez and the Reds was bitterly severed, and the former hero took sanctuary in Florida, where he eventually landed an administrative post with the expansion Marlins.

Felipe Alou, however, continued to do well in Montreal. Since his arrival in May 1992, the Expos had become one of baseball's strongest teams. This success carried into the 1994 season. Unfortunately for the club, the campaign came to a premature halt when the players voted to carry out a strike in August. By then the Expos had established baseball's best mark. This statistic was not overlooked by the Baseball Writers' Association of America when it bestowed upon Alou the National League Manager of the Year Award in November.

While the early Latin pioneers continued to make advances beyond the diamond, younger Latins enjoyed the fruits of their forebears' labors. Among the rising stars was Alou's own son, Moisés. His emergence made him the fourth Alou to play in the major leagues, a baseball first. Other baseball families from Latin America also flourished, such as Puerto Ricans Roberto Alomar and Santos Alomar Jr. Both brothers appeared in the 1991 All-Star Game. Their father, Santos Alomar Sr., a former player coaching for the San Diego Padres, also served as a coach for the National League squad. Predating the Alomars' arrival from Puerto Rico, Héctor, José, and Cirilo (Tommy) Cruz also emerged from that island to win major league jobs. José Cruz, in particular, was a standout player for the Houston Astros. However, well outside the media market, Cruz languished in obscurity. The Puerto Rican, who routinely led his club in various offensive categories during the eighties and batted over .300 six times in his career, rarely got attention. "I've had some good seasons, but sometimes I think the press underrates me," he once acknowledged.[24] Opponents, however, did not underrate him. In the 1980 divisional play-offs, for instance, the Philadelphia Phillies walked the dangerous Cruz eight times in the series, which established a big league mark. At that, he still batted a healthy .400 in a losing effort.

———————————

Other Latins, however, could not be ignored. In 1988, Havana-born José Canseco was the American League home run champ; Puerto Rican Luis Gonzalez won that title in 1992; Venezuelan Andrés Galarraga took the National League batting crown in 1993; and Puerto Rican catcher Iván Rodríguez, in 1993, at the age of twenty became the youngest player to compete in an All-Star game. Dominicans, too, were well represented. At the beginning of the nineties, thirty graced the rosters of big league clubs. By 1993, one out of every seven players was Latin.

Baseball academies, many of which started in the late seventies and flourished by the mideighties, contributed much to the Latin increase in the big leagues. Like American-owned companies of the late nineteenth century, major league organizations saturated the Dominican Republic, in particular, as a means to mill local talent. In 1985, the Braves, Astros, Dodgers, and White Sox had operations at San Pedro de Macorís, an area heralded by the *Sporting News* as "Baseball's Secret Treasure." "San Pedro de Macorís is not the best town in the world. That's for sure," pondered Ralph Avila, supervisor at the Dodgers' Las Palmas encampment. "But it's the best baseball town in the world."[25] Known to some as "Dodgertown South," the Las Palmas facility provided an opportunity for players with potential. Local heroes such as Rico Carty, Joaquín Andújar, Pedro Guerrero, Jorge Bell, and Tony Fernández largely contributed to the region's popularity among major league recruiters. Indeed, by 1985, the town on the southern Dominican coast boasted twelve big leaguers.

By the middle of the decade, big league clubs provided some equipment for the island's youngsters to replace the guava tree bats and rocks their heroes had used. But most former players who succeeded saw it as their duty to help future stars. "I could go to the beach and have a good time, but they dream of coming to the United States to play professional baseball," claimed Joaquín Andújar. "That's why I try to help them."[26] Pittsburgh catcher Tony Peña contributed $20,000 toward the construction of a baseball complex at Monte Cristi.[27] But although the camps primarily represented the long-term goals of young Dominicans, they also became temporary sanctuaries from poverty. Avila explained that "the Dodgers promise three meals a day, a bed, a physical examination, any necessary

dental work, prescription drugs and vitamins, classes in Spanish, an English teacher, transportation to and from the ball park and free laundry."[28]
By the end of the decade, nine other big league clubs set up camps in various regions of the country.

On the surface, this rush to the area gave the impression of impending
prosperity, but further analysis determined otherwise. Aside from the rel-
atively few opportunities Dominicans actually had in the big leagues (by
1990 49 Dominicans were on big league rosters while 325 toiled in the
minor league, 400 were in various academies, and 250 remained unsigned
in the Dominican professional league), sociologist Alan M. Klein revealed
that "for all the success that the Dominicans have enjoyed at baseball, 80
percent of the people are unemployed or underemployed, and the economic
benefits of baseball must be negligible."[29] To many, however, the various
major league encampments represented an opportunity to escape their
environs. "Everyday, some parents from the town will show up on my
doorstep and ask me to take two or three of their kids, all of whom, they
assure me, are tremendous prospects," reflected Avila. "I understand why
they try. Each one I accept means one less mouth for them to feed."[30]

The Latin special hunger did not diminish by the end of the eighties as
opportunities grew. Their path, of course, had been widened with the
achievements and turmoil of those who predated them. And they benefited from the baseball academies, club-sponsored language instructions in
English, and, most importantly, the experienced veterans who came to their
aid at a time of crisis. While many of their problems had faded, some of
the past continued to haunt contemporary players. As always, the language
barrier stood in the forefront. "I didn't speak a word of English," remembered Andrés Galarraga of his arrival to a minor league post in Calgary,
Canada. "I was completely lost and very scared."[31] Benito Santiago's experiences in Reno, Nevada, were not much different. "I don't speak nothing and we play in the snow," he recalled. "I used to run home from the
ballpark because it was so cold. I didn't speak a word of English, so who
am I gonna talk to?" he claimed.[32]

Aspects of the past also continued to haunt Orlando Cepeda into the
nineties. Residing in California and reunited with the Giants for player
development, the former slugger's reputation seemed to be on the mend.
By then, his supporters believed induction into the Hall of Fame was within
reach. Not only would it bring appropriate recognition to his distinguished

career but it would also erase the drug conviction that crippled his legacy in 1977. Sadly, their anticipated gala did not happen. In 1994, for the fifteenth and final time, the Baseball Writers Association of America denied him entrance. Though his seventeen-year career had included 379 home runs, a .297 batting average, unanimous choice as the 1958 Rookie of the Year and 1968 Most Valuable Player, and the 1967 Comeback Player of the Year trophy, his supporters were unable to garnish the necessary three-fourths vote needed for induction. "It's the narcotics thing," claimed journalist Nick Peters, who had voted for the Puerto Rican. "The only guys that did better than him are guys in the Hall of Fame. Why are [the writers] keeping him out? I've got to think there's some prejudice about it [concerning] the drug thing."[33] San Francisco columnist Lowell Cohn denounced those who did not vote for Cepeda: "Cepeda did not betray baseball and what he did never should have been an issue in his candidacy."[34] In the wake of this final rejection, the Baby Bull remained hopeful. "Maybe [when the Veteran's Committee votes] I will make it and my number will be there with Juan Marichal," he said.[35] With that, the wait continued.

Cepeda's plight, however, did not diminish his achievements during an era when Latins in the United States were virtually ignored. His success and the success of other pioneers in the face of language barriers, racism, loneliness, and exploitation all but forced big league clubs to address their needs and expand their recruitment of Spanish-speaking players. And each passing decade brought a new increase in their numbers. When Minnie Miñoso donned a Cleveland uniform in 1949, he was 1 of only 3 Latins in the big leagues. In 1955, there were 23. The next two decades averaged 60 Latins. By 1985, the numbers had risen to 110 and remained near 100 as baseball entered the 1990s.[36] Within that time frame, Mateo Alou, Bobby Avila, Roberto Clemente, Rico Carty, Rod Carew, and Tony Oliva won seventeen batting titles among them. Carew alone captured seven, while Clemente won four and Oliva three. In addition, Jorge "George" Bell, Rod Carew, Orlando Cepeda, Roberto Clemente, José Canseco, Guillermo Hernández, and Zoilo Versalles won distinction as most valuable players. Miguel Cuéllar, Guillermo Hernández, and Fernando Valenzuela won Cy Young Awards and Juan Marichal won twenty games in six seasons. And Luis Aparicio, Orlando Cepeda (who also was the 1961 home run king), Tony Oliva, Rod Carew, Fernando Valenzuela, Oswaldo "Ozzie" Guillén, José Canseco, and Benito Santiago all collected Rookie of the Year honors. Latins won awards in other facets of the game and distinguished themselves despite the trials and tribulations many faced.

The Latin contingency in America's national pastime altered the professional game. Their influx and subsequent success forced big league organizations to expand their scouting horizons. The pioneering scout of the past gave way to the academies of the contemporary period. During their first fifty years, American baseball observers amused themselves at the expense of the Latin players; in the second fifty years they groped to understand them.

As the twentieth century drew to a close, the impact and increase of Latin players in the major leagues reflected larger Hispanic society. In 1994, following an extensive study, a spokesperson for Nielsen Media Research announced that 10 percent of households in the United States tuned in to Spanish-language television stations. "The Hispanic universe is an extremely fast-growing segment of the population," announced the institute as researchers reflected upon the 23 million viewers worldwide.[37] A "forgotten people" of an earlier era, Latins could no longer be ignored by the United States or by professional baseball. By 1994, fourteen of the twenty-six major league organizations broadcasted games on Spanish-language stations. Moreover, the Atlanta-based Turner Broadcasting System introduced Spanish-language coverage of the Braves games in several regions of Latin America. When founded, the expansion Florida Marlins promoted itself as the "Team of the Americas."

Shades of earlier cultural conflicts, however, continued. To some, the polarization between Latins and white Americans had changed little throughout the decades. "There's a collective mentality in the United States that Hispanics aren't worth much," argued Clemente's old chum, Luis Rodríguez-Mayoral. "The Anglo culture is at war with the minority culture [in the United States], and that was the case 200 years before Juan González was born."[38] Still, while reactionary "English-only" proposals and "Save Our State" campaigns emerged as responses to the ever-increasing influx of Hispanics, by the nineties Latin people had clearly arrived. And their struggles, fortitude, and achievements, to be sure, were best profiled on the baseball diamonds. "We are survivors. We never give up; we never quit," pronounced Felipe Alou. "This is the spirit of the Latin. We are a hard people to put away."[39]

The saga of Latin ballplayers in the United States that began with Esteban Bellán in the 1870s continued into the 1990s. Indeed, the Latin stars of the late twentieth century represent only the most recent generation of a skilled and courageous group whose path to success was laden with loneliness, racism, and ridicule. The pioneers instinctively responded with determination and tenacity, virtues with which the Spanish-speaking communities in the United States could identify and traits that the players used to persevere against their long overdue notoriety in the big leagues. Thus, as the Latin players of today continue to captivate baseball audiences, each achievement is backed by a proud heritage and fueled by a very special hunger.

Notes

1. Heuer, "Latin Ballplayers," 23.

2. Ibid.

3. Art Rosenbaum, *San Francisco Chronicle,* Jan. 5, 1983.

4. *San Francisco Chronicle,* Jan. 14, 1983.

5. Robert Heuer, "Luis Aparicio: Breaking Two of Baseball's Barriers," Luis Aparicio file, National Baseball Library, Cooperstown, N.Y.

6. Ibid.

7. Jim Murray, *Sporting News,* Apr. 28, 1979.

8. "Baseball's Best Hitter Tries for Glory," *Time,* July 18, 1977, 55.

9. *Sporting News,* Apr. 28, 1979.

10. Mike Downey, *Sporting News,* Aug. 5, 1985.

11. Oleksak and Oleksak, *Béisbol,* 141.

12. Information compiled by author from 1989 media guides, National Baseball Library.

13. *New York Times,* May 4, 1987.

14. Few Latins involved with professional baseball criticized Campanis for his statements. A similar incident took place in 1982 when Pittsburgh Pirates scout Howie Haak, another whose association with Latin players reached back to the 1950s, uncharacteristically claimed that there were "too many blacks" on the Pittsburgh squad to win support of that town's fans. *Sporting News,* May 31, 1982.

15. Campanis, only weeks earlier, had accompanied outfielder Pedro Guerrero to Santo Domingo to attend the opening of a new Dodgers' baseball academy in the Dominican Republic. Guerrero, following the "Nightline" telecast, staunchly defended the beleaguered Campanis when he declared, "I still think he is a great man." *Los Angeles Times,* Apr. 10, 1987.

16. Ibid.

17. Taylor interview.

18. Peter Alfano, "Barriers to Advancement Thwart Hispanic Players," *New York Times,* May 4, 1987.

19. Ibid.

20. Alou interview.

21. *Los Angeles Times,* May 26, 1993.

22. *Los Angeles Times,* May 25, 1994.

23. Ibid.

24. Untitled, undated article, National Baseball Library.

25. Dave Nightingale, "Baseball's Secret Treasure," *Sporting News,* Aug., 19, 1985.

26. Janice Castro, "Harvesting Baseball Talent," *Time,* Sept. 2, 1985.

27. Nightingale, "Baseball's Secret Treasure."

28. Ibid.

29. Klein, *Sugarball,* 60–61.

30. Ibid.

31. Bob Kravitz, "Back in the High Life," *Sporting News,* July 5, 1993.

32. Newman, "Man with the Golden Arm," 62.

33. Peters interview.

34. Lowell Cohn, *San Francisco Chronicle,* Jan. 13, 1994.

35. Ibid.

36. Author compilation from Thorn and Palmer, *Total Baseball; Wall Street Journal,* Apr. 3, 1984.

37. *Modesto Bee,* Nov. 15, 1994.

38. *Denver Post,* Aug. 8, 1994.

39. Steve Marantz, "The Father and the Son," *Sporting News,* June 21, 1993.

Bibliography

Books

Aaron, Hank, and Lonnie Wheeler. *I Had a Hammer: The Hank Aaron Story.* New York: Harper Paperbacks, 1991.

Acuña, Rodolfo. *Occupied America: A History of the Chicanos.* 3d ed. New York: Harper and Row, 1988.

Aguilar, Luis E. *Cuba 1933: Prologue to Revolution.* Ithaca: Cornell University Press, 1972.

Alexander, Charles. *Holding the Line: The Eisenhower Era, 1953–1961.* Bloomington: Indiana University Press, 1975.

Alou, Felipe, with Herm Weiskopf. *Felipe Alou: My Life and Baseball.* Waco, Tex.: Word Books, 1967.

Ashby, LeRoy. *William Jennings Bryan: Champion of Democracy.* Boston: Twayne, 1987.

Baseball Register 1947. St. Louis: *Sporting News,* 1947.

Baseball Register 1956. St. Louis: *Sporting News,* 1956.

Bjarkman, Peter C. *Baseball with a Latin Beat: A History of the Latin American Game.* Jefferson, N.C.: McFarland, 1994.

Boswell, Thomas D. *How Life Imitates the World Series: An Inquiry into the Game.* Garden City, N.Y.: Doubleday, 1982.

Bosewell, Thomas D., and James R. Curtis. *The Cuban-American Experience: Culture, Images, and Perspectives.* Totowa, N.J.: Rowman and Allanheld, 1983.

Brown, Warren. *The Chicago White Sox.* New York: G. P. Putnam's Sons, 1952.

Brownstone, David M., Irene M. Franck, and Douglass M. Brownstone. *Island of Hope, Island of Tears.* New York: Penguin Books, 1979.

Burke, Art. *Unsung Heroes of the Major Leagues.* New York: Random House, 1976.

Burns, E. Bradford. *Latin America: A Concise Interpretive History.* Englewood Cliffs, N.J.: Prentice-Hall, 1972.

————. *The Poverty of Progress: Latin America in the Nineteenth Century.* Berkeley: University of California Press, 1980.

Carrion, Arturo Morales. *Puerto Rico: A Political and Cultural History.* New York: W. W. Norton, 1983.

Daniels, Roger. *Concentration Camps, North America: Japanese in the United States and Canada during World War II.* Malabar, Fla.: Krieger, 1986.

Dark, Alvin, and John Underwood. *When in Doubt Fire the Manager: My Life and Times in Baseball.* New York: E. P. Dutton, 1980.

Degler, Carl N. *Neither Black nor White: Slavery and Race Relations in Brazil and the United States.* New York: Macmillan, 1971.

Devaney, John. *Juan Marichal: Mister Strike.* New York: G. P. Putnam's Sons, 1970.

Dozer, Donald Marquard. *Are We Good Neighbors? Three Decades of Inter-American Relations, 1930–1960.* Gainesville: University of Florida Press, 1961.

Einstein, Charles. *Willie's Time: A Memoir.* New York: Berkeley Books, 1979.

Figueroa, Ed, and Dorothy Harshman. *Yankee Stranger.* Smithtown, N.Y.: Exposition Press, 1982.

Flood, Curt, with Richard Carter. *The Way It Is.* New York: Trident Press, 1971.

Gann, L. H., and Peter J. Duignan. *The Hispanics in the United States: A History.* Boulder, Colo.: Westview Press, 1986.

García, Juan Ramon. *Operation Wetback: The Mass Deportation of Mexican Undocumented Workers in 1954.* Westport, Conn.: Greenwood Press, 1980.

García, Mario T. *Mexican Americans: Leadership, Ideology, and Identity, 1930–1960.* New Haven: Yale University Press, 1989.

Garcia, Richard A. *Rise of the Mexican American Middle Class: San Antonio, 1924–1941.* College Station: Texas A&M University Press, 1991.

Grebler, Leo, Joan W. Moore, and Ralph C. Guzman. *The Mexican-American People: The Nation's Second Largest Minority.* New York: Free Press, 1970.

Gutiérrez, David G. *Walls and Mirrors: Mexican Americans, Mexican Immigrants, and the Politics of Ethnicity.* Berkeley: University of California Press, 1995.

Handlin, Oscar. *The Uprooted: The Epic Story of the Great Migrations That Made the American People.* New York: Grosset and Dunlap, 1951.

Higham, John. *Strangers in the Land: Patterns of American Nativism, 1860–1925.* New York: Atheneum, 1975.

Hoffman, Abraham. *Unwanted Mexican Americans in the Great Depression: Repatriation Pressures, 1929–1939.* Tucson: University of Arizona Press, 1974.

Holway, John. *Voices from the Great Black Baseball Leagues.* New York: Dodd, Mead, 1975.

Izenberg, Jerry. *Great Latin Sports Figures: The Proud People.* New York: Doubleday, 1976.

Keen, Benjamin, and Mark Wasserman. *A History of Latin America.* 3d. ed. New York: Houghton Mifflin, 1992.

Kerrane, Kevin. *Dollar Sign on the Muscle: The World of Baseball Scouting.* New York: Avon Books, 1985.

Kiersh, Edward. *Where Have You Gone, Vince Dimaggio?* New York: Bantam Books, 1983.

Kitano, Harry H. L. *Race Relations.* 3d ed. Englewood Cliffs, N.J.: Prentice-Hall, 1985.

Klein, Alan. *Sugarball: The American Game, the Dominican Dream.* New Haven, Conn.: Yale University Press, 1991.

Klugar, Richard. *Simple Justice: The History of Brown vs. Board of Education and Black America's Struggle for Equality.* New York: Alfred A. Knopf, 1976.

LaFeber, Walter. *The Panama Canal: The Crisis in Historical Perspective.* New York: Oxford University Press, 1978.

Levine, Peter. *Ellis Island to Ebbets Field: Sport and the American Jewish Experience.* New York: Oxford University Press, 1992.

Littwin, Mark. *Fernando!* New York: Bantam Books, 1981.

Marden, Charles F. *Minorities in American Society.* New York: American Book Company, 1952.

Marichal, Juan, as told to Charles Einstein. *A Pitcher's Story.* Garden City, N.Y.: Doubleday, 1967.

Mays, Willie, with Lou Sahadi. *Say Hey: The Autobiography of Willie Mays.* New York: J. B. Lippincott, 1979.

McWilliams, Carey. *Brothers under the Skin.* Boston: Little, Brown, 1951.

———. *North from Mexico: The Spanish-Speaking People of the United States.* New York: Greenwood Press, 1968.

Meier, Matt S., and Feliciano Rivera. *The Chicanos: A History of Mexican Americans.* New York: Hill and Wang, 1972.

Miller, Douglas T. *Visions of America: Second World War to the Present.* New York: West, 1988.

Miñoso, Minnie, Fernando Fernández, and Robert Kleinfelder. *Miñoso: Extra Innings: My Life in Baseball.* Chicago: Regnery Gateway, 1983.

Moore, Joan, and Harry Pachon. *Hispanics in the United States.* Englewood Cliffs, N.J.: Prentice-Hall, 1985.

Musick, Phil. *Who Was Roberto? A Biography of Roberto Clemente.* Garden City, N.Y.: Doubleday, 1974.

Myrdal, Gunnar. *An American Dilemma: The Negro Problem and Modern Democracy.* New York: Harper and Brothers, 1944.

Novak, Michael. *The Joy of Sports: End Zones, Bases, Baskets, Balls, and the Consecration of the American Spirit.* New York: Basic Books, 1976.

Noverr, Douglas A., and Lawrence D. Ziewacz. *The Games They Played: Sports in American History, 1865–1980.* Chicago: Nelson-Hall, 1983.

Oates, Stephen B. *Let the Trumpet Sound: The Life of Martin Luther King Jr.* New York: New American Library, 1982.

Okrent, Daniel, and Harris Lewine, ed. *The Ultimate Baseball Book.* Boston: Houghton Mifflin, 1981.

Oleksak, Michael M., and Mary Adams Oleksak. *Béisbol: Latin Americans and the Grand Old Game.* Grand Rapids, Mich.: Masters Press, 1991.

Oliva, Tony, with Bob Fowler. *Tony O! The Trials and Triumphs of Tony Oliva.* New York: Hawthorn Books, 1973.

Painter, Nell Irvin. *Standing at Armageddon: The United States, 1877–1919.* New York: W. W. Norton, 1987.

Pérez, Gustavo Firmat. *Life on the Hyphen: The Cuban-American Way.* Austin: University of Texas Press, 1994.

Peterson, Robert. *Only the Ball Was White.* New York: McGraw-Hill, 1984.

Rader, Benjamin G. *American Sports: From the Age of Folk Games to the Age of Spectators.* Englewood Cliffs, N.J.: Prentice- Hall, 1983.

Reichler, Joseph L., ed. *The Baseball Encyclopedia: The Complete and Official Record of Major League Baseball.* New York: Macmillan, 1979.

Riding, Alan. *Distant Neighbors: A Portrait of the Mexicans.* New York: Vintage Books, 1989.

Robinson, Jackie. *Baseball Has Done It.* New York: J. B. Lippincott, 1964.

Rogosin, Donn. *Invisible Men: Life in Baseball's Negro Leagues.* New York: Atheneum, 1985.

Roseboro, John, with Bill Libby. *Glory Days with the Dodgers and Other Days with Others.* New York: Atheneum, 1978.

Ruck, Rob. *Sandlot Seasons: Sport in Black Pittsburgh.* Urbana: University of Illinois Press, 1993.

———. *The Tropic of Baseball: Baseball and the Dominican Republic.* Westport, Conn.: Meckler, 1991.

San Francisco Giants Silver Anniversary Yearbook, 1958–1982. San Francisco: Wooford Associates, 1982.

Schlesinger, Stephen, and Stephen Kinzer. *Bitter Fruit: The Untold Story of the American Coup in Guatemala.* Garden City, N.Y.: Anchor Books, 1983.

Senzel, Howard. *Baseball and the Cold War.* New York: Harcourt Brace Jovanovich, 1977.

Sexion, Patricia Cayo. *Spanish Harlem.* New York: Harper and Row, 1965.

Seymour, Harold. *Baseball: The Golden Age.* New York: Oxford University Press, 1971.

Skidmore, Thomas E., and Peter H. Smith. *Modern Latin America.* New York: Oxford University Press, 1984.

Suchlicki, Jaime. *Cuba: From Columbus to Castro.* New York: Pergamon-Brassey's, 1986.

Taylor, Ronald B. *Chávez and the Farm Workers*. Boston: Beacon Press, 1975.

Terzain, James. *The Kid from Cuba: Zoilo Versalles*. New York: Doubleday, 1967.

Theroux, Paul. *The Old Patagonian Express: By Train through the Americas*. New York: Pocket Books, 1979.

Thorn, John, and Pete Palmer, eds. *Total Baseball*. New York: Warner Communications, 1989.

Tiant, Luis, with Joe Fitzgerald. *El Tiante: The Luis Tiant Story*. Garden City, N.Y.: Doubleday, 1976.

Torres, Angel. *La historia del béisbol cubano, 1878–1976*. Los Angeles: Angel Torres, 1976.

Tuttle, William M., Jr. *Race Riot: Chicago in the Red Summer of 1919*. New York: Atheneum, 1978.

Tygiel, Jules. *Baseball's Great Experiment: Jackie Robinson and His Legacy*. New York: Vintage Books, 1983.

Veeck, Bill, with Ed Linn. *The Hustler's Handbook*. New York: G. P. Putnam's Sons, 1965.

————. *Veeck—As in Wreck: The Autobiography of Bill Veeck*. New York: G. P. Putnam's Sons, 1962.

Voigt, David Q. *American Baseball: From the Commissioners to the Continental Expansion*. Vol. 2. University Park: Pennsylvania State University Press, 1983.

Wagenheim, Kal. *Clemente!* New York: Praeger, 1973.

Walton, Richard. *Cold War and Counterrevolution: The Foreign Policy of John F. Kennedy*. New York: Viking Press, 1972.

Wiarda, Howard J. *The Dominican Republic: Nation in Transition*. New York: Praeger, 1969.

Wiebe, Robert H. *The Search for Order, 1877–1970*. New York: Hill and Wang, 1967.

Wills, Garry. *Reagan's America: Innocents at Home*. Garden City, N.Y.: Doubleday, 1987.

Woll, Allen L., and Randall M. Miller. *Ethnic and Racial Images in American Film and Television: Historical Essays and Bibliography*. New York: Garland, 1987.

Woodward, C. Vann. *The Strange Career of Jim Crow*. 3d ed. New York: Oxford University Press, 1974.

Articles, Chapters in Books, Papers, and Theses

Alou, Felipe, with David Arnold Hano. "Latin American Ballplayers Need a Bill of Rights." *Sport*, Nov. 1963.

Arbena, Joseph L. "Sport and the Study of Latin American Society: An Overview." In *Sport and Society in Latin America: Diffusion, Dependency, and the Rise of Mass Culture*, ed. Joseph L. Arbena. Westport, Conn.: Greenwood Press, 1988. 1–14.

Beezley, William H. "The Rise of Baseball in Mexico and the First Valenzuela." *Studies in Latin American Popular Culture*, no. 4 (1985): 3–23.

Bjarkman, Peter C. "Cuban Blacks in the Majors before Jackie Robinson." *International Pastime* 12 (1992): 58–63.

———. "Hispanic Baseball Statistical Record." *International Pastime* 12 (1992): 87–95.

Bonilla, Seda E. "Social Structure and Race Relations." *Social Forces* 40 (Dec. 1961): 141–48.

Boyle, Robert H. "'El As' Is the Voice of America." *Sports Illustrated*, Oct. 14, 1963.

———. "The Latins Storm Las Grandes Ligas." *Sports Illustrated*, Sept. 19, 1966, 24–30.

———. "The Private World of the Negro Ballplayer." *Sports Illustrated*, Mar. 21, 1960.

Brandmeyer, Gerald. "Baseball and the American Dream: A Conversation with Al Lopez." *Tampa Bay History* (Spring–Summer 1981): 48–73.

Brown, Bruce. "Cuban Baseball." *Atlantic Magazine*, June 1984, 112.

Cantwell, Robert. "Invasion from Santo Domingo." *Sports Illustrated*, Feb. 25, 1963, 54–61.

Castro, Tony. "Something Screwy Going on Here." *Sports Illustrated*, July 8, 1985, 30–37.

Considine, Bob. "Ivory from Cuba." *Collier's*, Aug. 3, 1940.

Falls, Joe. "Far from Pappa Pedro's Finca." *Baseball Digest*, Sept. 1965, 56.

———. "It's Roberto Clemente." *Sport*, Mar. 1968.

Foreman, Thomas E. "Discrimination against the Negro in American Athletics." M.A. thesis, Fresno State College, 1957.

Frio, Daniel D., and Marc Onigman. "Good Field, No Hit: The Image of Latin American Baseball Players in the American Press, 1871–1946." *Revista/Review Interamerica* (Summer 1979): 199–208.

Furlong, William Barry. "The White Sox Katzenjammer Kid." *Saturday Evening Post*, July 10, 1954.

Garcia, John A. "Hispanic Migration: Where They Are Moving and Why." *Agenda* 11, no. 4 (1981): 14–17.

Gordon, Dick. "Twin First by a Twin." *Baseball Digest*, Dec.–Jan. 1965, 69.

Guernica, Antonio. "The Hispanic Market: A Profile." *Agenda* 11, no. 3 (1981): 4–7.

Heisler, Mark. "Fernando's Path of Glory." *Inside Sports*, July 1981, 13–14.

"Here Comes the Latino Era." *Nuestro*, Apr. 1977, 15.

Heuer, Robert. "Latin Ballpayers: Load the Bases." *Americas* 42, no. 2 (1990): 23.

Hirshberg, Al. "The Rough Rise of Juan Pizarro." *Sport*, Dec. 1964.

"Hispanics Make Their Move." *U.S. News and World Report*, Aug. 24, 1981, 60–64.

Johnson, Terry. "Rene Cardenas: Courage to Capture Dreams." *Dodgers Magazine,* Aug. 1989, 50–55.

Joseph, Gilbert M. "Forging the Regional Pastime: Baseball and Class in Yucatan." In *Sport and Society in Latin America: Diffusion, Dependency, and the Rise of Mass Culture,* ed. Joseph L. Arbena. Westport, Conn.: Greenwood Press, 1988. 29–61.

LaFrance, David. "A Mexican Popular Image of the United States through the Baseball Hero, Fernando Valenzuela." *Studies in Latin American Popular Culture* 4 (1985): 14–23.

Lewis, Franklin. "Sensation from South of the Border." *Saturday Evening Post,* July 15, 1955.

Mulvoy, Mark. "Cha Cha Goes Boom, Boom, Boom!" *Sports Illustrated,* July 24, 1967, 18–21.

"The Newest Americans: A Second 'Spanish Invasion.'" *U.S. News and World Report,* July 8, 1974, 34–36.

Newman, Bruce. "Man with the Golden Arm." *Sports Illustrated,* Feb. 11, 1991, 60–65.

Páramo, Fernando. "Jaime Jarrin: Profile of a Pioneer." *Dodgers Magazine,* June 1989, 6–9.

Phelon, Wm. A. "Baseball in Cuba: The Great American Sport as an International Game." *Baseball Magazine,* May 1912, 35.

Prato, Lou. "Why the Pirates Love the New Roberto Clemente." *Sport,* Aug. 1967.

"Que Viva Clemente!" *Major League Baseball 1993.* New York: Preview, 1993. 14–16.

Regalado, Samuel O. "Baseball in the Barrios: The Scene in East Los Angeles since World War II." *Baseball History* 1, no. 2 (Summer 1986): 47–59.

———. "'Dodgers Béisbol Is on the Air': The Development and Impact of the Dodgers' Spanish-Language Broadcasts, 1958– 1994." *California History* 74, no. 3 (Fall 1995): 280–89.

———. "'Image Is Everything': Latin Ballplayers and the United States Media." *Studies in Latin American Popular Culture* 13 (1994): 101–14.

———. "The Minor League Experience of Latin American Baseball Players in Western Communites." *Journal of the West* 16 (Jan. 1987): 65–70.

Rivera, Eddie. "Only Land." *Inside Sports,* June 1987, 44–46.

Rosenbaum, Art. "Leader of the Latins." *Sporting News,* Sept. 1962.

Ruck, Rob. "Baseball in the Caribbean." In *Total Baseball,* ed. John Thorn and Peter Palmer. New York: Warner Communications, 1989. 605–11.

Rustin, Dan. "The Spanish Market: Its Size, Income, and Loyalties Make It a Rich Marketing Mine." *Television/Radio Age,* Oct. 2, 1972.

Scully, Gerald. "Discrimination: The Case of Baseball." In *Government and the Sports Business,* ed. Roger G. Noll. Washington, D.C.: Brookings Institute, 1974. 236–39.

Shields, Mitchell. "Hispanics Step Out of the Melting Pot." *Madison Avenue* (Dec. 1984): 67–72.

Stann, Francis. "The New Mark of Zorro." *Baseball Digest,* June 1963, 41–42.

Stein, Steve. "The Case of Soccer in Early Twentieth-Century Lima." In *Sport and Society in Latin America: Diffusion, Dependency, and the Rise of Mass Culture,* ed. Joseph L. Arbena. Westport, Conn.: Greenwood Press, 1988. 63–84.

Sullivan, Prescott. "The Newest Alou Presents a Problem." *Baseball Digest,* May 1964, 9–10.

Wagner, Eric A. "Sport in Revolutionary Societies: Cuba and Nicaragua." In *Sport and Society in Latin America: Diffusion, Dependency, and the Rise of Mass Culture,* ed. Joseph L. Arbena. Westport, Conn.: Greenwood Press, 1988. 113–36.

Ward, J. J. "Gonzalez: The Cuban Backstop." *Baseball Magazine,* Feb. 1917, 33–34.

Weir, Hugh C. "The Famous Marsans Case." *Baseball Magazine,* Sept. 1914, 53–59.

Weisberg, Louis. "In Any Language, They're Still the Dodgers." *Advertising Age,* Mar. 19, 1984.

Williams, Edgar. "Sandy Amoros—He Got It!" *Baseball Digest,* Oct. 1954, 71–78.

Williams, Virginia. "Alternative Intellectuals and United States–Latin American Relations, 1910–1970." Paper presented at the North Central Council of Latin Americanists Conference, University of Wisconsin, La Crosse, Sept. 23, 1994.

Yzaguirre, Raul. "The Decade for the Hispanic." *Agenda* (Jan.–Feb. 1980).

Newspapers

Baltimore Review
Baseball Register
Binghamton (New York) Press
Boston Globe
Boston Herald
Boston Traveler
Brooklyn Eagle
Chicago Tribune
Christian Science Monitor
Denver Post
Eugene (Oregon) Register-Guard
La Opinión
Long Island (New York) Newsday
Los Angeles Daily News
Los Angeles Times
Miami Herald

Modesto (California) Bee
Newark (New Jersey) Star Ledger
New York Daily News
New York Journal American
New York Newsday
New York Post
New York Star-Ledger
New York Times
New York World-Telegram
Philadelphia Inquirer
Portland Oregonian
Rochester (New York) Times-Union
San Francisco Chronicle
San Juan (Puerto Rico) El Mundo
San Juan (Puerto Rico) Star
Spokane Chronicle
Springfield (Massachusetts) Daily News
St. Louis Globe-Democrat
Newark (New Jersey) Star Ledger
Tacoma News-Tribune
Troy (New York) Daily Whig
Washington Post
Washington Star

Interviews

Felipe Alou, taped interview with the author, May 31, June 1, 1989, West Palm
    Beach, Fla.
Alex Campanis, taped interview with the author, July 2, 1982, Los Angeles.
Orlando Cepeda, taped interview with the author, Aug. 8, 1982, by phone.
George Genovese, taped interview with the author, June 16, 1982, North Holly-
    wood, Calif.
Preston Gómez, taped interview with the author, Jan. 10, 1986, Anaheim, Calif.
Calvin Griffith, taped interview with the author, May 22, 1985, Minneapolis.
Monte Irvin, taped interview with the author, Apr. 1, 2, 5, 1982, New York.
Jaime Jarrín, taped interview with the author, July 2, 1982, Los Angeles.
Manuel Mota, taped interview with the author, Aug. 5, 1982, Los Angeles.
Tony Oliva, taped interview with the author, May 22, 1985, Minneapolis.
Tony Pérez, taped interview with the author, Sept. 25, 1992, San Francisco.
Nick Peters, taped interview with the author, Jan. 2, 1993, Stockton, Calif.
Luis Rodríguez-Mayoral, taped interview with the author, June 23, 1994, Anaheim,
    Calif.

Octavio "Cookie" Rojas, taped interview with the author, Apr. 26, 1996, San Francisco.
Chuck Stewart, taped interview with the author, Apr. 2, 1986, Spokane.
Tony Taylor, taped interview with the author, June 6, 1989, Philadelphia.

Archival Sources

Alex Campanis notes, author's possession.
Player Clipping Files, National Baseball Library, Cooperstown, N.Y.
Player Clipping Files, *Sporting News* archive, St. Louis, Mo.

Index

SAMUEL O. REGALADO holds a Ph.D. from Washington State University. He has published numerous articles on Latins in professional baseball and sport during the Japanese American Nisei era. Regalado was a 1994 Smithsonian Faculty Fellow and is currently a professor of history at California State University at Stanislaus.

BOOKS IN THE SERIES SPORT AND SOCIETY

A Sporting Time: New York City and the Rise of Modern Athletics, 1820–70
Melvin L. Adelman

Sandlot Seasons: Sport in Black Pittsburgh
Rob Ruck

West Ham United: The Making of a Football Club
Charles Korr

Beyond the Ring: The Role of Boxing in American Society
Jeffrey T. Sammons

John L. Sullivan and His America
Michael T. Isenberg

Television and National Sport: The United States and Britain
Joan M. Chandler

The Creation of American Team Sports: Baseball and Cricket, 1838–72
George B. Kirsch

City Games: The Evolution of American Urban Society and the Rise of Sports
Steven A. Riess

The Brawn Drain: Foreign Student-Athletes in American Universities
John Bale

The Business of Professional Sports
Edited by Paul D. Staudohar and James A. Mangan

Fritz Pollard: Pioneer in Racial Advancement
John M. Carroll

Go Big Red! The Story of a Nebraska Football Player
George Mills

Sport and Exercise Science: Essays in the History of Sports Medicine
Edited by Jack W. Berryman and Roberta J. Park

Minor League Baseball and Local Economic Development
Arthur T. Johnson

Harry Hooper: An American Baseball Life
Paul J. Zingg

Cowgirls of the Rodeo: Pioneer Professional Athletes
Mary Lou LeCompte

Sandow the Magnificent: Eugen Sandow and the Beginnings of Bodybuilding
David Chapman

Big-Time Football at Harvard, 1905: The Diary of Coach Bill Reid
Edited by Ronald A. Smith

Leftist Theories of Sport: A Critique and Reconstruction
William J. Morgan

Babe: The Life and Legend of Babe Didrikson Zaharias
Susan E. Cayleff

Stagg's University: The Rise, Decline, and Fall of Big-Time Football at Chicago
Robin Lester

Muhammad Ali, the People's Champ
Edited by Elliott J. Gorn

People of Prowess: Sport, Leisure, and Labor in Early Anglo-America
Nancy L. Struna

The New American Sport History: Recent Approaches and Perspectives
Edited by S. W. Pope

Making the Team: The Cultural Work of Baseball Fiction
Timothy Morris

Making the American Team: Sport, Culture, and the Olympic Experience
Mark Dyreson

Viva Baseball! Latin Major Leaguers and Their Special Hunger
Samuel O. Regalado

REPRINT EDITIONS

The Nazi Olympics
Richard D. Mandell

Sports in the Western World (Second Edition)
William J. Baker